INDIA MIKE

Michael Hendry

— THE PLEASE PRESS 2015 —

Typeset in Minion Pro

Printed and bound by Imprint Digital, Upton Pyne, Devon, UK.

ISBN: 978-0-9932018-0-6

India Mike is also available as an ebook

First published in Great Britain in 2015 by:
The Please Press
Culsh, Kildrummy,
Aberdeenshire, AB33 8RD
WWW.MIKE-HENDRY.CO.UK

The
PLEASE PRESS

A letter, in memorium, to Ian Grimble, author & historian: 1921-1995.

Dear Ian,

It was your misfortune in 1965 when you damaged your spine, lifting a heavy garden roller up that flight of steps. But for me, it was great good luck – for, in search of medical assistance, you consulted my surgeon father and came to visit our home, and by that string of circumstances, I came to meet you. By your kindly introductions, I went to the Himalayas, and in this book I relate what happened to me, and how it changed me. After India, my life moved quickly to other things; so rapidly indeed, that I never properly thanked you for what you did. So, this book is respectfully dedicated to your memory.

And with sincere thanks to...

Catherine, for her constant & loving encouragement,
Duncan Lockerbie of Lumphanan Press for every conceivable assistance,
Talis Archdeacon for editing,
Peter Ananin for suggesting I write 'India Mike' in the first place.

Contents

Foreword

This story of India is written from memory, with some contemporary notes and photographs. The events related are true, but out of respect for other people I have changed many names, places and times – and I have chopped up most of my characters and re-assembled them as other people. I have done this because I wanted this story to be an enjoyable read, rather than some cautiously written diary. I needed this freedom so that I could write what I wanted – but perhaps some souls from all those years ago might recognise a vestige of themselves that they would have preferred not to have been revealed. If this is the case, and an apology is needed, then I offer it wholeheartedly.

In 1966, the young voyager had no mobile phone by which he or she could call Mum from a far flung place… to call back in 10 minutes after she checks the web to find where her offspring can find a safe bed for the night in Nepal, the Solomon Islands or up a mountain in South America. It makes a big difference to the understanding of the traveller to know that he or she is truly on their own, equipped only with the instincts of their personalities to deal with situations in which the choice of one word or gesture could mean the difference between getting a knife in the back or an offer of assistance.

It was 48 years ago when I went to India, and my memory of events must be tainted by the self-protecting mechanism that covers up my own failings and exaggerates my small successes. I have not sought to make myself anything in this story – neither the rogue nor the saint: I am just the narrator.

Part One

1

Fears but good vibrations

IN 1966 I WAS 18. I HAD NOT MANAGED TO FORMULATE A CLEAR IDEA of what I wanted to do with life, except, vaguely, that the ordinary paths of university or a job were not for me. It was customary for senior pupils about to leave my school in Aberdeen to visit Aberdeen University for an open day – to get the feel of the place, to speak to students and to excite their ambition to get there. In the washrooms of the Student's Common Room, one of the toilet cubicles sported one of those metal and rectangular toilet paper dispensers which offers the user one measly sheet per one measly sheet. Above the letterbox-like opening for the paper, someone had neatly written, in bold blue felt-tip pen 'Arts Degrees – Please Take One'.

Of course, we had a great laugh about it, but somehow it had an effect on me and I decided that university was not for me.

Voluntary Service Overseas was an organisation that offered place-ments for young people around the globe, and I applied to them saying that I wanted to go to the Solomon Islands. Aberdeen is such a filthy cold place that the idea of wafting around a warm paradise for a year seemed appealing. It still does. I was invited for an interview in London but failed to impress, and so made further enquiries.

The next project was driving an ambulance in Kenya; this became a solid arrangement until, one evening at home when the family was dining together, the phone rang with the news that this adventure too, was, very sorry, no longer available.

It so happened that when I got up from the table to take the call, our family was at supper in the presence of a guest, one of my father's friends. The phone was in immediate proximity to the dining table, so everyone could hear me dealing with this negative piece of news. After the conversation ended, I sat down again and confirmed to everyone what the call had conveyed. I could feel my brothers, sister and parents looking at me with pained sympathy and an awkward silence followed.

It was a difficult moment in another sense because my elder brother David was due to leave soon for Calcutta, there to work for a French medical charity, so I felt like the last chicken on the shelf.

My father was an orthopaedic surgeon who had a wide circle of interesting and varied friends; our guest that evening was a rather dry, very tall, bony man, the author Ian Grimble. Although I did not know it at the time, he was a man of great adventure, having been in the Army Intelligence Services in India and later at Bletchley Park. In the war years of 1942 to 1946, he made several journeys into the Himalayas, there to play a part in the chess game of nations which had begun in the 19th century between Russia, China and Britain. His official role was in the rehabilitation of soldiers wounded in action, but it was always assumed that a man of Ian Grimble's unique talents were also employed in the shadowy world of skulduggery and intrigue.

It was not but a minute or so after the awkwardness of my phone call had passed that he put a question to me directly: 'How would you like to go to India?'

I was on the spot, everyone was looking at me, I was fed up with appearing to be directionless, so without asking any questions at all, I said yes. Truth to tell, India had never been one of the places I had wanted to go to. But that was it. Three weeks later I had a letter from Delhi from a Mrs Maheta who had arranged, via Ian Grimble, for me to work in a Tibetan refugee camp in the Himalayas, and but a couple of weeks after that I had my passage booked to Bombay onboard the Arcadia. More letters were written to an old family friend in Bombay who would meet me off the boat; after that, I would be on my own.

And the day dawned that I had to say goodbye to my family and to my father.

You probably know how it goes between many a father and son:

'Where are you going?'

'Out.'

'Who are you going with?'

'Dunno.'

'When'll you be back?'

'Late.'

Doors slam. You don't understand me. Leave me alone. Don't tell *me* what to do.

But it wasn't like that with my father. I'd adored him my whole life – child, boy and youth. And one cold and foggy Sunday night in late November 1966, my father drove me from our grand house in Aberdeen to the train station, and in both our silent thoughts was the anxiety that we might never see each other again. I was on my way to the Himalayas.

I did not have the courage to bring the adventure to an end because to have done so would have revealed me to him as a coward – and I could not do that. The fear of what I had got myself into was intense, but I disguised this with a camouflage of bravado even though I was quaking on the inside, unable to break out from the shell I had created and unable to stop the impending fall over a dark cliff's edge.

In those days, Aberdeen's streets on a Sunday night were almost entirely empty of people and traffic. There was still an oppressing Victorian gloom cast over 'The Sabbath' then, and if you did anything other than go to church or visit relatives for pancakes and tea there was a snooty judgement that you were not 'decent folk'. Every shop was closed, and by evening, curtains were drawn tight and it felt as though the street lights themselves shone less brightly than during the working week. The drive to the station was brief and not a word was passed between us. Because my father was a frequent traveller, we found my train and sleeper compartment so quickly that it seemed to me that I had hardly left the house. The berth was tiny, so we were in touching proximity to each other as we pushed my one heavy suitcase up onto the top rack. It made the impending farewell unbearable to me as the moment arrived that we had both anticipated – the goodbye.

'Well,' he said, 'take care of yourself.' It was all he said.

'Yes,' I mumbled, almost unable to form that simple word.

Our embrace was just the lightest, quick touch and as he turned his back to me, the ground opened up and he was on the other side of a dark and deep ravine. I sat down for a while in the warm, dim compartment and tried to accept or reject the temptation to run after my father – but when I stepped out to the platform, he had gone and I knew I had to go through with it. I fished out my cigarettes and strolled up and down the length of the train awaiting its departure to London. Just as the guard was waving his green light and blowing his whistle, my companion in the compartment arrived in a fluster of lateness and heaved his case onto the lower bed.

'Going to London?' I asked.

'Not quite, just to Peterborough… you?'

'India.'

The train clanked through the night and I was wakened early when my companion got up to disembark at Peterborough. The fields gave way to brick and concrete and London arrived hooting and busy, exciting and daunting. I made my way to St. Pancras and found the train for Southampton.

The SS Arcadia was as huge and as gleaming white as I had expected to be – I had passage to Bombay via Suez and Aden. I was escorted by a steward down into the bowels of the ship, deep down, darkly down, through narrow gangways and passages, into a cramped cabin which had four double bunks tight to its walls, and at whose centre was the mountain of luggage belonging to my seven fellow passengers.

We sailed the next morning very early – streams of paper from three decks connected the departing and those left on the quay; I had no-one to say goodbye to, but I was not concerned and not afraid.

I lived mostly in the second class lounge, making the acquaintance of fellow passengers, among whom was Dr Calder, an elderly and dour-looking Church of Scotland minister based at a seminary in Delhi. He was its principal, preparing the faithful to go out among the heathens. Always in a severe, itchy-looking jet black suit and starched white dog collar, he spent his time in a wicker deck chair, mostly behind a book; though he looked forbidding, I spoke with him a great deal and we

became friends. The result of this was an invitation to stay with him in
Delhi if this were ever required – a very welcome thing because I had
very little money and his hospitality might well save vital funds.

The Arcadia's second-class lounge had a small cafeteria of fawn
Formica and varnished plywood; milky tea was served in hefty Pyrex
cups and the food was mushy peas, custard and school dinners. There
was a juke box which broke and would only play the 'Good Vibrations'
by the Beach Boys. There were cow-eyed sons and daughters who congregated round the chromium and red plastic and who would come to
know that song better than most. I hardly mixed with them and kept
myself to myself.

As we steamed south, the air became warmer, then hotter, then hot.
We sailed over the seas and oohed at the dolphins and the flying fish
soaring just above the waves and through the shimmering hot air. The
ship made anchor at strange ports where even the lights ashore at night
seemed filtered by a wavy film of heat, to flicker and melt into the oily
black waters of their shores and sea fronts.

Weeks before, it had been arranged by an exchange of letters that I
would be met in Bombay by the widow of an old family friend with
whom I was to stay before heading north to Delhi. She would meet me
from the ship and take me to her flat, where she would leave me in the
care of her houseboy and his mother while she made a trip to Madras.

The voyage to India took two weeks, and when the Arcadia arrived
in Bombay it seemed to do so suddenly, as though there had been no
passage of time in which to adjust to the fact that I was away from home
and in India.

Leaning over the ship's rail I watched the tugs fuss the ship into its
berth then looked around at my new surroundings, the heat a wobbling,
shimmering film over the blinding blue sky and Bombay's dirty maroon
buildings. On the dock below the gangways were hauled to the ship,
and in obedience to calls over the Tannoys we went to our cabins to
collect hand baggage and disgorged unwillingly into the sudden gloom
of a roasting hot oven, a warehouse filled to its fullest capacity with
people shouting, waving sheaves of paper and running around to find
whatever was lost to them. My luggage was lost, there were messages
over loudspeakers, porters who bade me follow them and porters who

abandoned me. But two sweat-soaked hours later, I was in the arrivals hall meeting Madelaine Colquhonnie, and, after the briefest kissing of cheeks, we were swiftly into a taxi. This was achieved by the lady extending her right arm and hand (in which was held a pink polka dot silk scarf) and parting the throng of people trying to get taxis by the exercise of her personality only, like a terrific female Moses.

We had no sooner left the terminal and joined the maelstrom of bumper-to-bumper traffic than I was faced with my first shock of Indian life. A young boy, both legs amputated at the knee, propelling himself by bandaged hands on a small, wheeled sledge, held his hands up to the taxi's open windows when we stopped at traffic lights; 'Piasa Sahib! Piasa!' he moaned. And the heat was suffocating.

'Pay absolutely *no* attention,' said Madelaine, 'do you know, most of these beggars have been mutilated by their own parents… just so they can beg? It's unspeakable. Really!' As she spoke, her face was contorted as though she had bitten into a rotten apple. She held the polka dot scarf to her mouth and waved the boy away with less vigour than she used to disturb an annoying fly, which, unlike the boy, was imaginary.

Mrs Colquhonnie's flat was on the first floor of a sumptuous building directly facing sea and just a few hundred yards from the Taj Mahal Hotel and the Gateway to India arch. She introduced me to her houseboy and his mother, Sidir and Mangwa, Sidir being a boy of about twelve.

'Just whatever you want,' she said, 'just ask them… I have to go to Madras this afternoon and I'll be back in three days. Just relax and get the feel of the place. If you get lost, get a taxi back here, you can trust the taxi wallahs so be sure always to go out with some money. Get Sidir to go to the station to get timetables and fares to Delhi, and when I get back, we can chat properly.'

She left about half an hour later and I was left to my own devices. My first task was to write to Dr Calder in Delhi, saying that, yes please, I would be very grateful for accommodation for a few days, and I gave him my likely date of arrival.

My first full day in Bombay was spent in a state of glorious exultation; few activities excite me more than exploring an unvisited city for the first time – the absorbing of smells and sounds, the rush of surprises storming the mind and drenching it with new shapes, colours and textures. I wandered endlessly and aimlessly, without timetable or plan. The joy is the instant satisfying of an immediately aroused curiosity – the sight of a tower behind other buildings or the wafting of smells and shouts from nearby. Because you are not going to an appointment or are on your way to familiar work, you see the whole picture and its frame and the sources of interest are as comprehensive as your ability to see them. Aberdeen was never like this!

The excitement was the more intoxicating because the extent of the differences from home were not just the architecture but a whole culture, a new landscape of people in an order and organisation quite different from anything I had experienced.

I could hardly but turn to stare at some new street vista than a ragged human form would be before me, beside or behind me begging. Often these were children, arms outstretched, 'Piasa, piasa…'. I was at a loss to know how to deal with this and just shook my head. I was wrong, but I convinced myself that I couldn't afford to give them anything.

The shock of Bombay was considerable not in the existence of the ragged poor, because that was known and expected, but because nobody seemed bothered by it. Surely, someone ought to do something about it, as though there had been a catastrophe and at whose scene, properly speaking, there ought to have been a concerted community effort to save the victims. Not only were the poor ignored, it seemed they were despised, and despised by the very people who ought to have had enough of a conscience to be motivated to do something about it.

I had a few days of secure, happy wandering while Madame was in Madras. I had the use of a very grand apartment, meals when I wanted them and the luxury of two people looking after me. I couldn't even go to the kitchen for a lemonade but that Sidir and his mother would shoo me out.

I especially liked walking round Bombay in the evening and night. I would spend the daytime hot and footsore, come back to the flat for a cool shower and something to eat then go out wandering again until late.

There was a boy I met on a regular basis. He was about nine or ten, with roughly shorn, glossy black hair, barefoot, in shorts and a ragged vest. Not far from the Gateway to India, he habituated a street corner which was a sort of hub from which I would venture in different directions in my exploration of the city, so I saw him frequently. He was not a beggar but a tout.

'Sahib want drugs, girls? Nice girls? Sahib follow me...'. I always told him no, and by about our fourth encounter he knew me and would just skip in the air and give me a wave.

I was out late one night and had been around a street market enjoying the atmosphere of the Tilly lamps hissing brightly over stalls selling sweets and herbs, medicines, fabrics, jewellery and an abundance of things entirely unknown to me. In the half dark, a white European can mingle more invisibly than during the day, especially in a crowd – free to edge between people to peer at the goods on a stall, close enough to catch a tone of voice or understand what has made people laugh.

I had stopped in the market, puzzled by a smell which had a connection to something familiar but which I could not place. I stared at the ground trying to find the link. The smell was that of coke burning in a brazier; above its white hot coals was a wide shallow dish in which nuts were being roasted in sugar. I wandered slowly and aimlessly, digging into my mind. Then it came to me. When I was a boy of about five or six, we lived in a house in front of which, for a period of some weeks, major road works were being carried out. In those days, in the mid 1950s, a small corrugated iron hut no higher than five feet and a little longer in length was the sleeping accommodation for a night watchman, a common sight around Aberdeen. Inside the hut, along one side of its length there was a narrow bench covered in rough hessian sacking, and by its arched entrance was usually a brazier identical to the one I had been standing near. On the glowing coals in the cold Aberdeen nights, the watchman would warm his hands and boil a big black kettle for his tea.

The gassy odour of the burning coke was a smell I had entirely forgotten, and something in the success of having located the memory gave me a surge of pleasure as though I had found something homely and familiar. In the same moment, I had the understanding that a part of India was still mediaeval in ways that Europeans of earlier centuries would have found familiar. Perhaps my mind had scratched the memory of a painting in a gallery, a street scene by Breugal in which a fire at night illuminates the faces of the town's citizens gathered round it in the darkness. In great and high spirits, I realised it was late and time to find my way back home.

I would often get lost in Bombay, but with a general sense of heading east and finding the sea, I always managed to find my way, and always by foot. By the time I came to my familiar 'hub' it was late, and there, again, I encountered the young boy who would wave to me. He waved again and came over to me.

'Girls? Drugs Sahib?' he asked, and in his voice was irony rather than enquiry.

And I said yes.

'Drugs?' he said, taken aback.

'No, girls.'

He looked at me with a quizzical look for a moment, then jumped in the air.

'Sahib follow me... come, come, follow...' He grabbed my wrist and pulled me away.

An 18-year-old male, suddenly freed from the social and parental fold, and who has been mighty struck with the gorgeous beauty of Indian girls and women, is a sure candidate for temptation. Always ahead of me, the boy trotted through streets which I was a little familiar with from my explorations – and which later became unknown and strange – and which became alleys rather than streets – and which became darker and meaner and smellier. I was completely lost and it was dark, but my earthy temptations drove me on. The boy beckoned me.

'Just further Sahib... come, come... you see.'

We turned into an alleyway which led, maze-like, into a series of dark lanes in which I lost my sense of place and direction as well as my sense of being in control of events. I was on the point of abandoning everything when the boy stopped by a gate set into a high mud brick wall.

'Here Sahib... in here, come, girls, you go... go, come...'

I opened the gate and I could see a flight of rickety steep wooden stairs immediately before me which led to a door at first floor level and which was dimly illuminated by a single bare bulb above it. Behind me, the boy let out a loud whistle and threw stones or something at the general direction of the door. After a minute or so, the door opened and a man appeared; the man shouted something and the boy ran off. I swallowed hard.

'Come up, come…' said the man.

I hesitated at the bottom of the stairs.

'Beautiful girls upstairs sir… waiting your pleasure sir… come.'

I still hesitated.

'No afraid sir,' he said beckoning me with his hand, 'you see very beautiful girls… many.'

He edged backwards and partly disappeared inside, leaving the door open. I went up the stairs, my heart thump thumping.

I came directly into a dim and dirty cream-painted room at whose centre was an examination couch of the sort you see in hospital clinics, high and on a bent tubular metal base and with a thin mattress on top, this being covered in a green floral pressed plastic; it was torn at the side and a bulb of cotton wadding spewed out like a wound. There was nothing else in the room except one ceiling bulb above the couch. To my right and left were two doors, and the man stood by the door on my left. He was a short, stocky, thick-built man with a pock-marked face and stubby, spiky, grey ginger hair; he wore a filthy unbuttoned shirt, baggy pantaloons and sandals.

'See my girls… come,' he said turning and clapping his hands, 'such beautiful girls.'

Despite the lack of puffed silk cushions, gold tazzas brimming with pomegranates and tessellated bell pulls, I thought the clapping of his hands was a nice touch – just what you'd expect as the prelude to the delights of the harem and just exactly as anticipated from puberty onwards. Doesn't the eunuch clapping his hands just as the lute player begins his soft melodies signify the prelude to the entrance of the girls?

From the door behind him and on my left entered four women who positioned themselves in slow procession behind the medical examination couch. Three were Indian and, to my very great surprise, one was white. They were all aged more than a hundred, they were all fat and short and, to me, untouchable, ugly and repulsive. I knew instantly I was in trouble and my body went into protective mode – my limbs froze and the adrenalin surged through the skeleton in my chest in a full pounding spate of fear.

The man smiled at me and the women smiled at me, coyly, horribly and the only person in the room who was not smiling was me.

'Oh…' was all I could say.

There followed a silence in which the atmosphere tumbled in on itself. I was the first person to sense how acutely it had changed.

'Look,' I began, 'I, eh… I'm sorry, I don't think I can… I mean to say…'

As I spoke a staccato of incoherent utterances I could sense the atmosphere in the room becoming what my first fears had anticipated. The smiles on the faces of the women withdrew slowly and, as one, they looked towards the man.

'What trouble?' he said, taking a pace towards me, 'you no like beautiful girls? Fine young Sahib likes beautiful girls yes-no? My dollycats?'

'Oh yes,' I said, 'of course they are beautiful, but you see. Well, but…'

'You no want fucky fucky dollycats?'

The man took another pace towards me and the girls began to edge to their right towards the still open door from whence they came.

'You no want fucky dollycat girls?' said the man, his voice deepening as creases of his frown became dark and visible, 'but these are beautiful, beautiful fucky girls. They do any dirty thing you want… come.'

'No!' I shouted, 'I don't want to fucky fucky these… these…' and I just couldn't find the right word.

'Then fucky this!' roared the man, drawing a knife from somewhere behind his back. As he lunged forward with the blade pointing at me, the women screeched and instinctively formed into a single huddle, screaming as they all collapsed sideways into a heap on the floor.

I turned, wrenched open the door behind me and jumped clean out into the air, the fear of a blood red knife in my back propelling me like a charge of exploding gunpowder. Such was my panic that I missed the top steps and landed with a great painful thud halfway down the flight of stairs. I flung myself, half falling, half crouched, flailing down the stairs like a monkey, three and four steps at a time, yanked open the gate with an almighty bang, and ran and ran and ran into the dark for my life.

I was utterly lost in a labyrinth of alleys, and in that disorientating maze I could find no sense of east or west or how on earth to find my way back to safety. Eventually I came to a main road, clambering over a fence and through a deep ditch to get to it. The money I had planned to spend on a transport of earthly delight went on a long taxi ride instead – and in the circumstances, this provided more of a relief. I let myself into the flat very quietly and crept into bed, my ankle still rankling with pain.

By way of avoiding any thoughts about my narrow escape the night before, I busied myself the next morning with the serious matter of getting to Delhi and making contact with Mrs Mehta, my contact who was to give me details of where in the Himalayas I was to work. Sidir went off to the train station to get timetables for me, and my hostess arrived back from her trip to Madras.

On the afternoon of Madelaine's return, we went to the Willingdon Club and caught up with all the family news. Her late husband had been my eldest brother's godfather due to a family connection that went back to the War. I noticed that Madame referred to 'the War' frequently and always with an underlying affection.

'But that was before the War…' she would say, or, 'well of course, the War changed everything.'

She had adjusted to being a widow with difficulty, I think, but she had never come to terms with the changes that occurred to India after Independence.

'It used to be… to be so nice,' she said wistfully.

My mother and father had met in India – he a young army surgeon, she a nurse. In the operating theatre of their first day working together, he had thrown a kidney at her with the words '…catch that', and marriage, three boys and a girl were the result, I being the third of the boys.

'Of course David is in Calcutta,' Madame said, speaking of my elder brother.

'Yes, he came out a few weeks ago to work with Brothers to Medicine.'

'Really,' she said, trying to find some reference point that would give the information its proper social import, 'I don't know them. Will you be meeting up with him?'

'I haven't any plans, but I hope I can,' I said. She snapped her fingers at the one waiter who was far away ,who was busy serving somebody else and the only waiter not watching her in anticipation of her command.

'Well, you should,' she said, holding out her glass for a refill, 'families ought to stick together, you know. Gin with ice and Angostura… and plenty lemon.'

I swam in the swimming pool, and my emergence from its cooling delicious clean waters was awaited by elderly men in crisp white mess jackets attending with clean folded towels, iced drinks and a choice of skin tonics. These waiters and servants met all requests with a resigned willingness to please. In the changing rooms I caught some of the conversations between some of the younger members coming from the squash courts and thought that perhaps I was in an RAF officers mess during 'the War'.

'Good show old man…' and, 'those chaps…' and, 'I say Jupta, that was a cracking good shot!'

When I got back to the shaded gins where Madame waited, I checked the wine list to see if ginger beer was available in measures of lashings.

On my last day in Bombay, Madelaine took me shopping and most of the time was spent at a very upper crust chemist where she accumulated a large pile of medicines that she assured me were the necessary and usual accompaniments to travel in India. Water sterilisation and salt tablets, quinine, calamine lotion, anti-mosquito candles and lotions, pills and mixtures whose purposes would become known to me in good time.

'And I shall need two of your biggest boxes of Enterovioform,' she concluded to the chemist, and added to me in a confidential tone, 'and these are likely to become your best friend, because you will very likely have a runny bottom and the Indians have only a vague notion of defecating hygienically.'

Such was the volume of items to be packed for my journey that exceeded what my own case could accommodate that Madelaine forced upon me a small tartan suitcase to take the excess. I was not keen on this because I had sworn that travelling easily is best achieved with just one piece of luggage.

'Nonsense,' exclaimed Madelaine, 'the whole point of being in India is that there are people to carry things. What on earth has that father of yours taught you? Don't forget where you come from!' Madelaine's final contribution to my travelling effects was a tin of Del Monte asparagus spears. Offering this, she said, 'Michael, you may think this is an odd gift, but the day will come when you will bless the name of Madelaine Mary Colquhonnie because of it.' She seemed to attach a greater appreciation to the asparagus than I could understand, so I took it and expressed my sincere thanks without really understanding why it was such a big deal. In addition, I was very concerned that my luggage was becoming too numerous and heavy.

Of the experiences that complete the education of an adult, being a waiter and living in a squalid bedsit in a big city are the top two; a candidate for third place would be to travel for a few days on a train in India. In this circumstance, you are chin-close to humanity at the widest point of the pyramid of mankind. A rugby scrum is not as tough a place as the platform for the Bombay Delhi train, a sauna at maximum heat is not as hot, and the sinking, tilting deck of the Titanic not so fraught.

Despite the protestations of my hostess that such a move would not be proper, I insisted on paying for my own fare to Delhi, and by that insistence wedded my mode of travel to the third class. I had come to like my hostess more and more and regretted that I had been hasty and inaccurate in my first judgement of her. She was deeply disappointed that 'one of us' should travel with the hoi polloi. Like many of her ilk, she had little comprehension of life's choices being restricted by a shortage of cash and I had to pretend that I actually wanted to travel third class, 'to have the experience'.

'Well, so be it dear boy,' she said evidently exasperated, 'but you can upgrade any time by slipping the ticket collectors a few rupees; 10 should do it and don't go above 20. When they take the money, don't say anything, just follow them and you'll be shown to a higher class. Don't accept anything other than air conditioning. And for heaven's sake don't drink any of the drinks offered to you at station stops, they're all crawling with unspeakable filth.'

With these last words, the train whistle blew a series of piercing blasts, steam hissed and the engine huffed and we felt a series of violent jolts into motion; I waved goodbye to Bombay and my last contact with a safe and secure world.

2

Dark doubts in Delhi, but the Himalayas shine

THE TRAIN DREW ITSELF SLOWLY THROUGH DUSTY GREY SUBURBS and industrial zones of Bombay and gradually gathered temperature and pace through the heat wave of the day; the light was glaringly harsh, the sweat was oozing through every pore and the carriage became increasingly like a bulging suitcase as it filled with a crush of people, luggage, bundles, baskets and animals. I wondered how long the three young men hanging on to the door handles of the outside of the carriage door would last, and simultaneously understood why Madame had insisted we get to the train two hours at least before departure time. The three men lasted several hours, and then changed places with three others who were sitting on the roof.

That trip was the first of many train journeys in India. Eventually I became used to being stared at, but it was unnerving at first. I was, after all, a young European in jeans, a white shirt and linen jacket – there weren't many of me about.

The journey to Delhi was long and hot, and when we stopped at stations the carriages were assailed by sellers of fruit, juices, teas and sweets clamouring at the train's open windows and doors. Madame's caution about drinking unknown liquids rang in my ears, but I had run out of water and succumbed to fruit juices, arguing to myself that they, surely, would be safe. Madame was right, however, and I took permanent position near the toilet door. I watched the landscape race by, and when I could, I would stick my head out of a door window to get a blast of doubly hot smoky air: sultry, heavy and mixed with the coal smoke and dust belching from the engine pulling us ahead. The landscape, particularly its palm trees, awoke a deep-seated memory of 'far off lands', a phrase which often began the bedtime stories my mother used to read to me. I slipped into a mental whirlpool that drew me from my real surroundings through some kind of insubstantial tunnel into the very words and text of a book that now possessed me as a character.

In the books and comic annuals I had as a boy, there were often black line drawings of characters inserted into the text as illustrations to the story. At that moment I was reminded of 'Akbar the Terrible', dressed in a bejewelled turban and baggy silk pantaloons, one hand upon his hip and one holding a vicious looking scimitar.

In the dust-grained air of the Indian plains, which faded into vast great distances, it was not difficult to daydream that there were ivory smooth palaces nearby within whose exotic arched battlements were still being enacted intrigues and dramas more fitting to the 16th century than the 20th.

Whereas Bombay has a city centre and shore front that is dark, solid and old, and whose circumference fades imperceptibly into a dis-organised rabble of dirty habitations and streets, Delhi is altogether more dazzling white, bleached concrete and breeze block. There are strident glass-fronted hotels and office buildings, which pierce the horizon and declare the city to be modern and outward-looking and less burdened with a past – despite its colonial leftovers. Without any knowledge of the city, I had to resort to a taxi to find Dr Calder and the seminary building where he lived. The taxi deposited me outside a severe, slated, grey stone building sheltered behind a high formal wall at whose centre was a forbidding wooden gate. At the gate's side there was an old brass bell pull, a good heave of which produced the sound of a bell ringing in some far inside place.

It was himself that came to greet me; not at all the severe black suited gent on the boat, but a relaxed 60-year-old in tatty gardening trousers, an old Hawaiian shirt and a pair of pruning shears in one hand. With a warm welcome, he quickly showed me to my quarters and pointed to a shower room down the corridor.

'I should think you could do with that,' he said, 'it's the first thing I always do after a journey. Once you've relaxed a bit, just come to the common room and I'll be along; or if you can find the garden, I'll be there. The students are on holiday at the moment, so you have the place more or less to yourself.'

And so began a relaxed few days with a man curious as to my plans and my motivations. I would have the place to myself sometimes. On the chapel harmonium, I would repeat the one and only short passage of Bach I could play.

Most of my time was spent in tracking down Mrs Mehta, who was my contact to the Tibetans. With Dr Calder's help, I found where she lived on the city map and on my first afternoon after my arrival in Delhi I went there. Mrs Mehta lived in considerable style in a sprawling big bungalow set in spacious, well kept gardens; but though she lived there, she was not there – nor, according to the lady who said she was her daughter, was she likely to be there for some weeks. I explained my predicament and asked that Mrs Mehta be contacted at the earliest opportunity so that I might learn where I was to go in the Himalayas, when, and to whom I should present myself once there.

The lady I spoke to gave me the undertaking that she would convey this information to her mother and gave me her phone number with the suggestion that I should phone in two days. This I did, but there had been no contact with Mrs Mehta. On the fourth day, I phoned again and was asked to come back to the residence, where the information required would be available. I went immediately.

I was invited in and given a large white envelope on whose front was the imprint of the 'Express Sunway Insurance Company'. There was nothing inside it, but on the back was written an address – The Tibetan Camp, Palabir, Kulu Valley, Himachel Pradesh. And that was all.

'That's where you have to go,' I was told.

'But when?'

'I don't know.'

'And who should I see when I get there?'

'Mum didn't say.'

'Is there a phone number for up there?'

'I really couldn't say, I shouldn't think so, not up there.'

'Did she say anything about pay, or if I can get some expenses?'

'No, she didn't say anything about that either.'

'Did your mother say anything else? Did she have any message for me?'

'Yes, she said to say good luck and to get in touch next time you're in Delhi.'

'Well, thank you.'

I left with the envelope carefully folded in my pocket and went straight back to the seminary, perplexed that the sum total of paperwork supporting my voyage to India, and my commitment to give some time out of my life, amounted to an address hastily written on the back of a discarded envelope.

It was a tricky time. That evening with my host, we poured over maps to find out where it was I was supposed to go.

'Bloody hell,' said Dr Calder with uncharacteristic worldliness, 'that's *way* up in the Himalayas: you'll be at about 2,000 meters there!'

'What does that mean?' I asked.

'Freezing cold for one thing,' he answered, 'and for another, very isolated from the look of it.' I stared at the map. The town where I was going lay in a small heart-shaped extension of territory that protruded like an extra organ from the far north-west of India, almost to the border with Pakistan to its west and close to the border with China to its north. 'You'll get the mainline train to Pathankot, then there'll be the hill railway up into the mountains proper to the Kulu Valley, and then bus I suppose. Is anyone going to meet you?'

'No, I don't expect so,' I answered, 'but maybe. I just don't know if Mrs Mehta has organised anything.'

'Well let's hope she has. Got everything you need? Water tablets? Enterovioform?'

'Yes, my friend in Bombay got me everything. She even gave me a tin of asparagus, don't know why though.'

Dr Calder laughed. 'Sensible lady!' he said, 'which reminds me, I have a little present for you too.'

He went to his desk, took something from a drawer and handed it to me.

'Not quite in the league of asparagus I'm afraid, but you should keep these for some special occasion.' He handed me a tin of Libby's peach slices.

Before leaving Delhi, Dr Calder insisted I leave all manner of addresses and contacts with him.

'You'll be fine, Mike, but it's best I know how to contact your people if needs be.'

I was suddenly troubled at the prospect of travelling that far with so little money; I was worried that if I went there and found conditions utterly impossible, I would barely have enough funds to get back and would have to scream for help from all and sundry – in a place where screaming for help might be unheard. Such an outcome would be a blow to my self-esteem as well as an extreme botheration to those I would have to seek help from. It would be humiliating and shameful. Because it would make me look ill prepared and entirely the daft laddie, I had not ventured nor hinted at my precarious financial position to Dr Calder, so he assumed that money was not an issue and his advice to me was on that basis.

'I think you should go,' he said. 'If it's really untenable, you'll have had a good trip and I can ask a few people here to see if there's any other voluntary work you could do. I'm pretty sure I can fix you up with something and you're welcome to come back here for a while anyway. The students won't be back for another three weeks, and even after that we usually have room for a guest or two.'

I was unwilling to admit to him that I had assumed before making my trip that somehow I would get my keep and enough for minimal life from my efforts, because that had been hinted at in Mrs Mehta's first letter.

'Give it a day's thought,' said Dr Calder, and we left it at that.

That night, I turned over all the considerations in my mind and discovered that for the first time since I had the idea of 'working overseas', I was frightened. I could not gauge the degree of fear; I just knew I was facing a moment when some kind of determination was required, and that this was unexpected and troubling. Up to this point, there had been an unclouded simplicity in my leaving Aberdeen and my arriving in India: it had felt like the best holiday ever – I would go to x, I would do y, I would achieve A and B and C, and then it would end and I would glide seamlessly onto the next chapter. In this negative mental territory, I felt I had been fickle and light headed; first it was the Solomon Islands, then it was driving ambulances across Africa, now here was India. I was confronted with my own troubled reflection.

But I had to go, and deep down, I knew it all along. I bade my farewells.

About six hours from Delhi by train, en route to the Punjab and Pathankot, the temperature and the landscape became more comfortable as they became cooler and greener and hillier; where once there were vistas of dry dusty plains, here the rain fell on hillsides brushed with dark forests quilted into a patchwork of rich, neat fields, and my subconscious self felt easier at the sight of some familiar species of trees. But though the physical landscape was more temperately familiar, it became more alien in other ways and felt strange and far from home. It was quieter, too, in every sense. The villages and towns were poor and tumbledown; when the train stopped it was at small stations which sometimes were no more than a shed by the track. As the afternoon wore on, people drifted off the train and it seemed fewer were getting on. The train was getting slower and one could sense the engine huffing and puffing up the now steep inclines as we negotiated valleys tucked between high hills and mountains, and occasionally I had a glimpse of high snowed peaks in the far distance that foretold of the looming Himalayan ranges. I had left Delhi in the raging heat but Patankhot was almost cold and clouds had darkened the sky.

It was mid-afternoon when I arrived in Pathankot and I quickly ascertained when the next train would leave for Baijnath on the narrow gauge railway that winds its way through the Kulu and adjoining valleys. I had an hour to kill and wandered round, keeping near to the station, fearful that I would miss my train. Pathankot is an army town with more men in uniform visible than civilians; I knew it was one of the largest military bases in Asia. I was regarded, closely, with a neutral curiosity everywhere I went. I had my first taste of mountain Indian tea, which is made with boiled milk, and I nearly threw up. Up to this point, I had had no insurmountable problems in explaining my needs in English, sometimes with the help of a gesture: English is a universal second language to Hindi and widely spoken. But now my English was met with shakes of the head and looks of puzzlement and I had to resort to a basic pidgin and clear, theatrical gestures to get any meaning communicated. That way, it's not difficult to get a cup of tea.

By four o'clock on that gloomy rainy day, my mood was lifted by the sight of the small gauge train which was to take me further north and into the Himalayas proper. At first view, it seemed impossible that such a tiny train was a real thing – it looked more like a seaside miniature railway than a workaday transport capable of hauling carriages up a mountain. The impression of being a toy train was emphasised by the childish cream and baby blue of the carriages, as if the colours had been chosen by children and painted in a cosy English nursery on a blustery, wet afternoon. Even the engine seemed to have a face which at once conveyed both determination and, by the big buffers at its cheeks, a hint of a dimpled smile.

The misgivings that this quietly wheezing contraption provoked gave way to a sudden pleasure, because here was the first truly different thing from home. An antiquated object that had about it something of the fairground, the penny in the slot automaton which, above all, was a survivor that, had it been in Scotland, would long ago have been scrapped in favour of a characterless improvement. Its very existence triggered the immediate desire to share its discovery, as though I were a time traveller who had wandered accidentally into a past age and who was now anxious to convey the delight of what I had seen.

I heaved my cases into one of the carriages and sat down to wait for the train's departure to Baijnath, from whence I was to get a bus. At last, the engine tooted its high pitched whistle, and with an impressive show of steam hissing and smoke belching, the train pulled out of Pathankot and trundled easily out of the station as if to show me that, yes, it was perfectly capable of motion and that it had climbed its climb a thousand times and more. The drabness of Pathankot was left behind and the track weaved its way into woods and hills, climbing all the time. It slid seamlessly past precipitous gorges and rock cuttings, below which were sheer vertiginous drops of many hundreds of feet. There, the streams and rivers far below were but narrow threads of grey and white.

The air became cooler and somehow, contrary to the fact, more dense. The passengers of the train were quite different in character to those I had encountered further south. Their faces were tougher and more wrinkled, their clothes were woolly-thick and coarse, and their manners those of rural rather than urban people – expert in not looking at you and anxious not to offend. They were shorter and stockier, altogether tougher and more weather beaten; some of their items of clothing, such as caps and shawls, scarves and socks, were woven with a finely stitched floral work which was skilled and intricate. Some of the men wore what looked like coils of thick brown woollen rope wound diagonally around shoulder to waist. Though the light was a flat grey, now and again a close vista of a mighty snow-covered rock peak would emerge then disappear as the train puffed around the circumference of mountain spur and plunged from tunnel to steep cliff edge back into the dark of a deep-shadowed cutting. Sometimes the train was so slow and laboured, it would have been possible to step off it and walk comfortably alongside at an easy pace.

I had asked the ticket collector to make sure that I got off at Baijnath, and as he approached me with the indication we were near my destination the train slowed and stopped at a tiny platform. It huffed and sighed heavily and slowly, like a beast freed from strenuous exertion. I lifted my two suitcases out of the train and left them in the station hall under the eye of the man behind the ticket kiosk while I had a wander round to find the bus station.

Baijnath is typical of many small settlements in the foothills of the Himalayas; there is a small, narrow main street framed on either side by a jumble of low buildings made from crumbly mud or, occasionally, stone blocks that once were painted – they are mostly white, but some are a faded blue or orange or brown.

There are a few shops that have goods outside them – small cylindrical tin barrels of cooking oil, big square tins of fat or flour – all of them gaudily labelled in bright oranges and yellows. Some of the shops are only about four feet wide. An open gutter runs down the centre of the dusty street and some hens and a few goats wander about. I am once again viewed with intense puzzlement by the inhabitants and I am evidently a prize curiosity.

The bus station was at one end of the one main street, and there I had to find out how to get to my final destination. The light was that of a fading late afternoon and I brandished my envelope with the address on it to a group of drivers hunched on the ground. One took the envelope and passed it to another. He pointed to the bus beside which they are grouped, and there were already some people waiting inside. I pointed to my watch.

'Ten...' he says, 'ten times time.' He handed me back the envelope. The bus was an ancient Mercedes painted bright yellow, it's windscreen decked with a fringe of faded plastic marigolds.

I thanked him and went briskly back to the station and was back with my luggage in a few minutes. The group of drivers had dispersed and the bus's engine was now running. I boarded with my big case, but the driver at the wheel inside shook his head vigourously as I clambered up the step: 'No, no... not!' he said, and pointed up. 'Upsides!' he said. I dragged my case back out and he led me to the back of the bus and pointed to a tiny ladder that led to the roof.

'Upsides... up, up!' he said, pointing to the roof. He climbed up the ladder and I handed up my big case, which he flung roughly ahead of him to land among a heap of cloth tied bundles and trunks already there.

Back inside, the driver retook his seat and I showed him the address; he nodded and we negotiated the fare with fingers, nods and raised eyebrows. I was the last on board before the bus set off in the twilight. As the twilight became darkness, it became very cold. The bus weaved its way along a twisting, narrow, steeply-climbing road which clung to steep hillsides and ravines; its headlights would reveal steel protective barriers at the road verges and, from my train journey, I could imagine the drops which lay behind them. Although I was seeing my surroundings, my mind was racing with a mix of excitement and anxiety.

It was getting to be night, the air and the bus were cold and I was shivering; I am happy enough to approach people for directions or help at any time, but I wondered what I would do if I was dropped somewhere with no idea how to proceed from there. And that's about what happened about an hour later, after the bus had struggled upwards along a very narrow twisting and winding road.

The bus stopped and the driver motioned me that this was the place to get off; he got out and went to the back of the bus and climbed onto the roof. I went to the steps expecting to be handed down the suitcases, but he dispensed with this and threw the things onto the ground at my feet. He got back into his driving seat, there was a hiss of compressed air as the door closed behind him, and he drove off into the night.

I had feared that I would be abandoned in the middle of nowhere in the dark, but the bus had stopped outside a settlement of some three or four small houses. One of the houses had a light above a door, so I went and knocked, ready with my envelope and its address.

An elderly man came to the door, but drew back when he saw me. I said, 'Please sir...' and held out the envelope. He looked at it for a second, and then he passed in front of me and motioned me to follow.

'Tibet' he said.

He led me about 50 yards back down the road from his house and pointed first at a path which made its way through rickety outbuildings near to where we were standing. Then he pointed again as if to signify that I should go further back down the road. I gestured that I did not understand what he meant and he shook his head and pointed again energetically to the path. He said something which I did not understand and he left me and scurried back to his house.

Since leaving Aberdeen, I was facing my most difficult moment. The sky was the hue of a black-coated blue foil, luminous and lighter at the horizon but getting darker by the minute. And what got to me was the silence; very suddenly it was eerily quiet. There had been an accompaniment of noise and bustle from the moment my train had left Aberdeen; the ship reverberated, Bombay was hectic with people and traffic, bustling and shoving. The train to Delhi was a rattling, rocking, noisy journey, the toy train had puffed and clanked, the bus from Pathankot had whined and grunted and here, in the deepening gloom in a strange mountain place, it was silent. I felt alone and fearful.

I could picture my geographical location by remembering the map which Dr Calder and I had bent over – the camp being at a spot among wavy contours of buff brown and close to the whites which denoted the snowy high peaks, sparse of towns and villages and threaded with but few roads. It seemed unreasonably the case that there was not a phone nor even phone lines, my sense of self importance somehow expecting that there should have been one of those emergency roadside boxes that sit on poles and are in metal boxes with 'S.O.S.' written on them. And although silence does not echo, it felt so profoundly quiet that there was a sense of a mountainous, heavenly vastness in its extent and a feeling that any slight noise was a disturbance sensed by something looming and giant; something that did not wish to be disturbed.

I had no option but to follow the path. My first task was to gather my two suitcases and I got out my anorak because it was very cold – up to then I had just been wearing a thin jacket. I picked up the two cases and headed into the gloom that just barely revealed the path which lay before me. First, there was a strong smell of cattle as I passed through a small patch of open ground, walled on one side by a shape which I couldn't quite make out. The path then meandered through clumps of bushes and low trees on an upward incline that led me to a small area of flat open ground, ahead of which was a field of maize. The maize stalks were about four or five feet high and the path was visible as a dark gash that ran ahead of me and to the left hand side of the field. Before entering the maize field I paused to change the suitcases from one hand to another and cursed the weight of the big one, wondering why it had been necessary to take with me a large collection of taped music recorded onto big spools, four posters of Picasso's Don Quixote carefully wrapped in a thick cardboard tube, hiking boots, a radio, a camera, the Oxford Book of English Verse, a year's clothes and ridiculously, a tin of asparagus and a tin of peaches. I set off, the heavy case still biting into my hand. The sky had become a deep dark navy blue and my surroundings were shapes and forms of anthracite black. By raising my eyes to the sky, my lower field of vision could make out the path and I plodded on as my eyes became accustomed to the dark. The thought came to me that if something were to happen to me, the small headline in the Aberdeen newspaper, 'The Press & Journal', might read 'N.E. Man's Skeleton Found in Remote Himalayan Valley. City Mourns.'

I recalled what a joke my school friends and I had when we made up headlines for the local newspaper, which always described anyone from the North East of Scotland as the 'N.E. Man'. The paper was parochial in the extreme and an Aberdeen legend was that that its headline reporting the loss of the Titanic, declared… 'N.E. Man Dies at Sea.' below which, as the grudgingly reluctant afterthought, the line '1,200 Other Lives Lost'.

This thought cheered me up and changed my mood – I knew I had to go on in the hope of finding, finally, that which had inspired my whole trip in the first place.

The path through the field rose steadily, and after about a quarter of an hour I could hear water flowing near my left and I sensed the ground sloping down towards it. At the same moment I heard a distinct rustling and a heavy snorting noise on my right. I dropped my cases to turn and to find out what was coming near me and I could just make out a tall dark animal shape some three or four feet to my right. It was heading towards me and its breathing became clearer and more alarming. I yelled out, jumped in the air with my arms waving and challenged it head on with a lunge. Whatever it was, it paused and seemed to sway this way and that before turning away to crash through the maize back from where it had appeared. As I took a pace backwards in relief, I stumbled against a large protruding boulder behind me and fell headlong into a stream a few feet below my left. I lay motionless for a few moments, sensing a sharp grazing pain in my arm and the growing sensation of the water soaking my back and left side. As the cold shocked me, I scrambled up to my feet and clawed my way back up the sides of the ditch. I retrieved my cases, picked my way back over the ditch and up a steep bank. As I heaved myself to its top, I saw a light about 300 yards ahead of me. The path ended as it met a wide dirt track which was on my left; though it had quite a steep incline, it was much easier going. I carried on up the track and because my eyes were now fully adjusted to the dark, I could see my way without difficulty. As I neared the light, the track's incline flattened to a much gentler slope and I began to see many lights around me in the middle distance. The sight comforted me in the realisation that I was not entirely alone in a deserted world. As I walked wearily up the final 100 yards towards the light, I could see on my left a great collection of dim lights, the glow of some seven or eight fires and some moving lanterns – this must surely be the camp.

Directly ahead of me was the single electric bulb which had been my beacon; it shone from the wall of a building that was now immediately before me. There was an area of flat concrete in front of it, about the size of a tennis court, and the building was flat fronted, about two stories high. The lower two thirds were made of brick; the upper gable third was whitewashed. It had the appearance of a small warehouse or factory and the light was mounted above a small door on the building's right hand side; there were two larger, sliding doors to its left and far left. I went cautiously to the small door, put down my cases, rubbed my aching hands and brushed the mud on my jeans.

I knocked on the door and waited. There was no response, so after a couple of minutes in which the cold seemed to grip me, I pulled its latch and the door opened inwards. Before me, I could just make out that I was in a large high and dark space which smelled strongly of tea and at the centre of which was a high, pointed mound of something that seemed vaguely green and leafy. From the right side of this mound I could see a corridor leading away to the rear of the building, visible because there was a blade of light coming from what must have been a room to its right side. I edged into the dim entrance and skirted the mound, making out that it was a huge heap of leaves. I went down the corridor, cautiously through the gloom, towards the light. I came to the door, which was very slightly open. I stood motionless for a moment, and then I plucked up my courage, knocked on the door and pushed it gently open.

'Hello,' I said.

The room was about 10 feet square, with a low ceiling – the upper half was painted gloss brown and the lower a dull matt green; at its centre was a rough small table and seated at it were two European men. They had been eating but froze when I walked into the room.

The man on my right was about thirty or thirty-five, heavy-set, with long grey white hair tied in a bun at the back of his head. His nose was bulbous and his cheeks pudgy; he wore thick rimless glasses, one arm of which was held together by thick and dirty, vaguely pink, Elastoplast. His eyes were watery and he wore a thick heavy black robe. The hand which held a chappati close to his open mouth was rough and calloused and it stopped in surprise.

The other man was younger, in his early twenties. He had fine dark hair cut very short, with a shield-shaped face that terminated in a narrow aristocratic chin. He had a wispy small moustache and his very fair skin was rough with unshaved stubble. He was wearing a blue polo neck jumper, and draped over his shoulders was a brown blanket.

'I'm Mike Hendry,' I said.

'Sorry?' said the man on my right.

'Mike Hendry… from Aberdeen? Mrs Mehta arranged for me to work here?'

The two looked at each other, then back at me. The one to my right spoke again.

'No. Nope, I've never heard of a Mrs Mehta and I've been here six months. What did you say your name was?'

'Mike… Mike Hendry.'

'Sorry, never heard of you. Ross, have you ever heard of a Mrs Mehta?

'No,' said the other in reply, then to me, 'and you've come here to work?'

'Yes, from Aberdeen.'

'*Aberdeen*?!!' Both men received this information as though Aberdeen was a recently discovered human settlement on Mars.

'Well, I'm Ross and that ugly mug is Hugh,' said the one on my left. As I leant forward to shake their hands, they got up from their chairs.

'Well, you'd better get a seat. We'll have some tea in a minute. I'm afraid there's not much food about, you hungry? Hugh, tea up!'

'Yes,' I said, 'haven't eaten anything since Delhi except sticky cakes.'

'Got the squits?' asked Hugh.

'Yes, and how.'

'Join the club. Got it all the time here. Bring any Entrovioform?'

'In my case.'

'Appreciate a couple if you can.'

'Sure.'

'Come up on the train?' asked Ross.

'Yes, Delhi-Pathankot, Pathankot-Baijnath then a bus to… I don't know the name of the place I was dropped near here.'

'Ahju…' said Hugh, 'arsehole of the world. How come you're wet?'

'Oh, I fell in a stream walking up from the main road.'

'There is no stream on the way up,' said Ross handing me an empty tin mug.

'Yes there is, about half way up the path from the village. Nearly got breathed on by a huge cow or something as well… in that field of maize or whatever.'

'You didn't come up the track?'

'Only later, near the top.'

'And this animal, big was it?'

'Yes,' I said taking a seat at the table, 'it did seem to be, for a cow.'

'Here, sorry there's no milk, and you'll be pleased to know that your cow might have been a volunteer-eating brown bear.'

'Oh Lord, yes,' rejoined Hugh, 'it could have been; yes, it might have been the bear.'

'Well, Mike from Aberdeen, you may just have had the luckiest escape of your life. Dangerous animal that. Come to think of it, I wouldn't want to be that close to one of those bullocks, never mind a bloody bear. Cheers.'

Very suddenly, I felt an immense relief. I had reached the destination which had taken so many forms in my imagination over a period of months and I felt safe and secure. Enervated by the tea and by a fulsome sense of achievement, I had a million questions to ask and Ross and Hugh were happy to answer them.

Ross had been at the camp six months, Hugh for four. Ross was from Shropshire, son of a farming family. Hugh was not forthcoming about his past other than, vaguely, that he had been in London.

And so I had arrived.

I spent my first night in a sleeping bag swaddled and buried deep in the mound of tea leaves in the hall, and though my mind was swirling with excitement, I fell immediately and soundly asleep.

3

The Tibetan camp and its people – their health, its doctor

I AWOKE EARLY AND SAW SUNLIGHT FILTERING THROUGH THE GAPS of the tea factory's front door. I dressed, and with a prickling anticipation stepped outside into the quartz cold air. Before me was a range of round, peaked foothills which receded away into a great and far distance; glowing mist was lazing in their steep valleys. To my left, the sun had risen to just the summits of the hills and was outlining their patchy forests and catching the top layer mist to create sky-lakes of luminous light. I took a pace forward in wonderment, quite lost in the moment, then, almost absentmindedly, I turned to see what the sun was striking behind me. In a sensation that was like vertigo, I reeled backwards in shock as the true Himalayan Mountains swooped up immediately before me as if from the soles of my feet, through my bowels and into my tilted, dizzy head. The sight of their touchable closeness, their God-sized confrontational bulk and their astonishing sky-poking heights, was such that I stopped breathing.

'Not bad eh?' said Ross, beside me suddenly.

'Great God,' I gasped. It was all I could say.

After tea and chappatis, Ross volunteered to show me round the camp.

'That's the Rimpoche's house,' said Ross, showing me a small, very English looking post-war bungalow just behind the tea factory. 'The Rimpoche is the head man, the senior monk and the undisputed authority here. He's away in Dharamsala for a few days at some big pow-wow with the Dalai Lama. You know the basic story of the camps, don't you?'

'I know the background,' I said, 'but the specifics, no.'

'Well, there are 12 camps scattered round the area, and Dharamsala is the most important because that's where His Holiness is. This camp is a relatively big one – we've got about 700 at the moment.'

Ross and I wandered round the camp and I got the facts.

The camp was established late in 1965, just a year before my arrival. It was comprised of an old tea plantation which extended to about 100 acres. The estate was on a gently bulging fan-shaped hillside facing south and had the giant Himalayas rising immediately at its back. The estate could be said to have three distinct layers. The bottom layer, which abutted the tarred road from Ahju and was its south boundary, was made up of mud and stone hemispherical terraces where the tea once grew and where the old plants were being cleared. Above this level was a building site, which extended almost the whole width of the estate. Very simple houses were being built as permanent accommodation for the camp's inhabitants – when I arrived, some of the rows of houses had brick walls in place but most of the site was still at the stage of laying foundations. Above this level was a track which ran roughly straight, from the right to the left boundaries of the camp. At its extreme east, this track had a sharp angled turn which led it downhill towards the main Ahju road; it was at this right angle that the tea factory where I had entered for the first time was located. At a right angle, the track ran over a makeshift bridge of old railway sleepers, beneath which ran the stream I had fallen into the night before. Ascending, and above the building works and the track, was undulating ground, which rose towards steep screes that in turn became the mountains behind the camp. On this higher ground and occupying most of the westerly area was the camp proper – a township of tents. The tents were not arrayed in lines or avenues, but were a jumble of clusters. To their east was a small plateau, upon which was a building site where several big industrial sheds and a massive water tank were almost completed; the biggest shed was to be a woollen mill.

Below the woollen mill there was a wide, saucer-shaped patch of ground at the centre of which stood a tall flag pole, from whose top were strung some 15 or 20 outrigger lines pegged to the ground, all bedecked with prayer flags of many colours. This spot was the social epicentre of the camp. On the same level and a little further east were another three warehouses, one of which seemed completed; this was to be a chicken rearing unit. Close by this shed were four accommodation houses which were near completion. To the south of the chicken shed, and below the track, was a mud and stone building bedecked with prayer flags; this was the camp's monastery. Although the track formed the main artery of the whole camp, there were numerous small paths criss-crossing the estate.

The camp was home to some 700 people – the number varied because many of the men would leave the camp in search of work for months at a time; one of the aims of the camp was to create small industries by which the Tibetans could be more self-sufficient, obviating the need for the men to leave.

As Ross and I came to the site of the woollen mill, quite coincidentally and spontaneously some of the girls and women started to sing. From the monastery nearby blew huge 15-foot-long trumpet horns, which send out a low buzzing note like a fog horn blasting through the surrounding countryside, this accompanied by the clash of cymbals and the drone of the monks repeating mantras to the beat of a big drum and the tinkle of singing bowls.

There were two centres to the camp; the tea factory and the area between the monastery and the woollen mill. The tea factory was a functioning, productive unit which processed the small remaining tea production of the camp's tea plants into Tibetan tea bricks; these being made and consumed by the camp's inhabitants. Because the Rimpoche's bungalow was just behind the factory and because the factory was at the beginning of the track that ran through the camp, it was the natural place where visitors arrived and the factory had the feeling of being the administrative centre of the camp. If the tea factory was the 'office' for the camp, then the area by the woollen mill belonged purely to the Tibetans in the camp site. It was here that the women would gather and talk in the mornings, it was here in the late afternoon that the men would congregate and it was here that the gossip of the camp was created and disseminated. As Ross and I approached this spot, heads turned and I could feel the examination of myself just as surely as if I was on an operating table. It was very soon apparent to me that there was a cheerful mood among the Tibetans, especially the women. There was little shyness and some were quick to wave and smile.

'That's Tsongya,' said Ross, waving back to a woman, 'she's a bit of a lynch pin to the women. She knows what's going on and all the girls and women will go to her with their problems first.'

Ross was kind enough to devote most of the day to showing me around, explaining the plans that were in place, who was supposed to be implementing them and the difficulties of getting things done.

'What happens here is not like back in the UK,' he began. 'People will meet, talk, apparently decide something – and then nothing happens. You expect so and so to turn up at such and such a time, or something to arrive on such and such a date and it just doesn't happen. Actually, what's even more frustrating is that sometimes some things do happen as planned and it comes as such a surprise that you're not prepared for it. The nearest phone is in Baijnath and that's not always working; letters are hopeless and all we can do is try to fit in with the surrounding chaos and move things along with what we have to hand.'

He explained that his expertise was not anything specific, but that he had taken it in hand to assist in the building work as best as he could – supervising building when nobody from the contractors were present, ensuring works were done on time and so on.

'It drives me nuts,' he said, 'I'm pretty sure the builders are on the fiddle but I can't prove it, and actually I don't want to. All the organisations involved are very complex. You've got charitable agencies in Holland, America or Britain who have donated funds for such and such a project, but the funds are managed by representatives in Delhi or somewhere else, then some other party has the job to vet purchases and bids for work which then have to go through lawyers and when you try to nail somebody down to a specific question, you get passed on to somebody else who in turn denies any responsibility – so any work here is achieved by a process of muddle rather than by intention. I tried to implement a central planning system, but I gave up; it was just hopeless trying to knit everybody together, just hopeless.' Ross threw a stone in evident disgust.

It wasn't long into our walk through the camp that my fate was discussed.

'And if there's something to be done here that I could do,' I asked, 'what do you think would be the best help?'

'Have you any special skills? Horticulture? Weaving? Construction?'

'No, not a thing 'specially. I think I'm capable of most things if I get the chance to understand them.'

'Well, the first and really the only step is to talk to the Rimpoche; it'll be up to him.'

'What's he like?' I asked.

'Very easy going,' answered Ross with a smile. 'He's in Dharamsalah for a couple of days, which means he might be back sometime this week, and then again, he might not. You'll find the Tibetans don't reckon time the way we do. I'd give him a day back before we speak to him. And you'll meet Tenzin, he's our boy, normally does the cooking, and he's with him. Tenzin speaks fair English and we need him constantly to translate; you will need him when you speak to the Rimpoche. You're welcome to wander about wherever you like, but I wouldn't enter the camp proper until you've seen the Rimpoche. The Tibetans are very sensitive in the matter of manners and it would be considered impolite for anyone to enter into their territory other than by invitation, and certainly not until you had the blessing of the Rimpoche. If you stay, you'll find the camp a quite extraordinary place, more 18th century than 20th.'

'What about Hugh?' I asked, 'what does he do? Does he have a special skill?'

'Digging.'

'Digging?'

'Yes, that's mostly what he does. He's clearing out the old tea bushes – they're difficult to shift. Gets up in the morning, digs all day, comes back at night and does the same thing next day.'

'Does he organise the Tibetans to do it, or does he really do it himself?'

'Mostly he does it himself. Doesn't really like help I don't think.'

'Bloody hell.'

'I think,' said Ross confidentially, 'he's very slightly off his rocker. Used to be head of some big London advertising agency. One day, out the blue, decided he'd had enough, left instructions with his lawyers to tidy up his affairs and was on a plane to India within two days. Sold his house and everything. So I'm told.'

'Did he tell you?'

'Nope, and don't ask him. He doesn't like to talk much, especially about the past. Very nice bloke though and very clever too, got a double first at Cambridge. If you stay, you'll get to like him.'

'And is there a doctor, or medical care here?' I asked. 'From what I've seen, these people desperately need medical attention – I've seen some in a hell of a state.'

'Oh I agree. Just once a month we have a doctor who comes, a Swiss man, Dr Mittle. You can't see it from here, but we have a tent that the doctor uses as a sort of clinic. But it's not nearly enough for the camp – what we need really is a permanent medical centre.'

Ross suddenly gripped his stomach and bent in the middle.

'Oh my God, nature calls again… I'll see you later for the feast.'

Ross walked off, awkwardly, towards the factory and left me to wander as I wished.

~

I arrived in India in 1966, less than a year after the camp had been established. A brief background to events before these dates will help explain the reason for the camp and the predicament of the camp's inhabitants. To understand this in more detail, read APPENDIX 1 at the end of the book.

It's difficult to relate the political background of the region without casting the Chinese in a very poor light. Like a lump of malleable clay, the facts can be shaped in different ways, and certainly the Chinese would create a version which would cast them in the role of liberators rather than invaders. From a Briton's point of view, the risk of hypocrisy is a danger – at the invitation of the Chinese, the British invaded Tibet in 1904, though with the intention of exercising a 'suzerainty' rather than a sovereignty over the territory. But since the Tibetans are the people whose lives were permanently changed by the events of 1959, their 'history' is, here, the one that counts – and in their opinions and beliefs as to the events, they are unequivocal and certain.

On Ross's advice, I did not venture into the camp site proper, but wandered with a happy aimlessness that took me round the perimeter of the camp, down the main track to the public road, then back up towards the terraces where I spotted Hugh hard at work.

Hugh was digging and I ventured to speak to him.

'Finding your way around?' he asked, leaning on a spade and dusting his hands.

'Yes. Didn't realise it was so big.'

'Seen any bears?'

'No thank goodness. Do they come out in the day?'

'Not much, mostly at night.'

'What's going to happen here?' I asked, looking around the immediate vicinity of his digging.

'Well the plan was to plant vegetables, but they don't like vegetables.'

'The Tibetans?'

'Yeah.'

'What do they eat?'

'Well, not vegetables, not fish, not chicken, sometimes goat, but mostly it's tea they want – they seem to live on the stuff.'

'Could the tea grow here again?'

'Maybe sometime, but the ground's been wasted and it takes three years before you can crop from new plants. Some of the plantation is still good, over on the west side, and the Tibetans crop that to make their own tea, but most of the bushes are only fit to burn. Incidentally, you'll be offered some Tibetan tea sooner or later – I'd take only a small sip if I were you.'

'Why, is it horrid?'

'Well, you'll have to make up your own mind. They boil the black tea for several hours, 'till it's stewed to death, then they pour it into a narrow churn or barrel and add salt and rancid butter. They churn the mix with a plunger and that's Tibetan tea.'

'What does it taste like?' I asked.

'Well if you can imagine it, it's like a mix of Guinness vomit and sour cream.'

'That good, eh?'

'Hmmm. If you get offered a bowl, you must take at least two sips. And after each sip, the bowl is replenished. The best thing to do if you don't want to drink is to receive the bowl, place it in front of you with a bow, and, just before you leave, take your two sips.'

'I'll try and remember that Hugh, thanks.'

Hugh spat, as though the imagining of the taste of Tibetan tea was enough to warrant the action. Then he resumed his digging; he wielded a huge pincer like contraption with which he gripped the base of a withered plant and levered its roots up out of the ground by a few inches.

'That's the hard part,' he said to himself more than to me, 'I used to go through a spade a month before I made this thing.'

I left him to his hard labour and wandered back to the tea factory. Ross was up a ladder peering at an electric box in the front hall, so I retreated to the 'dining' room and wrote two aerogramme letters – one to my parents to say I had arrived, and one to Madelaine in Bombay thanking her for her hospitality and her wise gifts, and with the same news that I was safe and well and awaiting a final decision as to whether I would stay or not.

It was five days before the Rimpoche arrived back in camp, during which I had a chance to make several assessments in the calm of empty time. The first was in regard to my own state of preparedness for the camp, were it to come to pass that I stayed. I would need more warm clothes, but I blessed myself for having taken my walking boots; I had swithered about their weight and bulk in my limited luggage, but had decided in the end it would be sensible; the whole camp was muddy and everyone who could wore boots. I blessed Madelaine when I made a careful inspection of the medical supplies which she had thrust upon me; water sterilising tablets, many packets of entrovioform pills, vitamins, anti-malarials, a bandage, antiseptic ointments and sticking plasters.

I wired up an aerial for my radio and eventually managed to find a faint BBC World Service and I loaded my beloved Leica camera with its first roll of colour film. I realised I could survive here.

The second assessment was about my companions. I could see no reason why I wouldn't get on with them; they were similar to me in age and outlook and it was very comforting to have British language, British values and British company so far from home. In addition, Hugh and Ross had the experience of the camp and its ways and their knowledge would speed up my ability to achieve something if I were to have the chance of staying.

The third assessment was that food and diet was going to be difficult. In the camp as a whole there was an obsession with food. Essentials such as flour, cooking fat and sugar were rationed. If there happened to be some meat in the camp, it became general knowledge very quickly.

In the few days that I had been there, I had eaten only dhal (which are stewed lentils) and chappatis. There was plenty of tea though. There was word of some potatoes coming soon, and even tomatoes, but underlying these forthcoming treats, diet was meagre in quantity and variety. I decided that I would keep very much to myself both my medicines and my tins of asparagus and peaches.

My final judgement was about the Tibetans. In the few days I had been at the camp, I could see that the Tibetans were, taken as a whole, very likeable. I had never asked myself what my reaction would be if I found myself dedicated to helping people who, deep down, I might not like that much. But the more encounters I had with the Tibetans, the more I liked them.

When I had got past the stage of being self-conscious and overly aware that I should appear respectful and cautiously polite with the Tibetans, I could see past the man, woman or child who was smiling at me, or giving me a furtive little wave; I began to see that the Tibetans were in a very poor state.

Physically, they were filthy, particularly the men, and some smelt so strongly rancid that it was difficult not to wretch in their close proximity. It was the universal practice in Tibet to smear everything from hair to feet with yak butter as protection from the cold dry winds of their native country. Many had open sores on their hands and face, many limped and it was a common sight to see individuals walking very slowly and out of breath from the effects of TB. I never once saw a fat Tibetan.

Their physically poor appearance was compounded by their clothing.

Most of the men wore a tsuba. This is a very heavy, sleeved woollen robe with a wide flap at the chest which is held tight at the waist by a fabric belt. During the day, one sleeve is draped over the back and the void in the other side will carry food or other necessities. From the belt are hung knives, flint boxes and small silver shrines. Traditionally, under the robe is a long, white, high-collared shirt, and the tsuba will drape to just below the knees over the top of yak skin boots. This sounds romantic, and a Tibetan in his or her full garb is a magnificent sight. But in the camp, the clothes of the men were ruinously decrepit; covered in a greasy filth, torn and patched, threadbare and in tatters. These were the same clothes that they were still wearing when they fled across the Himalayas.

Some Tibetans had decent boots, but on many you could see that battered footwear had been poorly repaired or simply tied up with strips of cloth. Some had taken to wearing western jumpers and the like, but the majority still wore a tsuba. The women were a little cleaner than the men and some still wore the traditional apron of woven thin stripes of greens, whites, yellows and reds.

In contrast to the 'ordinary' Tibetan, the monks in their maroon and yellow robes and those who were based at the monastery were all better dressed, cleaner and in better health.

In the evenings, we three British volunteers would sit round our table, eating our dhal and chappatis. Ross never complained or fantasised about food, but Hugh, sometimes remembering his London days, composed dream menus: smoked salmon, fillet steak and a good Burgundy, bread fruit pudding and double cream, Stilton and port.

'Best lobster I ever had was at Trader Vics at the Park Lane Hilton,' said Hugh, 'it must have weighed at least four pounds, just cut into halves and grilled with butter. Still,' he added rather mournfully, 'they say lentils are good for you.'

The Rimpoche arrived back at the camp from Dharamsala and I saw him make his way from his jeep to his house by the tea factory. He was a big man, but not tall, and must have been in his mid- to late-forties. He moved slowly and with great ease and dignity. As soon as he arrived, he was surrounded by people anxious to help and carry. Anyone from the camp approaching him did so with a deep and reverential bow. Although it sounds like a contradiction, there was not the slightest element of subservience in this, just respect. With the arrival of the Rimpoche also came the return of Tenzin, of whom Ross had spoken much – all of it in praise. Ross introduced us. He was maybe a year or so younger than me and had studied and learned English during the years he had been in India. His parents had been killed by the Chinese and he had crossed the Himalayas to India with an uncle. He had a quick humour and a quicker smile, and he had adopted western dress. His hair was thick and black and flew round his head in waves; when he smiled three creases bracketed his mouth, and when he laughed there were more.

Tenzin's role in the camp was an important one – he translated between any western visitors or volunteers such as us and ran errands for the Rimpoche (and everyone else, too). He seemed to be at the centre of any activity, and it was he who knew who might have some potatoes, who was coming to the camp and what might be coming in the weekly post.

There is a complex background to the conditions or lineage by which a Tibetan man earns or is endowed with the title 'Rimpoche' – it is the title of a very senior monk. And since the Lamas (the monks) are the levers of most power in Tibetan society, a Rimpoche is the head of both a religious and a social group. In Scotland he would (nearly) be the clan chief.

Much rested on my first meeting with the Rimpoche because he had the entire say in whether I would stay in the camp or not. If he decided that I could not stay, I would have no option but to return to Delhi with my tail between my legs (and ready for a big bust up with Mrs Mehta). Before my meeting with the Rimpoche, Ross put me at ease.

'There are some niceties that Tibetans themselves observe at important meetings – wait for the tea to be served, bow receiving it and flick a couple of drops in the air before drinking, but with him, you don't have to worry, he has learned not to take offence when westerners do not observe traditions they cannot be expected to know.'

Because the Rimpoche had much to catch up on since his return to the camp, my first meeting with him had to wait for several days and this gave me to the chance to observe him whenever I could – at a distance, not overtly. I tried to see the wise and erudite monk that everyone said he was. His immediate persona came across as being that of a kindly bulldozer rather than a racing motorbike. He walked and moved as though every action was the result of forethought, and this was probably true. His gait was deliberate and unhurried and his posture conveyed the unmistakable impression that he knew that his authority was authentic, both in the sense of certainty that he possessed it and in the recognition of its supremacy over those who were subjugated by it. There was not a single Tibetan who did not greet the Rimpoche with a bow and body language that immediately conveyed both respect and liking. If this suggests that he was a bully, that inference would be entirely wrong. Although in apparent contradiction to the fact that the Rimpoche had a big, stout body, there was much about him in his movement that suggested that the man was engaged in a permanent dance or in the movements of yoga; there seemed to be some discipline at work behind each gesture, as though his whole life was the enactment of a choreography created in some other distant place and time. This may also have been true. In his dress, the Rimpoche did not rely on lavish robes to trick the eye into seeing an authority presumed by dress alone. As a monk he always wore the full length dark maroon skirt and a short sleeved, high collared shirt – but over this shirt was as likely to be a chunky knitted cardigan that had seen better days.

His face was a wide oval, his hair was very short and spiky and behind his eyes was a full courtroom of wise counsellors looking and listening attentively to the person before them. What scheme of thinking lay further behind the eyes and ears was well beyond my judgement. It was the pattern of most of his encounters, either with the entourage which usually surrounded him, or with the solitary, threadbare Tibetan before him, that within some period of time after the seriousness of life had been addressed, laughter would peal out as an antidote to the seriousness. If I had had any fears of meeting the man, they were dispelled by his proclivity to laugh.

On the appointed day, I met Tenzin at the Rimpoche's bungalow and we were shown in to the small front sitting room. Tenzin introduced us and as we shook hands I bowed my head. I felt my hand being gripped again as though the first touch was being reinforced with a second, more friendly and fatherly hold.

'Mister Mike,' he began, 'Tenzin says you are good man.'

'Rimpoche,' I replied, 'Tenzin says *you* are a good man, and, more importantly, so does everyone else.' He laughed heartily, slapped his sides and bade me sit down. Tea was served and Tenzin hovered in the background, translating when needed. There have been some men that I have taken a huge liking to almost immediately – and the Rimpoche was one of them.

The Rimpoche and I talked for about an hour about the world, about the war in Vietnam, about life in Europe and whatever came to mind. The Rimpoche asked me only a few questions about myself and my family, but he was not curious about what specific skills I had to offer the camp. Quite suddenly, and without any preamble he asked if I would like to stay. I noticed that just before he said this, he looked at Tenzin as if seeking his silent judgement on the matter. I replied that I would be very happy to stay, but, since I had very little money, I would need help with food.

'Not a problem,' he said, 'lentils we have, do we not Tenzin?'

Tenzin, smiling, said, 'Yes Rimpoche. Mr. Hugh and Mr Ross both *seem* to like lentils.'

'Then it is decided,' said the Rimpoche with a firm nod.

Of course, this was a great relief to me. I told him that if I could help, what I would like to do was somehow assist the health of the camp, and he agreed this would be a good use of my energies. He suggested that I should wait a week until Dr Mittle's arrival and discuss with the doctor what I could do.

Then the Rimpoche said 'then you go to Delhi and get money. You can do I think.'

'Go to Delhi?'

'Yes, I have names. 'Nited Nations. Merica. Horrand. Ingerland.'

I explained to the Rimpoche that an 18-year-old, and one that didn't have a suit nor even two pennies to rub together, was unlikely to be successful in 'getting money' from the United Nations or from anyone else.

'You go,' he said with finality, 'you get money!'

He would have none of my objections and when our meeting was over, I was inexplicably disappointed. I had had a picture in my head,

for a long time, a very physically coloured, animated image in my head
– something along the lines of me lifting the cup to parched lips, or ad-
ministering the healing injection, and it seemed that the Rimpoche had
other ideas of what I could do. As I left my first meeting with him, I felt
both very happy *and* a little disappointed. That night I wrote a second
letter home confirming that I would be staying. I had just licked the
gum and folded it up when Ross came in.

'How'd it go?' he asked.

'Just grand, he said I could stay.'

'Great,' said Ross, 'really I'm pleased.' We shook hands.

'But he wants me to go to Delhi to raise money for the camp. From
the United Nations for God's sake.' Ross smiled thinly and stroked his
growing moustache.

'I wondered if he'd ask you. He tried it on me, and Hugh. I just told
him no.'

'What about Hugh?' I asked.

'Same thing. No way.'

'I don't see myself doing this,' I said, 'I just don't.'

'Well, just keep telling him no. He'll keep at you, you know… 'Merica,
Horrand. Get money!'

Despite this odd development, I felt a great weight slide from my
shoulders – it was the culminating moment that had taken months of
deliberation, preparation and travel to achieve. I was in India, I was in
the Himalayas, I was with people I liked and who were showing me a
great friendliness. I was filled with that top essence of happiness that
is glee. By the second week at the camp, I had walked all I had wanted
to, I had seen all I wanted to see and I felt I knew the basic running and
routine of the camp to the extent that I had begun to feel redundant and
a little bored.

Christmas came and for dinner we had dhal, three chappatis instead
of the usual two and some blessed potatoes; the day passed with virtually no sense of celebration.

I joined Ross, sometimes, to try and get to grips with the ins and outs
of the construction side of things and to offer Hugh my services, but
though they expressed themselves glad of help, I had the impression
they would rather be on their own. I was glad at last when a brisk and

business-like Dr Mittle arrived one morning from Dharamsala, on the
dot at 9:00 precisely; Tenzin had told me a week before that he was
due to arrive, so I was near the Rimpoche's bungalow when he drove
up in his car. I joined Tenzin, the Rimpoche and the doctor and the
introductions were completed. My position was explained to the doctor
and, should it concur with his wishes, that I should be regarded as
someone who might, with experience, be able to supervise the progress
and treatment of his patients between his monthly visits.

'Ah, this is very good' said the doctor, 'but you are young, you have no
qualifications?'

'No, none at all,' I said – I did not mention the first aid badge I got in
the Boy Cubs.

'But Mister Mike's father is doctor, a *surgeon,*' said Tenzin, hopefully
but not helpfully. The doctor, for once, smiled.

'Well, we can try,' said Dr Mittle, and we set off to a tent which was on
its own by the middle of the camp, where a lengthy queue of patients,
under the watchful eye of Tsongya, was waiting for us.

Dr Mittle was as neat and organised as the Swiss at their most Swiss; he
was a clean cut, balding, middle aged man in a light tweed suit, and he
peered at life through rimless round glasses. He spoke perfect English;
he was curt in his manners and briskly expeditious with the patients.

His patients were mostly women who regarded the whole episode
of seeing the doctor as a matter of great hilarity. Tsongya, the camp's
'matron', ushered each patient into the tent and acted as an intermediary
between Tenzin and the doctor. I couldn't understand why the patient
couldn't communicate directly with the doctor through Tenzin, but I
was told later that it would have been improper for any woman to be
without Tsongya's support during the consultation.

The diseases and ailments which afflicted the Tibetans were often due
to the differences between their old and new domiciles; in Tibet most
people lived at very high altitude and in very cold temperatures. Living
at lower altitudes and at higher temperatures brought upon the Tibetans
a wretched concoction of ailments – widespread TB, malaria which was
drug resistant, a tendency to suffer tropical ulcers and skin disorders,
and widespread dysentery. These were worsened by poor nutrition, a
susceptibility to infections caused by insanitary conditions, and an

ignorance of the necessity in new surroundings to practise basic hygiene. In Tibet, when yak butter was smeared onto the skin to ward off the rigours of a biting cold wind, the habit was beneficial, but in India this practice caused widespread skin infections. In Tibet, the natural facial colour is a ruddy, wind beaten brown-pink; in India it became a pallid sickly yellow.

The patients presented themselves with a selection of sores, pains, difficulties and problems, all of which Dr Mittle dealt with efficiently. Where pills were to be given, he simply took a handful and handed them to the patient with instructions via Tenzin. For sores and skin disorders, the doctor's common treatment was a dab of gentian violet, an antiseptic liquid with a deeply staining vivid purple colour. The patients always seemed delighted to receive this treatment, and some, even though they didn't need it, mentioned that they would like some of it. Within the camp, treatment by gentian violet was regarded as powerful medicine and had an effect far beyond its physical capabilities.

I would make my own notes as Dr Mittle treated each patient, and occasionally he would address me with a comment or advice. By the end of an intense and exhausting morning, we had a short break for tea and chappatis then began the round of visits to the sick in their tents; it was my first and my most severe introduction to the campsite proper. Dr Mittle knew his way round the camp intimately and did not flinch nor pale at the squalor in some of the tents and he entered them without announcement or preamble.

'Always establish your authority over the patient,' he explained, 'if you knock and ask permission to enter, the patient will not respect your treatment of them. You must learn to walk straight in.'

My conscious observations were towards the patients and their treatment, but my obverse senses were taking in the camp itself; I remembered Ross's description that it evoked the dark and domestic filth of the eighteenth century, and on that day I saw the reality of the Tibetans' predicament close up.

By four in the afternoon we had finished, and the doctor and I returned to the factory for tea as Tenzin departed for other tasks.

'Well, do you think you can do it?' asked the doctor. 'Some of it is not pretty.'

I confessed I had found some of the sights and events difficult.

'Just remember that even if you can't help a patient in a direct sense, it's a great benefit to them to know that some kind of help is available. You can always help by improving their hygiene – get them to wash, show them a scrubbing brush and teach them *how* to wash, especially after defecating. Even if you do that, you'll be doing something. And keep distributing the vitamins, we have a big stock of them at Dharamsala and you can hand them out as much as you like, especially to the children: they're the ones that get the greatest benefit from them. Watch that the TB patients are taking their pills – some sell or exchange them for food, so you might want to introduce a regime where you see them actually swallow the things. Lastly, if you have someone you think is in genuine danger of dying, try and get them to the hospital at Palamjong; they know me and have agreed to take emergencies. Now, we need to go over the notes you've been taking…'

We were an hour discussing and confirming what each patient needed – checking that medicines were being taken, wounds that needed regular cleaning and dressing, monitoring the temperatures of some, making notes of progress on others. At 5:30, the good doctor left as briskly as he arrived, driving off in his shiny clean ambassador's car.

My circumstances changed for the better that day – I had something to do that was mine. At the feast that evening, Tenzin came to our room with food – in addition to dhal and chappatis, he proudly produced boiled potatoes: two each – it had been a good day in every sense.

4

Home in a tent and dinner with the Count

WITH MY TENURE NOW FIXED, IT WAS TIME TO MAKE MY RESI-dency more permanent. I had been sleeping on the floor in a tiny cold room at the tea factory and I was living out of my suitcase with my clothes and effects in disorder. Via Tenzin, I got the Rimpoche's permission to take one tent from a batch of 20 which had arrived as a gift to the camp and to set it up as my home. The tents were about 10 feet by 6 feet high, enough to stand up in comfortably, and, though not grand in any sense, it had space for a bed and perhaps a small table and stool. To my surprise, Ross ventured that he would like to join me as co-habitant in this new abode; I didn't enquire as to the reason why, nor suspected that there might be tension with Hugh. I think he just wanted a change.

Ross agreed with me that it was better to be more detached from the factory and the Rimpoche and all things to do with the administration, since it made us seem more neutral in the eyes of the camp's inhabitants. We searched for a suitable site and picked a spot very near to the camp proper, well away from the tea factory but near to the woollen mill and chicken shed. The place had more of a feeling of being at the camp's centre of gravity and was a few yards below the camp's main track. With Hugh's willing help, the three of us dug into the sloping ground to form a recessed rectangle about a foot deep that the tent would just sit into – this to keep out draughts and to make a flat floor. As we laid out the tent for erection and were humming and hawing about what poles and lines went where, Tibetan men and women gathered, watched, hesitated and muttered amongst themselves. Then the men edged us out of the way and had the thing up in a few minutes. We three applauded the Tibetans and they, in turn, laughed and bowed. Ross and I were still pacing up and down inside the tent, getting a feel for its space and tramping the ground smooth, when the same men who had erected the tent arrived in a small procession bearing two charpois, a small table, a tilly lamp, and a camp chair, these having been purloined from we knew not where. The charpoi is the standard bed in India – a wooden frame on short legs about 6 inches high, the open frame being woven with a diamond lattice of strong scratchy string. As long as the string is really tight, the charpoi is comfortable and easy to get used to. With a bottom blanket and sleeping bag, a good charpoi can be adequately comfortable. I tested the strings and knew there was work to be done.

Ross and I made our quarters with our beds under each of the tent's eaves, mine with a small table in front of it, Ross taking the camp chair. I found some old electrical flex at the factory and rigged up an aerial for my radio and we were set. With my suitcases under the charpoi, a radio next to it and a camp-stove outside, we were well pleased with our new home. Our first night together did bring to light a new slant on Ross's character. We had been chatting amiably about home and food when the time came for bed. I clambered into my sleeping bag; Ross climbed onto his bedknelt on his knees, put his hands together and started praying out loud.

'Oh Lord, thy humble servant begs thy strength and forgiveness; help me with strength to carry out your word and work – forgive my sins and those of the world. Grant me peace and… and, Our Father, which art… in Heaven.'

The next day, I encountered Hugh on his way to the terrace.

'How's it going in the new home then?' he asked, a smile on his face.

'Oh fine,' I said, 'I'll need to speak to Ross about his…'

'Praying?' Hugh interjected.

'Yes. He can pray as much as he likes, but I don't see why he can't keep it to himself.'

'Sent by God,' said Hugh, 'thinks he's been sent by God.'

'Oh.'

'Ross is off his rocker you know. Well, back to the digging – not far to go now.'

'You nearly finished?' I asked.

'Yes, only got about 50 more plants to go and that's them cleared – at bloody last.'

'Then what'll you do?'

'Oh, I'll be moving along in a few weeks.'

'Oh Hugh, I didn't realise.'

'Yup, I'm going to Dharamsala. I've decided to join a monastery there, become a monk. I've been thinking about it for a long time. Come to think of it, that's what I've been digging for. Yes. I'll wander round for a few weeks first. I haven't taken any time to see this part of the world – did you know there's a 13th century temple at Baijnath? 13th century! And I've been digging since nearly the first day I arrived here, the very first day! Oh well, see you tonight maybe.'

Hugh sauntered off, and for the first time I heard him whistling to himself, a man happy, and at peace.

I went to seek out Ross at the factory to tell him the news.

'No, doesn't surprise me. He hasn't said anything but I had the feeling there was a change afoot. I'll miss him though.'

'So will I,' I said, and then had the thought that perhaps it would change my status at the camp.

'Will that affect us at all?' I asked.

'No. Hugh won't go until he's undertaken what he set out to do, and with the terraces cleared maybe someone will realise they're a great potential source of food. No, we'll be fine. If I could only capture Mr Battacharia [the building contractor] and tie him to a chair and force him to get the electrics in the chicken shed finished...'

From the time of moving into the tent and having a sort of a permanent home, my life very gradually and slowly settled into a routine. I would open the dispensary tent each morning with Tenzin, and from our notes we would hand out pills, clean and dress wounds, and generally play at being doctors. I use those words intentionally because the more patients I saw, the more I realised that what I was doing was of only minor importance. As the Tibetans became used to me, new patients would appear – very nervously at first, often accompanied by a supportive friend or with Tsongya. As I listened to symptoms and watched the patients illustrate their ailments with animated body and facial gestures, pointing to their groin or waving their hands to communicate feelings of pain, I knew they had ailments and needed treatments far beyond the simple first aid I was dispensing. I took notes on each case in the hope they would ease Dr Mittle's workload at his next visit, but it was distressing to face my shortcomings so forcibly. I did what I could, and where there was distress, there was gentian violet and vitamin pills. After morning 'surgery', Tenzin would prepare some food at our home tent, after which we would do our domiciliary visits to those bedridden in their tents. As these visits became more regular, so the Tibetans began to emerge as individuals. I was learning names and relationships and beginning to get an insight into their circumstances, past and present. The difference between their lives and mine was not a subject that my young mind could make much sense of. But I did understand that whereas I would certainly return to my home, the Tibetans I was living with never would. They were human beings cast out from the security and friendliness of their own homes and were adrift in circumstances where there was a very small gap between life and death. The more I learned about their circumstances, the little help they were getting seemed to me to be too little, and too late.

As my first weeks became my first month, I had a sense of what lay behind the setting up of the camp. The Tibetans were in very urgent need of seeing *how* they could rebuild their lives – this by the small industries that were planned for them once the building of the various sheds and industrial units had been completed. It was crucial that the Tibetans had a means to support themselves by weaving and carpet-making and so on. What was much more important was that they had something to hope for. The intention was to introduce them to business. This might seem a simple lesson to learn for people brought up within a well-developed capitalist society. But the Tibetans had to begin learning right from scratch – even though a very few were natural and cunning traders.

Tibetan society was rooted in a culture that was long in its evolution. The value system inside the Tibetan head understood trading and money, but it did not understand the all-consuming importance attached to these activities and the concomitant lesser value attached to spiritual and communal wellbeing. Tibet experienced no industrial revolution, yet many of its inhabitants were violently shoved over a cliff to land in a life where their survival would depend on mastering 'manufacture and markets'. *Whereas I used to weave to clothe my children, are you telling me that I must sit at a loom for 8 hours a day making 30 copies of the same garment? How strange.* The camp was a cheerful place, genuinely full of spontaneous laughter and a great sense of unity, but there was a look in many eyes that, in unguarded moments, was despairing and told the observer that the soul inside was lost. It was easy to see that a focus of hope was needed, but that hope seemed a long way off.

As my routine began to emerge, so did the problems. The first was that Tenzin's time was so much in demand that his ability to co-run the dispensary with me was becoming limited. The Rimpoche had endless tasks for him to perform, yet I needed him increasingly. The second was the Rimpoche kept reminding me at every meeting of his wish that I go to Delhi to raise money from international agencies.

"Merica' he would say, holding up a finger to remind me of his wishes.

I tried as much as I could to persuade him that I had just got the dispensary in operation and could not justify being away – he would have none of it. 'Horrand, Ingerland, Nited Nations!'

As December became January, the weather became colder and colder; the days were tolerable, but the nights were miserably cold in the tent. I had only a sleeping bag and a blanket and I would mostly sleep with a layer of clothes still on. This led me to a state of personal uncleanliness I was not used to. There was cold water to wash in; Ross and I would heat a big old tin can to get hot water sometimes, but there was no question of a bath or shower. The first day of snow came, with huge flakes like scraps of tissue paper drifting silently down to layer the camp with white. I was comforted by a letter from home and by catching music sometimes from the BBC World Service. I asked Ross whether prayer that was silently mouthed might have the same effect as prayer spoken aloud, and he took the hint.

By the middle of January, Hugh had packed his things and left; he had insisted there be no ceremony or fuss – one day he was there digging, and the next, he was gone. He said goodbye to us as though he were just leaving for the day, but we never saw him again.

On the same day as Hugh left, I was walking back to our tent when Tenzin came running towards me.

'Mister Mike! Rimpoche want you. Tonight, you eat Rimpoche.'

'You come too,' I said.

'Yes, I come. No eat.'

I knew it was Delhi time.

I had been in the Rimpoche's bungalow often enough that I was at ease there and had got to know his wife and children.

'Mister Mike,' said The Rimpoche, flourishing a letter, 'welcome. Read letter, new volunteers come, come soon, two and chicken man.'

I was handed a letter from the Tibetan Rehabilitation and Relief Agency in Delhi and read that three volunteers were to be joining Ross and I at the camp. There was no more information other than that the three comprised of a chicken man, a nurse and an ex army officer. I was bidden to sit.

'Now you go Delhi,' said the Rimpoche, pouring me a bowl of chang. Tenzin was not offered the same. Sensing that I had to put up a fight I spoke in a firm voice.

'No Rimpoche. With every respect, I do not think this is wise.'

'You go.'

'Rimpoche, how can I expect to do this? I have no money, I have no clothes. How am I going to do this?'

'Money not difficult,' said the Rimpoche, 'and you use words. You have 'Merica words, and Horrand.' Tenzin sat quietly, paying attention but not speaking (other than, occasionally, to translate).

The Rimpoche and I drank a lot that evening. We began with chang, which is a mild rice-based wine; it's only vaguely alcoholic, but a few bowls make the cheeks hot and merry. After we had finished the chang and I judged it time to go, the Rimpoche lent back on his chair and called to his wife, who left the room and returned just a minute later with a bottle containing a most peculiar looking liquid. It was vivid orange colour, more like a chemical dye than a beverage.

'Arrack,' said the Rimpoche, rubbing his stomach, 'very good.'

The effects of the change and my self confidence with the Rimpoche emboldened me to ask how it was that he, a senior Buddhist monk, could drink. The Rimpoche began to tell a tale and spoke to Tenzin, who translated such words as the Rimpoche did not know.

'When The Buddha was formulating the rules by which monks should adhere to the faith, it took him a period of several days. The first precepts he laid down were four in number; the first was not to kill, the second was not to steal, the third was not commit sexual infidelity and the fourth was not to lie. The Buddha made these known to his followers, who saw and appreciated their wisdom. It was the practice for monks to travel the countryside for alms, and one day a monk arrived in a small settlement and there met a young woman. She was very beautiful. She had the fairest skin and her fine clothes were of pure white. From one hand she led a goat by a tether of woven silk.

After the woman had given the monk a small coin, she said, "I am going to make sacrifice of this goat, and I must find someone who will kill the goat for me, which will be my sacrifice. Will you perhaps kill the goat for me, for you look so strong?"

Remembering the first of the Buddha's rules, the monk said, "no, Lady. By my vows, I cannot take a life."

"Then, since you are a handsome man, will you sleep with me to give me pleasure so that when I make my sacrifice my mind and body will be more prepared to receive enlightenment?"

The monk was terribly tempted, but recalling the Buddha's teaching, he disciplined his desire and said, "No, for if I were to do so, I would be taking something that is not mine and therefore I would be stealing."

"Then if you will come to my house, will you take a drink of arrack as part of my sacrifice?"

The monk pondered this and decided that it was part of his duty to assist the faithful in their sacrifices, so he agreed to the Lady's request.

"To do you honour Lady, I will partake of the arrack."

They entered a house and the monk partook of the arrack. He enjoyed the sensation and he drank more and became drunk. In his drunkenness, he lost the discipline of his mind, killed the goat and made love to the woman.

It was seeing the moral consequence of this episode that made The

Buddha add to his determinations that a monk *shall not* partake of alcohol.'

'... so you are a disciple of this monk?' I asked the Rimpoche after Tenzin had finished translating.

The Rimpoche raised his glass to his lips, and said to me directly in his own English, 'partily.' Then, after savouring another small sip of the liquor, he said 'and if it serves a greater purpose, it may be permitted.' Like the monk, I drank more than I should have and sometime later I was persuaded to go to Delhi.

'Alright,' I said, 'I will go, but I want to take Tenzin with me.' Tenzin looked at me with a great big wide smile and nodded his head vigourously – in our exchanged glances we both foresaw that we would have fun in Delhi.

'No, defferntly not,' said the Rimpoche, 'Tenzin here. Tenzin do medicine. You go. 'Merica money. You boys in Delhi together not safe thing. I think you boys in Delhi are trouble, too much fun.'

I was carried back to my tent that night, drunk. Tenzin and three other men laid me out on a charpoi and hoisted me shoulder high in procession to my tent, where, unknown to me, they put me to bed and zipped me up in my sleeping bag. It took several days for my hangover to restore my head back to its usual place, and it was too late to try and reverse the plot. A couple of weeks later, I was on the toy train to Pathankot and in Delhi the next day.

Delhi was at least a relief from the cold. The journey had been easier now that I was a little accustomed to Indian travel, and also because I travelled with a rucksack borrowed from Ross; no more lugging awkward suitcases about. I had made the assumption that I would be able to stay with Dr Calder and made my way from Delhi station to the seminary, but was met at its gate by an old woman who said that Dr Calder was away for several days. She was a cagey old biddy who clung to the door and spoke through the narrowest possible opening; I did not feel it proper to press my acquaintanceship with Dr Calder and the associated free bed and board. I retraced my journey back to Delhi's centre and got myself into the Y.M.C.A., where the accommodation is cheap, clean and sparse, and where, deliciously, I had my first shower in weeks.

The date of my first day in the city was January 26th, and that was Republic Day. At that festival I stood among the crowds and watched the parades and the elephants and felt like a relaxed tourist again.

My first assignation was to go to the offices of the Tibetan Rehabilitation and Relief Agency, where I was to introduce myself as a new volunteer at the camp. But I was tired after my journey and took a bus to Delhi's epicentre, Connaught Square, where I wandered till early evening, enjoying the feeling of being at the heart of a great city with its buzz and bustle, its crowds and hooting traffic energising me as if with an injection of adrenalin (and the palliative to the cold isolation and discomforts of the camp). I went back to the Y.M.C.A., fell in with four Australian girls and went out for a meal with them that made up for many weeks of dhal and chappatis.

The T.R.R.A. offices were near an industrial development and their building was big, white and dull. After explaining myself to the receptionist and after waiting an hour I was led upstairs and shown into a long, windowed room filled with filing cabinets. At one end and directly beneath a ceiling fan was a plain post-war oak twin pedestal desk piled with two heaps of files on either side. In the gap between the mounds was the man I had come to see, Mr Reginald Starling, head of operations of the T.R.R.A., the organisation responsible for most of the Tibetan camps in India. He was fat Anglo-Indian with a cheerful look about him, about 50, and, judging by the crucifix behind his desk, a Catholic.

'Ah, the Rimpoche!' he said when I had outlined the task I had been sent to do. 'How is my dear friend? Always the optimist, thinks money grows on trees, thinks he just has to ask and he'll get what he wants, you see. We've had most of you volunteers through these doors and we say the same thing to all of you. It can't be done – and especially it can't be done quickly, you see. We have to share out the money between all the camps around Dharamsala and beyond. Do you know how many camps there are? We have 23. Twenty-three! All of them need clean water, all of them need medical and dental facilities, all of them want schools and teachers… look, look!' He swivelled in his chair round to face a map pinned to the wall behind his desk, got up and started pointing to green paper stars pinned on the map.

'At Ravangdoh we have 700 people and they don't even have enough tents – here at Palchuba we had about 50 new arrivals last month alone, you see, and they've all got dysentery, and at Ponkham there's been a murder – a murder, you see!' He sat down after his exertion and dragged both of his hands front to back through his hair.

'We are at full stretch,' he said leaning back in his chair like a man under siege.

Both Ross and Hugh had warned me of the response I would likely get from Mr Starling. I was with him for a generous half an hour, in which time I understood much better the background and anticipated future of the camp, who had been donating the funds, and how they were spent. It was as complicated as Ross had first described. As secretaries floated into Mr Starling's office and left files on his desk with an occasional quiet aside, I knew my time was nearly up.

'I hear we're getting new volunteers at the camp,' I said.

'Oh yes,' he said pulling out a file from the pile on his right side, 'here we are. Major Adrian Allingham, from Basingstoke, good organiser it says here… and Hazel Schelmerdine, she's a paediatric nurse, she's from Rossborough and, yes, here we are, Jay Naseer; he's a veterinary graduate of Lewes College, near Brighton I think, specialises in chicken rearing.'

'Do you know when they're coming?' I asked. He referred to the letters in his file.

'Mr Naseer will be at the camp in just two weeks from now, which reminds me that the Rimpoche needs to prepare accommodation for him; will you do that? For the major and the nurse Schelmerdine I do not have definite dates.'

'And one last question…' I asked, 'have you ever heard of a Mrs Mehta? She's the lady by whose offices I came to India.'

'Mrs Mehta?' Mr Starling looked up to the whirring ceiling fan for a moment. 'No. No, I've never heard that name.' He called out to the secretary who had been bringing files to his desk, 'Mrs Jupta, have we come across a Mrs Mehta?'

The secretary came in and said 'No. I've never heard that name. And sir, you have a meeting…'

'Ah yes, you see, Michael, I must be leaving now.'

'If you want my advice,' he said, 'if you really want to help these people, you could do more by raising money in your home countries than here in India, you see. I do not think you will get anything from the agencies in Delhi – we are working on them all the time – but good luck. Now we have met, you see, you know where I am.' We shook hands and I left.

My next destination on that first day in Delhi was the British Embassy. Both Ross and Hugh had advised me to visit the Embassy to let them know who I was and where I was; there was no official arrangement whereby British citizens were especially listed or noted, but there was an unofficial understanding that it was wise for long-term visitors to have some contact there.

In the refreshingly cool British richness of the Embassy hallway, I explained my purpose at the front desk and waited on a lavish leather button-back sofa reading Punch and Country Life, enjoying the sheer prosperity and splendour of the place. At length I was approached by a man in his early 30s in a grey silk suit, white shirt and a George Watson's old school tie, polished black shoes and neat, closely cropped black hair.

'Mr. Hendry? Tom McKillop. From Aberdeen I'm told.'

'Yes. You must be Edinburgh,' I said, gesturing at his tie.

'Yes, George Watson's, know it?'

'Not directly – played rugby against you lot, once. Got hammered. Just the seconds though, never made it into the firsts.'

'What did you play?'

'Wing forward. You?'

'Reserve. Never liked the game, avoided it like the plague.'

'I didn't like it either actually. Heresy.'

The pleasantries over, he confirmed that the Embassy had no facility whereby long-term visitors become officially registered in any formal sense. But he wrote down my name and where I was and my home address in Aberdeen. I asked him for any guidance as to how I could make realistic contact with any agencies that might be in a position to help the Tibetans.

'Well there's no-one at the Embassy with any function of that sort here. All questions of overseas aid are decided by the F.C.O. in London. We know the agencies of course, but I couldn't give you any introduction – and besides, it wouldn't do you any good. If I can help in any other way, you know where I am.' It was a brief, businesslike meeting. Tom

McKillop shook my hand and departed. I left the Embassy in low spirits, having had not the scintilla of the suggestion that I might learn how to raise funds for the camp. I left the swish and cool gilt marble of the Embassy by its front door and headed towards the entrance gates when I spotted a car in the Embassy car park that attracted my attention, an old Italian Lancia car. I had always loved fast and interesting cars, an appreciation inherited, I suppose, and shared with my father, who was an avid enthusiast.

I diverted my path from the gate to the car and was peering inside its window when a man approached.

'You like?' he asked.

'Oh yes, very much. The Aurelia was the best Lancia ever made!' The schoolboy still in me shone out.

The man was in his mid 40s, very tall with long black wavy hair, and he was immaculately dressed. His suit was light blue silk woven with thin cream stripes, and his shirt and tie were almost as dazzling as the crocodile shoes. He spoke fluent English with an Italian accent.

We talked about the car in particular, and about cars in general, and about Italian cars versus French cars, and racing drivers and carburettors and engines and our conversation went on for a good half an hour.

'Et si,' he said finally, 'why don't you join my wife and I for dinner this evening, if you can manage it, and we can continue our conversation?' He handed me his card. '… say about seven? There is no need to dress, it is just my wife and I, it is simple, we would be delighted!' He took a card and a lacquered pen from his pocket and he wrote an address on the back of it.

I looked at the card and read that this was Le Count Guido Del Assantio, Attache Culturel to the Italian Embassy.

'Why yes,' I said, 'but I really would appear dressed as I am now, I am sorry...' I gestured to my jeans.

'No need. This is my home address. You come as you come, you have just as we eat, very simple... about seven?'

He slid his tall frame into the Lancia in a series of elegant movements, started it up with a roar, and with a 'Ciao!' he drove off.

I had neither the spirit nor the self confidence to further politic that day, and in my weak and defeated state took to my habit in a new city:

to wander. In my meanderings, I turned over in my mind how I could further the Rimpoche's interests and I could see that I was in an unfavourable position. It was quite clear that this young man was not going to succeed in raising money for the camp, and that the Rimpoche's expectations were unrealistic and naïve. But the problem was that I was at the camp at the Rimpoche's pleasure and if I were to lose his support my position there could become untenable. There was also the issue of the new volunteers; I was very pleased at the news that there was to be a nurse because this would greatly improve the Tibetans' prospects for better treatment. That there was to be soon someone who could get the chicken rearing unit going was also a great step forward; the building was nearly ready – it needed just the chickens and the expertise to rear them. As to the major, I could not make any estimation, but my instinct told me that neither the Tibetan personality nor the general ethic at work in the camp would respond well to a military mind. The Tibetans are the reverse of the military. They are instinctive and spontaneous. Their organisation is the consequence of their disorganisation and I didn't think they would have it any other way.

With these troubling thoughts churning round my mind, I wandered and walked and by late afternoon found myself back at the YMCA, where I discovered that the main consequence of the day was a severe bout of homesickness. I sought the Australian girls, but they had left and I felt more alone than ever. Out of boredom, curiosity and hunger, I decided I would risk a visit to my Italian acquaintance.

On the dot of seven, I was outside the gates of a huge colonial house set in extensive wooded grounds that must have extended a couple of hectares, which were fenced in by high, ornate iron railings. The gates were a massive three to four metres high and were open to an immaculate gravelled driveway that led to a flight of stone steps which ascended to a porticoed double door. I walked up the driveway in some disbelief that this was the address to which I had been invited.

I climbed the steps to the door hesitantly. Before I had rung a bell, one half of the great door was opened by a man dressed in an orange and white tunic and trousers, on whose head was a green silk turban.

'Good evening Sahib,' he said, bowing, 'the Count and Countess are expecting you. Please enter.'

I followed the man into a great hallway floored with black and white marble, and our footsteps echoed in the vastness.

'If you care, Sahib, there is a washroom to your right...' I took the hint and washed and cooled myself.

As I re-entered the hall, the Count was there, striding towards me. I noticed with relief that he was wearing jeans, as I was.

'Ah, my young friend, please come in, please... I am glad you could come.'

The count led me from the hall into a huge sitting room lavishly furnished with suede sofas and solid glass side tables sumptuously assembled round a fireplace of baronial proportions.

'My wife...' said the Count. The Countess, dressed in an impression of floating spotted yellow silks, was seated on a sofa fingering an emerald necklace; I took her offered hand gently and bowed slightly. Her mouth opened like a pale pink rose opening at dawn and she smiled graciously – nevertheless she gave the slight impression that she had been asked to give a coin to a vagrant.

'You like the cars... like my husband?'

'Yes, I'm afraid so...'

'You boys...' she answered, shaking her head.

'Oh come my darling, they are things of beauty,' rejoined the Count, 'they are not only transport!'

Perhaps seeing that she had little to contribute to the mutual interest of the Count and myself, the Countess rose from her seat in a shimmering of bouffant. 'I shall check the dining room,' she murmured.

I was on my second Cinzano when dinner was announced and the Count led me to an adjoining room; this one was panelled in mahogany, and at its thirds and corners were broad breakfront grooved pilasters decorated with gold swags at their capitals. It was very grand. In the centre of the room was an English triple pedestal mahogany table about 15ft long, upon which rested a magnificent silver and silver gilt candelabra embellished with Neptune and swirling mermaids, carefully counterpointed by massive square vases of white lilies. Places were set at the table's centre and ends. The Count and Countess sat at the ends and I was placed at the middle, and I was faced with an array of silver cutlery that caused me some concern.

As soon as we were seated, a servant wheeled in a trolley laden with domed silver tureens, which were placed on a serving table behind the dining table; the servant was no less magnificent than that which he bore – he was dressed entirely in white, his pleated hat bearing a tall gold fan at one side.

Conversation around the table was almost shouted because of the distance separating the three of us, but it was affable and easy until I was presented with an artichoke, something which I had not encountered before. In Aberdeen in the sixties, a green pepper was considered an exotic.

The Count and Countess dealt with their artichokes as one does, but because of the candelabra and the vases of flowers I could not see, and therefore could not understand how to deal with this vegetable. The artichoke lay before me with its adjacent silver bowl of vinaigrette and its accompanying crystal finger bowl of warm lemon water, but the next line of cutlery in gave no clue as to the simplicity of eating the thing. In these situations, honesty is the best policy, so I asked what this vegetable was and how was one supposed to eat it. Thankfully, I had not yielded to the previous, passing inkling that the liquid in the fingerbowl might be a garnish.

Had I ever stood a chance with the Countess, the artichoke dealt such an opportunity its death, and thenceforth she was distant and sullen. I forget how many courses this meal comprised, but I do remember soup, lobster, veal, pheasant and sorbets; sometimes a dinner remains a long time in memory. I asked in passing where on earth in Delhi one could acquire a lobster.

'Oh, the diplomatic bag,' answered the Count. After dinner, back in the sitting room and quite the young lord – with two smooth cognacs under the belt and delicious coffee swarming its caffeine around my swimming head – I chatted with the Count alone and raised the subject of the Tibetans, explaining my difficulty in raising funds.

'Ah yes,' he said, 'that is difficult; it begins not here in India, but with well meaning ladies in Milan, Amsterdam or New York or London. I do not think you will get funds in Delhi. But maybe, perhaps, I will see what I can do. Some people I can speak to. But now, I want to show you something, something I think you might like…'

He got up and I followed him. He led me through the hallway and down a long right-angled dark corridor at whose end was a small door. This door gave onto a narrow set of service stairs, which spiralled slightly inwards on its one-flight descent. The stair ended in a dark, small, stone-floored hall in which there was a single arched door. I was briefly very frightened. I sensed the headline – 'North East Man's Skeleton Found in Delhi Mansion; Black Magic Ritual Suspected. City Police Investigate.'

'Come,' said the Count, opening the door before him.

As he pushed the door open, the space beyond it was temporarily completely dark, then neon ceiling lights stuttered on as the Count touched some switches just inside the dark space to his left. What we had entered was a vaulted, brickwork stable about 10 metres square; the floor was concreted into small squares where once the horses stood – what was now there took my breath away; next to the Lancia was a red Ferrari.

There are some things to some young men that comprise, in physical form, the poetic essence of all their dreams – of testosterone, of achieve-ment, of fulfilment, of pleasure in its purest, unadulterated form. And for this young man, a red Ferrari was such a thing of incomparable excitement.

The Count opened the car door, clambered in and turned on the igni-tion; there was a brief whirring, then the engine caught and 12 cylinders began to sing a hallelujah chorus to the male ego. The chatter of men and young men talking cars is dull to those not afflicted, but the Count and I indulged our love of that peculiar language until the Ferrari's attributes, aesthetics, speed, potential and promise were fully exhausted and we could say no more and do nothing but gaze over its liquid luscious lines.

'But where on earth in India could you drive it?' I asked.

'Mon Diamo! I never drive it, I just look at it!' he replied.

The Count and I parted good friends, and despite his invitation to stay the night I felt the need to get back to reality and made my way back to the YMCA. I dreamed the happy sleep of a man driving a red Ferrari at great speed up tortuous twisting Alpine roads in circumstances which included an Indian Princess, some fine drama, and the conclusion of which was rich in praise and adulation. I think I saved the object of my dreams from pirates and her father gave me the Ferrari.

I spent one last day in Delhi and found the United Nations Association building so that I could tell the Rimpoche I had at least made a start to getting millions from America and the United Nations. I went into the building, rifled a stash of leaflets in the hallway and asked at the Reception desk for the name of someone I could write to. This was to create a camouflage so that I could tell the Rimpoche that I had been to the 'Nited Nations' and that I had a name of someone I could contact. In fact the lady at the desk was very helpful, asked me a million questions and insisted that I *should* write.

'You never know,' she said. Nevertheless, I felt guilty of a subterfuge.

After dealing with the affairs of state, I then used the last of my time to get myself to the offices of an organisation called 'Brothers to Medicine'. This was the outfit for which my brother David was working. I thought I might get some news of him and, as luck would have it, he had been there but a week before, but had returned to Andrahpur. I was very upset that with a change to my timetable I could have seen him. My homesickness had been getting quite severe and I was deeply hurt at having missed him. But at least I had found the place and met the people there and in that exercise found free and pleasant accommodation anytime I happened to return to Delhi. My last assignation of that day was to return to the house of Mrs Mehta. There, and this time informed by that lady's son, I learned that she had returned since my first visit but had left again – she was now in Dehra Dun, up in the foothills. I was at her door but three minutes receiving this information, then I left.

I decided that my work was done in Delhi and took the bus back towards the YMCA with the ambition of pleasing myself for the remaining hours of that day with a wander. Two stops before I was to get off, onto the bus boarded an instantly familiar figure: Finlay Cruikshank.

'Finny!' I cried as he came down the aisle. 'What on earth are you doing in Delhi?'

'On my way to Oz. Going to see my girl.' He slung his rucksack onto the rack and sat down beside me.

Finny and I had been at school together and were good friends. He and I had undertaken a 10 day winter trek across the Cairngorms just the year before, during which, in a cramped tiny tent, we vomited simultaneously after eating a packet of 'Surprise' dehydrated peas that we had boiled and eaten and had neglected to soak in water beforehand.

'And what are *you* doing on a bus in Delhi?' he asked me.

'Long story. I'm working up in the Himalayas and came down to try and raise money for the camp I'm in.'

'Done any climbing?'

'No, I only got to India a month ago.'

'Lucky bastard.'

'Not really, camp's freezing, I'm living in a tent and there's bugger all to eat but lentils, can't you tell?' I tapped my stomach.

'Better than dry peas,' he answered.

'Oh Lord, here's my stop... good luck in Oz.'

'Same to you, see you at the Blue Lamp.'

'Mine's a MacAllan.'

'You'll be paying then,' he shouted. I got off the bus and waved to him as the bus disappeared into the Delhi traffic.

After a day's train journey in the sweltering heat from Delhi to Pathankot, and then on the small gauge train to Baijnath, I was glad to be back at the camp despite the fact it had received a hefty covering of snow since my departure. The bus from Baijnath to Palabir had slithered and gasped up the hill road and took twice as long as normal. The Rimpoche was well pleased with my reported progress in Delhi and especially at my meeting with the 'Itarrians', whom he was sure would produce vast quantities of aid. I gave him back the balance of the money he had provided for the trip and graciously he let me keep fifty Rupees.

'So how'd it go?' asked Ross.

'Waste of time. Like we both knew. I went to the British Embassy, the United Nations Association and I met someone from the Italian Embassy, but they're all saying the same thing – don't waste time trying to raise money in India, do it in Europe and America.'

'Thought so. Have a good time though?'

'Yeah, had a shower anyway. Fab.'

'Oh yes, and what's that like? I've forgotten.' I leaned close to him and sniffed.

'Yes, you have rather.'

I got back to my routine with a new sense of seriousness. In my absence, Tenzin had continued treating our patients and there had been no major setbacks to our regime; I was heartened by the prospect that the camp was to get a nurse, and that Dr Mittle's next visit was not far off.

By the beginning of February, our dispensary tent had become a focal and fixed point in the camp; each morning by about 10:00 there were old and new patients waiting outside. We had a system of record-keeping that logged each patient, their symptoms, any medications and so on, and these began to accumulate into a record of the camp's general health. The women were gradually becoming used to us, but the men seldom presented themselves unless dragged there by concerned family members.

One dull morning, a truck arrived and bumped its way slowly along the slush-covered track towards the tents. By the time it came to a halt by the flagpole near the woollen mill, word had spread and a crowd gathered to investigate. The back tail of the truck was lowered and the driver heaved out huge soft bundles which contained we knew not what, wrapped up in old blankets tied at their tops in big knots. When the truck had gone, Ross and I undid one bundle and found that it contained old clothes.

'Ah, I know now,' said Ross, 'these are from Holland. There's a women's group near Amsterdam who collect old clothes for us and send them over!'

It didn't take long for the Tibetans to savvy what was going on, and within minutes the area was swarming with people, scrabbling through the piles of sweaters and trousers, blankets, hats, scarves, old shoes and trousers. Ross and I watched one elderly man who had picked up a round flat black object out of the pile of clothes and was examining it intently. He looked at it this way and that, turned it upside down, held it at a distance from his short sighted eyes trying to work out what it was. In a fit of mild frustration, the mat hit this thin black round thing against his thigh and it suddenly transformed itself into a top hat. It was an old Victorian hat which had a springy circular wire around its inside that enabled the hat to be squashed flat. The hat fell from the man's hands and he leapt back in fright. He leaned forward and peered at it as though it were some unknown small animal. I picked my way through the crowd, picked up the hat and put it on the old man's head. He laughed and laughed and hobbled off. He met a man with a sombrero and they raised their hats to each other and they roared with laughter.

There were clothes in the shipment that I would dearly liked to have had, but Ross and I decided it would be inappropriate for us to take anything. The most sought-after items were woollen sweaters and blankets, and those who had been successful in fighting for clothing that fit would run off with their spoil like naughty children.

It was about a week after this that we welcomed a new volunteer to the camp – Jay Hassan. Jay was a British born and educated Bangladeshi, 25 and just finished with his veterinary exams at Lewes in Sussex. He was a tall, handsome man with heavy black framed glasses, fine hands and quite an upper crust accent. He arrived sharply dressed as if for a new job, but after the first day he joined the rest of us in the slow decline into natural scruffiness. As the camp's 'chicken man', his arrival had been eagerly anticipated – not least by us volunteers. We recognised that where there were chickens, there would not long afterwards be roast chickens, and Jay was welcomed with more enthusiasm than he perhaps appreciated.

As prompted by Reggie Starling in Delhi, Ross and the Rimpoche had one of the houses being built for the Tibetans temporarily and minimally finished off; the windows were glazed, a front door was fitted and the roof sheeted with corrugated iron. The house chosen for Jay was very near to the tent that Ross and I lived in; Ross and I had a look round the concrete floored, bare-breeze, block-walled shell of the house that Jay was to have and judged our tent to be the superior accommodation.

The day Jay arrived at the tea factory, he immediately saw the Rimpoche and Tenzin for the first introductory meeting, and then Ross and I showed him around the camp proper. Naturally, he wanted to see 'his' chicken shed and he was very pleased with the unit, but bemoaned the lack of electricity, which was vital to its operation. Then we showed him his 'house', which he looked at with dismay and later chose not to use in preference to the small room at the tea factory that had been Hugh's.

The next day, Mr Bhattacharia, the Indian building contractor, was on site and I was party to a blazing shouting match in which Ross surprised everyone with the force of his appeal to Mr B. to 'bloody well' get the electricity into the chicken unit and to the woollen mill, 'otherwise…'. The 'otherwise' we never knew (nor did Ross), but the flare up had the desired result and within a week the electricity was brought to the shed and, miraculously, within three weeks the unit was full of chicks. Demonstrating great foresight, Jay had armed himself with the knowledge of where in the North of India he could get chicks for rearing before he came out from England, and in this preparation he earned great admiration for his planning. Within one week of his arrival he had written to whoever had the chicks and within two he disappeared on a trip, to come back a few days later in a truck. This disgorged a heap of sacks of feed and a thousand caged chicks into the warmth of the chicken shed.

The Rimpoche was very impressed.

'Very good man,' he said, wagging his finger at me in particular, 'very good.'

The Tibetans are curious as cats, and the chicken shed and its contents were a major attraction for many weeks; it was appealing to all of us because it was a warm place in a cold climate, and it became so popular that Jay had to fit a lock to its doors and bar everyone from going inside except those who were to play a part in its operation. The rationale of the chickens was that the Tibetans would learn how to rear them and process them and, in that repeating cycle, create regular income. Jay had it all worked out.

Before the chicks had arrived, Jay had put the word out via Tenzin that the chicken-rearing unit would need an initial six trainees from within the camp. To begin with, only men came forward, but Jay made it known that he also wanted some female help and finally four men and two young women were chosen to be the first chicken wallahs. During the first few weeks, these Tibetans showed themselves to be very good at everything to do with the chicks because they seemed already to know naturally what to do – the only thing they did not understand was the necessity of filling out the feed sheets. They asked why the sheets were necessary when all of them knew anyway exactly when and how the chicks had been fed. No explanation could satisfy their other logic.

I had been at the camp for two full months. The weather had been cold, there was a thaw and it became wet and miserable but I was very happy – except for one thing. The dispensary tent was the focus of my life, but the feeling that I was doing very little persisted and grew. I could see plainly that patients were describing symptoms that were indicative of ailments far more serious than my first aid could affect. My frustration was the worse because of an incident which made me seem more able than I was.

Ross and I had settled in our tent one evening and were about to turn off the lamp to sleep when Tenzin stuck his head through the flaps.

'You come Mike! Come quick. Yeshe very very sick. You see her now.'

It was precisely the circumstance I had been dreading. .

I quickly dressed, as did Ross, and we followed Tenzin to a tent at the heart of the campsite; there, Tsongya was waiting very anxiously along with a small crowd, and as I approached I could hear screams of agony coming from inside the tent. I went in and a young woman of about thirty was lying on her side, her knees doubled up into her stomach; she was rocking from side to side with her arms clenched tight around her middle, moaning for a few seconds then screaming out very loudly as spasms of pain hit her. Her eyes had that far away look of someone in intense agony. She was not a lady I had seen before at the dispensary, so I knew that what was happening was something very sudden and very serious; there is no mistaking the authenticity of someone in great pain. I ascertained first that she was not pregnant, and then asked the husband if the pains had come very suddenly or whether there had been any precondition in the hours and day preceding. The husband was equivocal about this, saying that she had complained of some stomach and bowel pain for two days previously, but that the woman herself thought this was due to some bad food she had eaten. I could make no sense of it and decided that this was a patient that had to be got quickly to the hospital in Palamjong, some 20km away.

I got the husband to get blankets to wrap her up as much as possible and Tenzin and I ran with torches to the Rimpoche's bungalow, where the jeep's keys were given to me without hesitation; the Rimpoche was jealous of his jeep and we had tried for weeks to get the use of it to no avail – but on that occasion he relented immediately. Ross bravely stayed with the patient. With much screaming and yowling, we got the woman into the back of jeep, swaddled in blankets: it was a very cold starry night and a frost was icing the slush.

Tsongya sat beside the patient in the back, while Tenzin was in the front passenger's seat beside me. I drove down the dark track, trying to avoid the deep potholes as best as possible, but each time the jeep lurched into a rut, loud screams from the patient would follow. As we approached the tea factory I had to negotiate the sharp right-angled bend that takes the track towards the main road; there, there was a makeshift bridge of railway sleepers over the stream. The outer two sleepers had collapsed sideways over time and had left a deep dip layered with protruding rounded boulders. In my haste, I went too close to that edge and the jeep jolted downwards with a violent and metal-to-rock thump. A massive and heart-rending bellowing came from the back of the jeep amid shouts and gasps, but the jeep had enough momentum to lurch onwards. I was shaken and embarrassed but I could only drive on to try and get to Palamjong as quickly as possible. I headed onto the main road at the fastest speed I could manage. My greatest fear was that the patient would lose consciousness and that I would be the one who would have to make the decision either to stop and give artificial respiration or drive on in the hope she survived the journey. The road was slippery with ice and it was pitch black. I closed my mind to everything but the driving, but I became aware that Tenzin was hitting me on the shoulder.

'Mike! Stop! Stop!' he shouted, 'Stop!'

I brought the jeep to a skidding halt in the middle of the road thinking some dreadful catastrophe had befallen the patient; I was very nervous and I was shaking. If something was happening to her that needed skilled medical attention, I knew her life could be at risk. But the oddest thing happened.

'She okay!' shouted Tenzin, 'she okay!'

The two women had got out of the jeep and were holding each other; the patient was crying, but not from pain. What had happened medically, I don't know, but the woman was, apart from a minor soreness, recovered enough to speak and move normally. I asked her through Tenzin if she wanted to go on to the hospital, but she was adamant that she wanted to return to the camp and to her husband. Greatly relieved, we drove back in great good spirits and all was well.

The consequence of this event was that I was credited by the Tibetans of having a medical competence that I did not have. The patient perhaps had some bowel obstruction which the jolting of the jeep had dislodged, but her cure was pure accident and none of my doing. The next day, word had spread throughout the camp of the previous night's events and the dispensary was very much busier in the following days and weeks. I noticed that my 'patients' were listening to me more attentively and looking at me differently too.

In my first attempts at running the dispensary, I had been ignorant of, and had taken no account of, the long tradition of Tibetan medicine; I had the simple and singular understanding of ailments that my Western background had given me. An ailment or injury could be explained and therefore treated according to the manifested symptoms – a clear case of cause and effect. Tibetan medicine has a different perspective and understands the human body as something that functions by the interaction of three different forces – Phlegm, Bile and Wind. When I worked in the dispensary, I would almost always have Tenzin and Tsongya with me and at any time, any one of us would be bandaging, or cleaning wounds or dishing out TB medications. When the occasion did arise that I needed Tenzin to translate an instruction to a patient, I noticed he would often converse briefly with Tsongya before speaking directly to the person before us. I didn't see any significance in this to begin with, then I asked Tenzin once what it was, precisely, that he had said to a patient.

'Well, I told her the pill would help equal the force between Tsen Bah with Hui Bzen,' he answered, casting a glance at Tsongya.

'But I said that she should take one pill three times a day Tenzin.'

'Oh, I said that too,' he replied.

So I began to understand that the Tibetans viewed Western medicine with a scepticism which I had previously not had the wit to see; they were more likely to believe in the efficacy of a pill or ointment if it could be described as having an effect within the language of their own traditions. So I began to ask Tenzin to translate Tsongya's interpretation of my treatments to the patients so that I could begin to understand how it fitted into the scheme of Tibetan medicine.

Quite how the incident in the jeep could be described within the terminology of Tibetan medicine I don't know, but it was ultimately good that came out of the whole event – it brought people to the dispensary who previously had been reluctant to do so. We also had many more children brought by their mothers for vitamins, and this enabled us coincidentally to push the necessity of washing and personal hygiene. The scrubbing brush was not a common object in the camp and scrubbing was not a common habit.

In preparation for the arrival of our nurse and, later, the major, it was time to re-arrange our accommodation. Jay had voiced his reservation of sharing the room at the factory with a woman and we decided it would be best if the new nurse took over that space. I was cold but perfectly happy in the tent with Ross, but I had the chance of moving elsewhere and this allowed Jay to move from the factory to the tent and to share space with Ross. Like Jay, I did not like the half-finished house that had been intended for him, even though that was the obvious spare accommodation.

About 100 yards to the east of our tent was an old mud shed that had once been a store; inside, it was about 10ft square and about the same high; there was a small, low timber door and the floor was just smoothed mud. It had no windows except for one small glass pane set into the roof, but it did have one very great asset: an electric light powered by a line which ran by poles from the east of the camp. It had been occupied, as a special privilege, by one of the camp's older ladies; she had become so frail and unable to look after herself that she moved to another camp at Dehra Dhun to be with her daughter. There was considerable competition for the shed, but the Rimpoche offered it to me without even my asking. The shed was my first home with solid walls since I had arrived at the camp and it was a great relief to move in to someplace that had a door. I would be able to have my Picassos on show again. It was luxurious accommodation, apart from the drawback of being infested with scorpions. These were not the black ones of common knowledge but small pink-brown ones that could scuttle with great speed into tiny crevices and corners. Ross and Jay and I had a morning squashing those we could find and an afternoon ensuring we had found every possible nest. I had a terrible fear of being stung, even though I had been assured by one of Tenzin's friends who had suffered the event that the result was 'only' 45 minutes of very intense agony and that that was the extent of it. I had known of the scorpions before I moved in, but I had been so cold in the tent that I was prepared to try anyplace to be more comfortable. Among the comforts of home, I stashed my tinned asparagus and peaches under my charpoi and covered them with an old sack; I had still found no occasion worthwhile of their indulgence.

A few days before my 19th birthday in mid-March 1967, Hazel Schelmerdine arrived at the camp late in the afternoon, on a day which was particularly cold and miserable; the clouds were low and thick brown and a freezing drizzle drifted over the camp. Hazel was a woman in her late 20s and had immediately about her that air of personal virtue which, though a moral quality, is physically apparent. She wore a thick fawn sweater, workaday jeans and walking boots. She had clear, almost transparent fair skin and had gold-brown Goldilocks hair that was slightly curled; it grew naturally and seemed unlikely to have ever received the attention of many hairdressers. For luggage, she had but a rucksack, and when she was shown her meagre accommodation in the tea factory she simply put her pack on the charpoi without comment, apparently unconcerned with her surroundings. After meeting Ross, Jay, the Rimpoche and Tenzin, I showed her round the camp. The dispensary tent was our first destination; there she looked closely at the facilities and she asked me a torrent of questions. She very quickly fathomed the thin extent of my knowledge and I felt my little world was under siege.

That evening, Ross, Jay and I extended such hospitality to our new guest as we could and helped Tenzin create a decent meal to welcome her to the camp. Some buffalo meat and potatoes had come our way – they had been acquired with a bottle of gentian violet, a small jar of vitamin pills and some currency.

At the end of March, the snow slowly melted and for weeks the camp was miserable with mud: everyone reluctantly shuffled around hunched up against the cold and it was impossible to find any daytime warmth other than in the chicken shed. There, the chicks had matured surprisingly quickly into a herd of uniformly white-feathered chickens, and I had the idea that since they would soon be ready for killing perhaps we could sell some of them to the British Embassy in Delhi. I remembered my acquaintance Tom McKillop had said he would help in any way he could. I therefore wrote to Tom and suggested he might like some Himalayan chickens for the Embassy freezers.

By the time I had been at the camp for three months, I could see that progress in completing the woollen mill, the houses, the water tank and the three other industrial sheds had amounted to practically nothing. The chicken shed had been completed as a result of fiercely raised voices, but no other force seemed capable of speeding the building works. I could see Ross was becoming increasingly depressed; he would wander about the camp, head down, lost in his own thoughts. I didn't believe he was ill in any sense, but, like me, he doubted his ability to influence events and felt a bit useless because of it. At the woollen mill, the looms had been installed even before my arrival, but they sat there useless because the rest of the building work and the installation of water and electricity were nowhere to be seen. The contractor, Mr Battacharia, would appear on site irregularly, trucks with breeze blocks or bags of cement would arrive and depart, and sometimes a gang of Indian construction workers would labour for a few days then disappear, often furtively bearing sacks filled with the very stuff they were supposed to be building with.

I suggested to Ross that a trip to Delhi to see Reggie Starling would be good in the two respects of giving him a break and of giving him the hope that some pressure could be brought to bear on the contractors by some means or other. Ross said he would think about it, but I suspected bigger thoughts were going on in his head than just a trip to Delhi.

Since my first emergency use of the jeep, the Rimpoche had been much more willing for Ross, Jay and I to use it, and we had gradually taken advantage of this to make trips to nearby Baijnath and Palamjong. At Palamjong there was a post office and a telephone; there were shops and a pharmacy, food to be bought, and even a bookshop where the 'Times of India' newspaper could be had, so the use of the jeep gave us access to more of the small things in life which made our existences a little more comfortable. By the beginning of April I had used up all my medications in the constant battle against diarrhoea, so the trips to Palamjong became essential.

Ross left for Delhi at the end of the first week in April, and at the dispensary Hazel proved herself to be far superior in treating our patients.

Like many experienced nurses, she had knowledge of medicine that, in some circumstances, approached that of a fully qualified doctor, and in others exceeded it. It was not long before I began to feel redundant. Hazel began as the listening, attentive assistant to Tenzin, Tsongya and I, but it was just a matter of weeks before Hazel was being assisted by the rest of us and I was the one who was needed the least.

Ross returned from Delhi after a week and seemed refreshed by the change of scenery. He had had little success with Reggie Starling at the T.R.R.A., but held out hope that his visit might bear fruit eventually. Reggie was, according to Ross, furious at the catalogue of failures reported to him – these, apparently, were at odds with the reports that Mr Battacharia had been sending him.

We decided that there was little we could do, either collectively as volunteers or as individuals, and that our only option was to bide our time. Ross had tried his best to assist the building and construction work and had at times physically mixed up concrete, laid foundations and taken up a saw and hammer. But there were a hundred houses to be built, so it was hopeless to think that one man's efforts could materially bring the project forward. There was some clause in the building contract that prohibited the Tibetans from undertaking any of the labour themselves, though what reasoning lay behind this neither Ross nor I could fathom.

For my part, I had also reached a watershed, because although I assisted at the dispensary I was becoming more and more redundant. I therefore had more time on my hands, as did Ross, and we both reacted in the same way – by taking time off.

This was not to say that we were suddenly freed of tasks, because there was always some job to be done, but there was a new pattern of time that saw us both free to do as we pleased from about the mid-afternoon.

I took to walking among the hills and valleys around the camp. I would find small reasons to make trips either by bus or jeep to Baijnath, Palamjong and to some of the surrounding towns and villages. I found in this new regime that I became more acquainted with the Tibetans because I had more time to spend with them, and as a person rather than the male nurse dabbing them with gentian violet. Nevertheless, time and circumstances left me with the feeling that I was not doing enough that was useful, though I had no sensation that the Rimpoche was in any way grudging that I was still there. I had written my letters to the United Nations Association in Delhi, but their reply was in a voice that was slightly offended that such a direct approach should be made and that 'official' agencies were already looking at projects and schemes for the Tibetan settlements as a whole.

It was during a blank-minded day in the afternoon that, driving the jeep back from Dehra Dun, I stopped in response to a man thumbing a lift; he was white, young, in jeans and tee shirt and he had a red rucksack slung over one shoulder.

'Hi man, going my way?' asked the man, leaning his head into the jeep.

'I'm going to Palabir, to the Tibetan camp,' I said.

'Hey, cool, that's just fine, I'm not far from there, just about a mile.' He threw his rucksack into the back seat and got in beside me.

'Thanks man, thanks.'

This was Howie, and he was with the American Peace Corps.

Following his directions, I went beyond the track that led up to the Tibetan camp and drove about another two miles before turning down a wooded lane on the right hand side of the road. This led downward for about a quarter of a mile and ended in a clearing, in which stood an orderly little wooden chalet. The building was a complete surprise in that it was almost purely Swiss in character and neatly built of smooth finished planks, unlike any other building anywhere in Northern India. There was a central door flanked by double-glazed windows, and from a single chimney on the right gable wall blue smoke curled into the still air. Perhaps the oddest anomaly was the pair of blue gingham curtains that lay behind the windows. I drew up by the front door and Howie invited me in.

'Sure, come on!' he said, 'you've time for a coffee.' The prospect of a cup of coffee was very exciting. I hadn't had coffee for months.

Howie led the way into the chalet, which was immediately warm and cosy. On a sofa, playing a guitar, was a very tall, lanky young man with long black hair.

'That's Ritchie...' said Howie, 'Rich, this is Mike, he's from the Tibetan Camp... you know, the one back at Palabir? Up the road?' Rich waved from the sofa.

'Hi man… what's it like up there… we've never been.'

'Well, it's okay.' I said, 'living's been a bit hard, but I suppose I've got used to it.'

'Yeah, I know what you mean,' said Ritchie struggling with a chord, 'India sure ain't Oklahoma, that's for damn sure. Have some coffee why don't you… and where are you from?'

'Scotland.'

'Hey, I been to Scotland once, when I was a kid with my parents. We stayed in Dublin.'

As the mugs were gathered, I looked around me. The chalet consisted of one main room with two doors set into the back wall – it was just like any student residence anywhere in the Western world. On shelves on the side walls were unimaginable and forgotten comforts such as a hi-fi and rows of LPs, stacks of books, college flags and baseball trophies and, on the opposite shelves, food; packets, boxes, bottles, jars, stacks and stacks of food. I realised I must have been staring at the bottles of ketchup, corn relish, Dijon mustard, barbecue sauces, tortilla dips and packets of crisps. A cup of hot steaming fresh coffee was thrust into my hand, poured from a pot which sat on top of the wood burning stove.

'Oh thanks,' I said to Howie; he must have sensed my thoughts.

'Hey, no problem, we get pretty well looked after,' he said. 'We get a delivery from Delhi every three months. We're kinda low right now. How d'you do for stuff?'

'You mean food?'

'Yeah, and the rest.'

'I've lived on lentils and chappatis for over three months now,' I said meekly, vaguely hoping this might produce sympathy and a bottle of ketchup, '… and sometimes we get potatoes.'

'Naw! That ain't none too good. You gotta eat.' There was disbelief in Ritchie's voice; he put the guitar to one side and sat upright, curious. I sipped my coffee.

'God that's good!' I gasped. 'Well, I can't say I wouldn't like more food, even a change would be welcome. But I don't think about it so much now.'

'Yeah, right,' said Ritchie, 'right,' and he leaned back on the sofa again.

'And what about you guys,' I asked, 'how long have you been here?'

'Nearly a year now for me,' said Howie, 'Rich… you been here, what, six months?'

'Yeah, just on I guess.'

'And what do you do?'

'Well we kinda go round the villages, make reports on health clinics, family planning, that sort of thing; we kinda offer help to them, see what they might need, that sort of stuff. But we don't have a jeep no more, so we're kinda grounded, have been since January, right Rich?' Rich picked up the guitar again and studiously set his fingers to a chord, head bent.

'Rich trashed the jeep' added Howie.

'Weren't my fault,' said Ritchie defensively, 'god-damn fuckin' cart in middle of the fuckin' road…'

'Don't matter a fuck man, you trashed the fuckin' jeep. Goddamn knows when we'll get another… fuck…'

I was there about half an hour and realised my head was slightly swimming with the coffee and the warmth. I invited them to come to the camp anytime, but warned them we wouldn't be able to offer much in the way of hospitality.

'Sure, we'll come. Like to see the place. So how many people you got?'

'About six hundred at the moment.'

Howie whistled. 'You don't say! I never knew it was that big, but yeah, we'll come on over some day, look forward to it.' Rather awkwardly, I shook hands with them both and drove back to the camp.

I related my meeting to Ross that night.

'And how long have they been there did you say?' he asked, eyebrows high.

'Well one of them's been there for a year.'

'Blow me, I never even knew they existed. D'you think they'll come and see us? We might get some stuff from them.'

'Don't know Ross, but I'll certainly ask them to bring some ketchup if they do.'

'And did you say Dijon mustard?'

'Yes, proper Meaux mustard, in one of those big white clay jars with the red wax on the cork.'

'And the coffee was fresh coffee, not instant?'

'Columbian fine ground.' Ross let out a long low whistle.

5

A routine settles, and back to Delhi

A FEW DAYS AFTER ROSS HAD GOT BACK FROM DELHI, HE CAME TO my shed one morning bearing a copy of the 'Times of India'.

'Meant to give you this,' he said. My stomach had been in uproar and I was still in bed.

'Thanks Ross. I'll read every word from back to front.'

'That's what I did. How's the stomach?'

'Heaving both ends.'

'Well, take it easy, maybe see you later.'

'Thanks.'

The newspaper was welcome, a rare thing for us. In the months I had been at the camp, there had only been two or three occasions when we had any sort of newspaper by which to keep abreast of world events. I read the first few pages and leafed through the rest, and by midday I had put the thing on my bed for later reading – I then got up and went to whatever task it was to occupy me for the day. In the evening before bed and by the luxury of the electric light bulb, I continued reading. I was just about to turn into sleep when I came across a story that stirred my intense and anxious interest. It was on one of the back pages and occupied just three or four inches of a single column. Its heading said 'British Aid worker killed in Andrahpur' and I immediately sat bolt upright. The story was about an incident that happened to a British man working for the 'Brothers To Medicine' charity. This was the organisation my elder brother David was working for, and I knew he was working in or near Andrahpur.

The story reported that a Land Rover with four passengers – two British and two Indian – had been involved in an accident in which the Land Rover had collided with and killed a cow in the middle of a crowded town. A mob had gathered round the Land Rover, which had become immobile because of the accident, and the villagers had smashed the windows of the vehicle and dragged all four occupants onto the ground to beat them up. The mob became further incensed as each of the four victims resisted the attacks and attempted to escape. One Briton was so seriously injured that he died. Of the two Indians, one was very seriously injured and both were in the hospital in Haramabad, which was the nearest big hospital. The remaining Briton was unaccounted for. The story ended with the statement that the British Embassy in Delhi had been informed and were seeking to contact the families of the Britons involved. I had an eerie feeling that my brother was one of the Britons. I don't know if there was some kind of fraternal communication 'in the ethers', but, as I tried to sleep, I was sure he was involved. I checked the date of the newspaper and it was five days old.

The next morning I rose very early and had to intrude on the Rimpoche's breakfast to beg for the jeep from him to go to Palamjong so that I could phone the Embassy. A sleepy and grumpy Rimpoche denied me the jeep because it was to transport someone important later that day, but turning from the door and coming back just a second later, he handed me a set of keys and said that there was a motorbike in one of his back sheds which I could use 'carefully'. I did not enquire about this new arrival but went straight away to Palamjong as fast as I could. By 10:00, I got through to the Embassy and found out that David had been the Briton unaccounted for in the attack. But the news was that he had made his way to safety and, furthermore, that he was on his way to Delhi, where he was to report to the offices of 'Brothers To Medicine'. Beyond these facts, the Embassy knew nothing else concerning my brother. I concluded my conversation with them by asking that, should they speak to him in the near future, would they please convey to him that I would be going to Delhi within the next couple of days and would hope to see him there. I was given the number of the 'BroMed' offices and the matter was left at that. I phoned the 'BroMed' offices, but the line was engaged continually and I rode back to the camp having decided I would anyway go to Delhi.

I explained the situation to the Rimpoche and he was not only understanding, but generous by providing some help with the fare.

I left the next morning. In the very late evening of the same day, after a very anxious journey to Delhi, I met my brother at the 'BroMed' building. I was more relieved to see him alive than I can express. He had vivid bruises around the side of his head, neck and wrists, but otherwise, physically, he was fine.

I had but a few hours with him the next morning, and before I had even begun to speak to him properly he was called to meetings, and by early evening was on his way to the airport and Calcutta.

Although the affair had lasted but three days or so, I was utterly exhausted. I had been unwell before I left, but the circumstances had overcome this and I had found ample energy to deal with my trip. But the aftermath of that energy imposed a severe lethargy on me, such that I asked my hosts if I might rest for a day or so before heading back to the hills. They were a friendly group of men; there was plenty spare accommodation in the residence and I was encouraged to stay as long as I liked. I slept for a night and day and another night and awoke not understanding the loss of one day of the week.

The 'BroMed' headquarters was a large, square, anonymous, white-washed building that was part offices, part hostel and part club. It was the Indian centre of operations for 'BroMed' and was run by Patrice, a balding, plump, middle-aged Frenchman.

'Ah, you are awake, young man,' he said as I appeared from my slumbers, 'you must have been tired.'

'Yes, I suppose I must have been. Any news of David?' I asked.

'I spoke to him last night and, really, he's fine. Of course, he has had a big fright. But I have asked our staff in Calcutta to keep a close eye on him for the next few weeks. Your brother is a strong man inside I think.'

'I hope so.'

'And what of you, what are you doing in India?'

I told him my tale of the camp and what I was doing and what the camp was trying to achieve.

'Well, you are welcome to use this place any time you wish. All I ask is that if we are full, not to displace any of our own staff – but that is unlikely, we are in a calm period. We have some people coming this evening, but they are only four, so we have plenty of room.'

I ventured into the blinding Delhi heat for the day and made for Connaught Square, from which point I relaxed by wandering around the city centre. I took the time to get my hair cut as it had become very long and searched out more medication to take back with me. By mid-afternoon, I had planned to visit Mrs Mehta's house for the third time, but the heat got the better of me and I went back to the 'BroMed' Centre to shower and sleep.

Apart from the occasional and distant voice of Patrice in the office below me, the house was hot and quiet. As the late afternoon became evening, I ventured up a narrow flight of stairs on the upper floor and found myself on the flat roof, where there was a cafe-type table and deck chairs positioned so that they looked over the front of the building and out over the city. The orange red sun was setting and I was suddenly lonely and homesick. In going to Delhi to see my brother, I had anticipated nothing other than seeing of him. That had been satisfied, but deep down I was miserable and disappointed that I had spent only a short time with him. He had been nervous and over-talkative and there was no point at which we had had a chance to speak of our parents, about home and perhaps other things. Deep down I was very homesick and his abrupt departure left me feeling worse. This dark mood deepened and spread. Although at that point I was not facing up to the fact that my presence in the Tibetan camp was becoming tenuous, my innerself probably was wondering what my choices could be in the event of that circumstance becoming fact.

That evening, the house was filled with the animation of the arrival of four of the 'BroMed's' field workers. There were three men and a striking blond woman. Like me, they were all young volunteers in their 20s or early 30s, giving of their time to various aid or health projects, some directly with 'BroMed', some just because the 'BroMed' Centre was a sort of hub for people like us. It was the first clear instance I had experienced that somehow, maybe even mysteriously, there was a community of volunteers in India, and that events and places brought members of that community together. It was in places such as the 'BroMed' Centre, or the YMCA, or at some odd street corner that one learned of other, cheap places in India to stay.

'If you're ever in Bangalore, be sure and go to the... whatever,' or 'I hear that UkAid is looking for help at a centre in Kerala'. It was at gatherings such as this that one began to hear the mythology that told of the time, the place and the people.

'Well, I came out with Dan Smith. We drove a VW to Afghanistan, sold it for 500 dollars and hitched the rest of the way to here.' Or, 'Did you hear about so and so – managed to get from London to Delhi on 25 quid, overland, all the way. Rode the trains mostly, climbed on to the roof when he could!'

It was by these stories that one began to feel part of something; it was not a brotherhood, nor even a coherent, definable grouping – but there was definitely a feeling of belonging to something. The members were mostly young, mostly white and almost always from backgrounds that the British understand as the 'middle' or 'professional classes'. The Americans and the British were by far the biggest groups – it didn't matter what outlandish location you were in, but that a white face ventured a 'Hi' or 'Hello'. There were also many French and Swedes, some South Africans, few Germans, but no Japanese or Chinese. It was the time when the term 'hippy' referred to someone who had opted out of the mainstream 'back home', be that college or a job. Use of the description of the term 'hippy' brings to the mind's eye an image of long hair, drugs, garlands of flowers and sexual promiscuity. But that was only one part of the story. There were some of that type – mostly American, and they were usually a touch older – but the majority were clean cut, clean living individuals who exhibited no extraordinary quality of appearance or behaviour.

I could fathom three common factors. The first was a desire to travel, and to experience the challenges that travelling always throws up. You get stuck in strange places, in odd situations, often with a language barrier and always without a solution that would be easily achievable on home territory. There were some people who 'just' travelled – hitch hiking where they could or otherwise travelling by the cheapest means possible – in a spirit of adventure.

Another factor was a mix of two things – a cynicism of the West's values and, as the result of that, a desire to do good in the world for reasons other than money. I am not mixing up dried milk in Bombay because the rate of pay is $1 higher than digging roads in Utah or Surrey.

As to the cynicism towards the 'West', it was widely and variously expressed. When one listened to people talking about why they were in India or just bumming round the world, the rejection of 'home' values was never far below the surface. It came in several forms: going to university or starting a career was a dull option when there was so much more of the world to see and experience; hell, getting a job in midtown America is just so boring compared to jumping trains, getting stranded in the Afghan desert or trading used Volkswagens for native jewellery. And there were those who took a much more calculated approach and articulated the moral complexities contained in knowing that the rejection of Western values usually begins in people who are from prosperous families and who are in good health. And there were those who seriously believed that the ultimate conclusion of the post-war generation would be a life of communes, free love and an end to all wars – and that those who had seen other lives in other countries (i.e., us) would be the ones to start the changes that would bring this about. The Americans were by far the strongest proponents of this idea.

In the middle were people like me – vaguely uncomfortable with the orthodox choices of life and vaguely uncertain as to what to do when faced with making a*ny* of life's big choices.

Such was the sample of people who might at one time be congregated in places such as the Brothers to Medicine Centre in Delhi; it was a small world and one where its participants learned and talked a lot. At the practical level, meeting other people in these circumstances helped disseminate information – who might be looking for volunteers in exchange for basic keep, who to speak to in such and such an organisation, how to get from this city to that city by a cheap or free means few would know about. The 'BroMed' Centre was a place for all this.

I was in the lounge and I had my head buried deep in a mound of old 'Paris Match' magazines when the Landrover arrived, late in the evening at about 10:00, and it disgorged four very tired and dusty people. They spoke minimally as they dumped their luggage in the hallway, pulled out sleeping bags and wash-bags, and gathered briefly in the kitchen before going to bed.

There was Robert and Daphne, a husband and wife team of doctors; there was Xavier, a Frenchman about 25 or so, lean faced, wiry and with penetrating sharp blue eyes. Lastly was an Englishman, Kim Fairweather. Kim had driven from Madras in his Land Rover and had picked up his passenger friends along the way. He was a tall, distinguished young man with chaotic curly straw-coloured hair, an oval freckled face and big feet which poked out of his sandals like two odd, caged animals. Kim had a prosperous father who had provided his son with a Land Rover with which to explore India to broaden his horizons. Kim sometimes helped out at aid centres, hospitals and the like, but he was under contract to no one and pleased himself as to how long he would stay at any one place.

As he explained it, 'I didn't fancy getting a job, didn't like the atmos-phere of university and my Dad kindly offered me the Landy if I fancied doing some travelling… so here I am.'

We spent most of the day together, just chatting and relaxing, and I got to like him. I told him of my work at the Tibetan camp and of my feelings that perhaps my time there was coming to an end. He said, 'I know there are people in Bihar needing help if you want to think about that. I've heard there's genuine famine there, no rain for years. Patrice has been very kind and has said I can use "BroMed" as a sort of base, so you can always get in touch with me eventually by contacting him.' He said that he hadn't been to Bihar, nor knew anything first-hand about the place seeking volunteers, but he knew how to contact them if ever I wanted to follow it up.

'And where are you off to next?' I asked.

'Dunno really. I need to rest a bit, maybe help here a while to repay Patrice for his hospitality, then maybe Kerala, maybe Nepal. I'll certainly be in India for another nine months or so – at least till the end of the year, then I'll see.'

The next day, Kim drove me to Delhi station where, once again, I made the long journey north to Pathankot, to Palabir, and to the camp. I was tired of that journey and hoped that I would not soon have to repeat it.

When I got off the bus at Ahju in the late evening to walk up the track to the camp, the night was mild and clear and wonderful. As I neared the top of the slope at the tea factory and headed for my shed, the sound of singing coming from the camp reached my ears and I was in love with the place all over again.

In my absence, there had been a delivery of post. It included a letter from home and a letter in a very imposing crested envelope from Tom McKillop at the British Embassy in Delhi. It read:

'Dear Mike, I have spoken to our catering manager and he says he would consider an order of up to two hundred chickens if these are reared to a high standard and have not been fed on fish meal; these must be plucked, eviscerated and free from any feathers or stubble and clean to the extreme. If the giblets can be supplied, these must be packaged separately within the carcass and each chicken must be individually packaged. We've not discussed exact costs, but let us know your price per unit delivered, chilled, to the Embassy. If this is of interest, please let me know. Yours aye, Tom McK. PS: I was glad to learn that your brother David survived unscathed from his ordeal.'

When Ross, Jay, Hazel and I were discussing the potential of this order for the Embassy, it came to light that the preparations and execution of this enterprise would be more complex than we had at first assumed.

The first task was for Jay to train some of the Tibetans in the slaughter and processing of the chickens; it wouldn't take long to show them, but it was a preparation that had not been, at that stage, thought of. Jay's trainees had proved themselves dedicated and efficient at the rearing of the chickens, but they had had no training in the slaughter and preparation of the carcasses. Other questions needing answers were: where would we get packaging for the chickens? Where would we get ice to chill the chickens on their journey to Delhi? How would we transport the chickens from Palabir to Delhi? How would we package the consignment so it was fit to travel? We discussed these questions and a hundred others and embarked on finding the solutions. I was glad of the tasks presented because I felt useful again. My part was a) to find large baskets into which the packaged chickens could be ice packed and b) to find a trailer for the jeep by which the chickens could be delivered to the train at Ahju, thence onward to Delhi. Although the identity of the person to accompany the chickens to Delhi had not been delegated, I had suspicions the task would fall to me. Jay was the main protagonist in getting plastic bags in which to pack the chickens, and in finding a source of ice. He also had to find more Tibetan volunteers to train for the packing of the birds. Ross was to prepare one of the buildings next to the chicken shed to be the slaughtering and packing station. Jay advised us that we would need large quantities of hot water in which to dip the dead chickens prior to their plucking, and Ross set about this task too.

Hazel gratefully acknowledged that there was not much she was qualified to do, but volunteered to prepare the paperwork by which we counted and recorded the chickens as they were slaughtered, plucked, eviscerated, packed into plastic bags and finally packed into the large baskets.

I had replied to Tom with the news that we would be delighted to supply the chickens, and in an unworldly way, assured him that we would be happy to accept his catering manager's valuation of them once they had been received. I thought it safer to initiate the deal on that footing rather than enter into protracted negotiations of price by letter. I thought of it as the first tentative step on the route to a long and profitable association with the Embassy.

Our first setback came within two days. Tenzin had been given the job of asking among the Tibetans if any were interested in helping with the project, but all had refused to have anything to do with the slaughtering or cleaning of the birds. We were all frustrated by this and Jay asked Tenzin to please find people who would help. It was at this late juncture that we found out something we should have realised before.

'Mr. Jay,' said Tenzin, wringing his hands in regret, 'no one will help'.
'Why not?'
'They, we... are Buddhists, we cannot kill any living thing. Not an insect, not a worm and not even one chicken.' Tenzin replied.

Jay clasped his head in his hands.

'Tenzin, this does not make sense. Yes, you are Buddhists, but from what I have heard you do not seem to have a problem killing Chinese. How come you can kill a human being but not a chicken?'

Tenzin tilted his head and thought for a moment.

'The chicken has no thoughts of harming me or anyone in this camp'.

He might as well have said 'up yours', and he left Jay where he was, defeated.

It became very suddenly obvious to us that at no time had the two words 'fore' and 'thought' been placed together in any adjacent sense. It was blindingly obvious that the Tibetans would not kill the chickens, but no-one, in all the planning and all the discussions, had thought of this simple but insurmountable obstacle to the plan.

Ross and Jay pressed ahead with the tasks that were possible, and within two weeks they had all the facilities ready in the unfinished house adjoining the chicken shed. This bare breeze block construction was just the outside four walls of one of the houses; Ross had managed to get enough roofing sheets to have it temporarily covered and he had rigged up hooks from the roof for lamps, should we need them. The floor was just rough flattened mud. At either end of the rectangular interior space there were two small enclosures of chicken wire, each about six feet square by some four feet high; these were to be the pens into which chickens from the big shed would be placed prior to being killed. Ross's preparations had also accumulated some tables, knives, two old oil barrels and pots to boil the water that would fill them; outside there was a large pile of firewood and Ross had made three fire pits with ingenious stands for hanging the pots over the fires.

Jay had proved himself to be the master of scrounging and had located a supply of ice from a bottling plant some sixty miles from the camp, and he had already received polythene bags for the packaging. The ice was going to be very expensive as it had to be delivered by truck; the Rimpoche was of the view that the price was too high. He thought on it for a few days then agreed that, in the long-term interests of the camp, the price was worth paying – but with the condition that future arrangements would have to see this side of the equation much improved. The Rimpoche was very adept at working out costs and profits.

For my part I had the wonderful excuse to drive the jeep around the whole area surrounding the camp in my search for big wicker baskets. These I eventually found in a market displaying vegetables and from the trader I found out who had made them. The next day I came back to the camp with 20 of them piled high and tied down at the back of the open jeep. The Rimpoche had used his extensive network of contacts to find a suitable trailer for the jeep in Dharamsala and, joining in the spirit of the enterprise, went to collect it himself.

It was now late in April and the chickens were three weeks beyond the point at which they should have been slaughtered. We were completely without Tibetan help and decided we had no option but to try and do the whole job ourselves. I had to let the Embassy know an approximate date of delivery, so we decided to bite the bullet and agreed a day. I wrote a letter to Tom in which I proposed a date for delivery, and in which I managed to convey the impression of a slick, hygienic operation without having to resort to anything as awkward as the actual facts.

In preparation for our tasks, we set everything up to practice what we were going to have to do. We lit the fire pits and set water to boil and caught about six chickens from the big shed and put them in the holding pens in our abattoir.

When we had enough hot water to conduct our trial, Jay showed us how to strangle a chicken.

'You've got to find the right balance between pulling too hard and not pulling hard enough. If you pull too hard, you'll pull the head off. If you don't pull hard enough, you'll stretch the chicken's neck and cause it great pain, but you won't kill it. When you pull the neck, you should do so with an outward twisting motion, like this.' Jay grabbed a chicken and in one smooth, practised twisting movement, pulled its neck. The bird twitched briefly and died.

'Once you're sure the chicken's dead, you plunge it into water that is very hot, but not quite boiling.' He plunged the chicken into the hot water pot, pulled it out after a few seconds and began to pluck it.

'You must pluck cleanly, especially for a quality client like the Embassy. Don't ever think 'oh that'll do'. If you don't pluck cleanly from the skin, you leave stubble which is difficult to remove.' In a flurry of feathers, he proceeded to pluck the chicken and after about ten minutes it was done.

'Now, you cut off its head right at the base of the neck then you push any remaining stump into the neck area. Next you cut its legs, just at this point.' Jay pointed to the exact spot then chopped the legs with a small cleaver. He had to make three attempts, and turned to Ross.

'This table is not good enough – we'll need something like thick chopping boards, otherwise we can't make a clean chop.'

After this, he opened up the bird's rear with a knife, inserted his hand inside and pulled out the entrails.

'We want the heart and the liver only. Some people add the neck as part of the giblets, but since we have so much to do, heart and liver only will be okay. Just separate them out making sure there are no odd bits of guts and pop them into one of the small plastic bags.'

Jay stood back from his work and drew a hand across his sweating brow.

'Next, you *must must must* clean the inside of the bird. We should use a hose, because the jet will dislodge any bits of gunge that are hanging about inside – but we don't have a hose, so just dip it in a bucket, slosh it about as much as you can and shake out the water to finish, but look inside carefully once you've done that to check. If there's any odd loose stuff, you must pull it out and dip it in the water again. After that's done, put the small polythene bag of giblets inside the cavity.

'Once the giblets are in the cavity, try to cross the birds legs together then put the whole thing, legs first, into one of the big plastic bags. Clear?'

Ross and I exchanged glances. Hazel, like a schoolgirl, put her hand up.

'What about the water we dip the carcasses into, to clean out the insides. Shouldn't that be sterile? We should at least use water purification tablets shouldn't we, or salmonella might develop?'

'Good point' said Jay, 'have we got any?'

'We've got some at the dispensary, but we better get more.'

'Mike?'

'What about the offal? The heads and entrails, shouldn't we have something to put them in? We can't just chuck them on the floor. We'd all better look for buckets or something.'

'Ross?'

'I think I've got it,' he said, 'but I'm not convinced I can pluck as fast as you Jay, you've had lots of practice. We have 200 chickens to process, and we have to have them finished by, what time Mike?'

'The Baijnath train to Pathankot that connects to the direct overnight Delhi leaves at half past nine, it'll take us an hour and a bit by road to

Baijnaith so we'd better be ready to go, all ready here, by seven at the very latest.'

'Is there a later train to Delhi after the one planned, just in case?' Ross asked me.

'I think there is,' I said, 'but I'll have to check.'

We worked out that each chicken would take a maximum of 10 to 12 minutes each to process. We had 200 to do, and we had four people to do it. This meant a work time of more than twelve hours each. With breaks for food and rests, it came as a surprise to all of us that we were in for a marathon that would need to start early in the morning.

'I still don't think we can pluck 200 chickens in that time without plenty of practice,' said Ross.

'Well, you're about to get plenty of it,' said Jay who seemed quite pleased with himself.

We gave ourselves a week extra to prepare for our day and I immediately wrote to Tom at the Embassy with the confirmed delivery date. I went to Palamjong the next day to post it by express mail so that he would get the information before the due date. Our plan was to order the ice the day before and store it under covers so that we could make a very early start. We worked out that if we had the ice ready to hand for the very early morning, we could get all the chickens processed and packed on ice by between 5:00 and 6:00 in the evening. By taking the birds by train to Delhi, the most time that a chicken would be exposed to the degradation process was 36 hours, and that would be packed in ice. The weather was heating up, and by the time the chickens would be on the train to Delhi beyond Pathankot, they would be exposed to some very high temperatures. That was the risk, but our plan gave us the best opportunity of success – and by acknowledging the problems which had to be faced, we reckoned we had good odds of achieving a safe delivery of 200 fresh and chilled chickens to Delhi.

The day of days was a Tuesday, and on the Monday Hazel almost chopped off one of her fingers with a cleaver whilst having a last practice on a chicken. Holding up a mammothly bandaged hand for all to see, Hazel declared herself absolutely and without doubt unfit to help. At about 4:00 in the afternoon, the ice arrived in a truck. We were relieved to see that it was crushed ice and that it was packed in long galvanised tubs, like old hip baths. These we began to stack up in our abattoir until the driver insisted that the containers had to be emptied of their ice and retuned with the truck.

We had no option but to make two big piles of ice on beds of hastily pulled grass. We covered these with old sacking.

I awoke so early on that Tuesday morning that it was only twilight, and even before I had ventured out of my shed I knew by the heavy pattering on my roof that it was pouring rain. I dressed and headed for the chicken shed, where I knew there would be activity, tea and chapattis. Ross was nearby, kneeling in front of one of the fire pits, blowing furiously in an attempt to kindle a fire out of soaking wood.

'Wouldn't you just know it,' he fumed, 'I've tried paper, I've just about used up all the kerosene and still it won't take hold.' A ghostly vestige of smoke drifted thinly through the pile of wet wood. I left Ross and went inside the chicken shed to join Tenzin and Jay for tea and chapattis. I declined the chance for the remains of the chicken stew we have made ourselves the previous evening.

'Tenzin, can you help? Ross is having difficulty in getting the fires going. I've seen the fires in the camp burning when it's raining, can you get someone to get the fires going?' Tenzin finished his tea and left.

The thousand or so chickens in the shed normally made little noise but I could plainly hear that they were making a terrific racket, and instead of moving slowly around the shed, pecking here and there, sections of the flock would suddenly charge into rapid motion and in noisy cacophony sweep through the shed, causing fear and confusion among the others.

'They know,' said Jay.

Tenzin came back.

'Lobsan Gompo will help you with the fires,' he said. I went outside to watch.

The man knelt by the first fire and from a bag he carried, stuffed some dry grass and some small fragments of wood into the base of the first fire pit. He motioned to Ross for a match and in just a minute, a strong, very yellow flame was licking through the bonfire. He repeated this to the three fires, and by the time he had got the third one going, the first was burning hotly.

I understood the dry grass, but not the small bits of wood that had been placed on top if it.

'Tenzin, would you ask Lobsan what he put on the fire?' Tenzin spoke to the old man.

'Roots,' said Tenzin, 'full of resin.'

With the fires going and the water heating, we caught the first batch of chickens from the big shed and took them to the pens in the abattoir. Ross, Jay and I were sharpening the knives when the Rimpoche arrived.

'Chickens,' he said, 'embassary chickens. Good but not good,' he said mysteriously. He wagged a finger at us and left, taking Tenzin with him.

By about 8:00, the light was as good as it was going to get; the sky was leaden with thick pewter-coloured clouds which hung coldly about the high peaks behind us, concealing their summits. Inside the abattoir, the mud floor was wet from the water seeping from the piles of ice and thick with smoke from the bonfires outside. Even before we had started on the chickens, the place was unpleasant.

'Come on Jay, you go first,' said Ross. Ross had adorned himself with a makeshift apron that gave him the air of a battlefield surgeon.

We began our slaughter.

In my practice for the day, I had processed about five chickens and had mostly succeeded; such difficulty as I had was in the matter of wringing the neck. Mostly I judged the action correctly, but I had two that I misjudged; I had found pulling a chicken's head off to be off-putting and I don't suppose the chicken was too pleased either. In our attempt to create a production line, we tried each performing a function, which resulted in the chicken being processed by the three of us; Jay wringing neck and plunging into water, Ross plucking, and me eviscerating, washing, stuffing in giblets, bagging and placing in large wicker basket. We tried changing the order of production because Ross was not good at the plucking and caused a delay in the line. But no matter how we tried to find the best formula, we ended up as we had begun, with each of us performing the whole operation.

In the first hour, we had managed 20 or so chickens – these filled only the bottom quarter of one of the 20 baskets waiting to be filled. The inside of the abattoir was already a mass of feathers, mostly layered into the muddy floor but sticking too to the rough texture of the breeze blocks of the walls. The bucket we had for the discarded guts seemed to have filled very quickly, and when flinging entrails into them we often missed – this added to the inhospitable floor, which was already ankle deep in feathers and the odd accusing chicken head.

The big barrel of hot water did not stay hot for long and needed frequent top ups from the pots heating over the fires. Getting the water in the barrel up to the necessary very hot temperature meant partially emptying the big barrel so that the new hot water would have an effect. The consequence of this was that we were scooping buckets of lukewarm water from the barrel, which contained a nasty mix of feathers and guts. The discarded water, when thrown outside from a bucket, left the guts on the ground as the water flowed away. Although there were no dogs in the camp, two appeared as if from nowhere and took up station nearby.

By 10:00, we had managed a total of about 50 processed birds. Although we were far short of a speed that would see us complete the 200 birds in good time, we knew we were speeding up. The problem that was slowing us was the supply of hot water to keep our barrel at a good temperature; the water was heating slowly and we could see we would run out of firewood.

By midday, we had found a good rhythm and we had a break for tea and to check our progress. The count was just over 50 and comprised of five full baskets, there being 10 chickens per basket, neatly layered with crushed ice and sacking.

The inside of our abattoir became a hideous, unpleasant, smoke filled scene of carnage. In our speed and haste we became careless of where and how we threw the offal. The floor was an ugly thick layer of muddy compressed feathers, and such work space as the tables comprised was a chaos of blood, entrails, the odd complete head and neck, and bloodied knives and cleavers.

Having finished her dispensary, Hazel and Tenzin visited our battlefield and Hazel called an immediate halt to operations.

'This is absolute madness!' she cried as she peered into the dark, stygian interior.

'You will stop this minute! Come out, all of you.' Ross, Jay and I had never seen Hazel in this forceful mode and we obeyed meekly. She disappeared while we re-stoked the fires, and she returned a few minutes later with a container of disinfectant. Hazel stepped into the abattoir and washed down the work surfaces and our instruments, scrubbing them vigourously.

'And you will do this at least every hour. Do you understand? And, you will replace my disinfectant at the end of this absurd exercise. And when did any of you last wash your hands? Jay, come here right now...'

Hazel made us hold out our bloodied and be-feathered hands and, saint like, washed us.

We got back to work as Tenzin raced off to summon help to procure more firewood for the fires.

Since our operations had been behind closed doors, the Tibetans were mostly unaware of what was going on. But some stood by in the rain watching the comings and goings; they would stand and watch for a few minutes and then drift off, shaking their heads.

By mid-afternoon, we had processed about 100 birds, and the pile of completed baskets was growing. Although we were not conscious of it, the rain eased off and the air warmed slowly. Inside our hell, we had passed through that stage of reckless humour which is the result of tiredness and anxious pressure, and we worked silently and sullenly. The 'take that!' and the 'off with your head!' comments faded as exhaustion set in. We pulled and plucked, we ripped and we poked, we stuffed and we huffed. Our hands were alternately cold then scalded. Our fingers were numb and grazed; there were feathers up our noses, in our ears and in our hair. When we took a break, we emerged into the open air like victims of a tarring and feathering, and feathers would blow off us in a stream into the breeze.

Hazel appeared every hour and repeated her disinfecting; Tenzin had a constant supply of tea for us and began to help by catching arm loads of chickens from the big shed and bringing them to the slaughter house.

'I'm not killing them, am I?' he said by way of justifying his action.

By 5:30, we had 15 baskets packed with a total of 150 birds, and we all acknowledged that we were getting careless. We found that our tiredness meant that we were losing our sensitivities – and this meant mistakes at every stage. We still had 50 birds to do and wearily we set to it after a final cleaning session by Hazel.

The floor of the abattoir was a foul nasty mass of compressed feathers and had reached a springy depth of at least a foot; even though we were walking on top of it to compress it, each footstep became harder and we were stumbling and tripping frequently. Our last hour was spent in a state of such utter exhaustion that it stimulated a vague nausea; we could barely speak and our limbs were aching. My fingers had begun to stiffen in a painful outstretched numbness that made them incapable of further action. By 7:00, the light was fading; we were about 10 chickens short of our requirement, but we decided we could do no more. The tally was 18 baskets and they contained 190 chilled chickens. We gathered in the dim light of the big chicken shed and slumped on the bare floor, quite unable to speak.

Ross was to accompany me in the jeep and trailer to Baijnath; there, he would help me unload the baskets at the station and return to the camp. I was to accompany the baskets all the way to Delhi, the plan being to get ad hoc transport at Delhi station to get the chickens to the Embassy.

Although I was desperate for rest, I decided that the risk of falling asleep was too strong, so I went to my hut to change and to pack my bedding role in preparation for my trip. I went to the tea factory and got the jeep and trailer and drove it along the track to the chicken shed to load the baskets. Ross roused himself from rest and together we heaved the baskets into the trailer and roped them down.

The last train from Baijnath to Pathankot was due to leave at 9:30. We had a long hour's drive and needed at least another half an hour to load the baskets into the baggage car, so we didn't have much time to spare.

'Come on chum,' I said to Ross, 'let's get going. The sooner we're done, the sooner we can rest.'

We set off into the darkening evening, Ross driving, me slumped and half asleep in the passenger's seat. We arrived at Baijnath without incident. We drove to a gate that opens directly onto the platform. As Ross began untying the baskets I went to the ticket office to get my ticket and to arrange for the baskets to be loaded into the baggage car. I was given a single consignment note for the baskets and I put it into the pocket in my bedding roll to keep it safe.

We got a porter to help load the baskets, and on the dot of half nine the last one was carried on board and the whistle blew for the train's departure. I ran to a carriage, found a seat and dumped my bedding roll; Ross was waving goodbye on the platform.

The small train chugged through the night towards Pathankot and I settled back for an hour's respite from my day's labours. I dozed and awoke in that suddenly reawakened state that all was quiet around me. The train was stopped at the Pathankot platform and the few passengers had disembarked. Under the meagre platform lights, I went to find a porter to help me offload the baskets and to my surprise discovered that they were already stacked up at one end of the platform.

I went back to my carriage to retrieve my bedding roll, which I took to the waiting room before going to the ticket office to get my ticket for Delhi. The whole station was quiet, but I found the station master in his office and I followed him to the ticket office, where I explained that the baskets also had to go to Delhi on the night train.

His English was meagre, but eventually, with much explaining, I got my ticket and paid for the transport of the baskets through to Delhi. I had an hour to wait for the overnight train, so I went back to the waiting to room, where I was glad to find I was alone. The night was cool and I pulled a jumper out of my roll and settled down to wait. On the wall opposite the bench I was lying on was a clock so I could keep a check on the time.

When I awoke from a deep sleep, it was an early, sunny dawn. I leapt up from the bench and raced out onto the platform, rubbing the sleep out of my eyes and shielding them from the low, rising sun. Even as I ran to the end of the platform, I knew from the first blurred observation of my surroundings that all the baskets of chickens were gone and that I had missed the train. I stood like a statue posed mid-stride in front of the spot where they had certainly been, unbelieving but still trying to summon their presence back from the unknown. I ran to the other end of the platform, hoping that my senses had been deceived, but I knew I was wrong and the hot panic of my predicament swept through me with a gush of dread. I walked back to the spot where I was certain they had been and, by the considerable puddle of water that lay there, I had to face the fact that, yes, they were gone.

I went straight to the station master's office, but it was locked; I looked at the platform clock and it read 6:00. I went back to the waiting room and my corner on its bench and proceeded to smoke 10 cigarettes, one after the other, so that my fuzz of panic was compounded and further heightened. I could not settle nor think and for the next hour created a circuit of short quick paces which saw me variously check the station master's office, look through the station entrance in the hope of identifying the station master, return to the waiting room, peer down the tracks, and pace up and down the platform as if desperate to leave. The day was getting hot and the sun had changed from its delicate dawn warmth to a much more strident heat.

Soon after 7:00, a ticket collector came into the station hallway and let himself into the small room that was the ticket kiosk. I immediately pleaded with him for information about the 18 baskets of chickens that I had accompanied the previous evening.

'Baskets!' I said, 'baskets? Delhi?' I pointed feverishly in the direction of the platform.

He shook his head in a circular sort of motion that conveyed the meaning of both the affirmative and the negative, combined in one moment to convey complete indifference.

He pointed to the clock in the hallway and shrugged his shoulders. 'Precisely 7:15, Sahib,' he said, and for further emphasis presented his wrist watch to me and tapped it.

'Seven fifteen?' I asked, not understanding his point.

'On time,' he said, 'Motorway junction.'

After I had packed up my bedding roll, the waiting room and the station became populated with people, and at 7:15 a train puffed slowly up the platform and stopped. As the passengers boarded and the station emptied again, I went to the station master's office and found it open and occupied.

The man at the desk that faced me was an elderly, thin man in dhotis. He was on the phone when I entered, but as he spoke he motioned me to sit down on a chair. When he was finished, he said, 'How can I be helping you sir?'

I explained that I had arrived the previous evening with 18 large baskets that I was supposed to accompany to Delhi.

'Let me be looking now,' he said, and looked in a large old ledger, which he drew towards him. He peered at its entries.

'Yes, 18 baskets to Delhi on the 11:00 overnight to New Delhi Central.'

'It goes direct to Delhi, yes?' I asked.

'No, the overnight Delhi is going to Chakki Bank then Sirhind, then Ambala. You change at Ambala for Delhi, going via Karnal.'

'Not direct?' I asked.

'On Fridays, the Delhi overnight is not direct, Sahib, it is going to Chakki Bank and Ambala. On weekdays it goes to Chakki Bank, then Jalanda City then Ludhiana. You have to change at Ludhiana to catch the 0500 hours to Delhi. If you don't change at Ludhiana, the train is going to Narwana.' He looked up at me. As I digested this confusing information, the train on the platform blew its whistle and I could hear the rumble and clank of its departure. The man behind the desk looked at his watch and said, 'On time.'

'So the baskets – they go to Chakki Bank first?'

'Yes, Sahib, they will be going to Chakki Bank then Sirhind and Ambala.'

'But what happens at Amabala to my baskets, they go to change at Delhi?'

'If there are proper consignment labels on the baskets, they will be changed, you have my word for that, sir. We are being very efficient.'

As he spoke, I realised with a further sinking feeling that the baskets were not properly labelled; I remembered I had simply put the paperwork into my bedding roll.

'And if no labels are on the baskets for Delhi?' I asked.

'Oh. Then sir, maybe they will be at Ambala. If there is no label, I am asking you how will they know to put these baskets onto the 0500 for Delhi? I am thinking they will maybe certainly be at Ambala if they have no proper labels.'

'What is the quickest way I can get to Ambala?' I asked.

'First you go to Chakki Bank, then you change at Jalander City and get the 1123 to Dhuri; the Dhuri to Jind train stops at Ambala. You have just missed the 7:15 to Chakki Bank, and the next one, I am telling you, will be departing at 12 noon sir.'

'What time does the noon train from here get to Chakki Bank?'

'It is arriving at 1430 hours sir.'

'And gets into Ambala?'

'That will be at 1945 hours. The Chakki Bank train stops at Dhuri and has a stop in Jind for one hour sir to attach the carriages from the 1245 from Nangal Dam.'

'And when is the next direct train to Delhi?'

'From here, sir?'

'Yes.'

'The next direct is the Karnal express. It is due to be leaving here at 1100 hours this morning.'

'But it doesn't go via Ambala?'

'No sir, the express is not going via Ambala. It is going via Jakpal.'

'So when I get to Ambala, I get the Karnal train to Delhi?'

'Yes sir. The Ambala train to Delhi via Karnal is an early morning train, and departs at 0500 hours sir.'

I thanked him profusely for his help and returned to the waiting room to think about what to do.

I sat in a mood of deep despair. Returning to the camp to admit to my mistake and the utter failure I had precipitated was out of the question. There was no point in going directly to Delhi, because the chickens would be elsewhere. Even in my befuddled mental state, I realised I had only one course of action – to go to Ambala to try and find them. I persuaded myself that if I could get there, there might be some hope of salvaging the situation. I went back to the platform and peered at the national railways map to get a sense of where the different geographical points were; in particular, to find out the distance from Ambala to Delhi. I was fermenting the idea that if Ambala was not too far from Delhi, I might be able to hire some transport, perhaps a truck, which would enable me to get the chickens to Delhi faster than the trains. Ambala was easily found and seemed a biggish junction, but it seemed a long way from Delhi (though I could not easily work out the scale of the map to be certain). There were many things to detract from the optimism of my plan to hire a truck. Firstly, there was the cost. I had no idea how much it would cost to hire a truck and driver; I had money with me, but I had absolutely no clue as to whether it would be enough to meet the expense of a truck delivery. Secondly, my arrival time in Ambala would be in the evening, about 8:00. Any assumed difficulty in finding a truck and driver would be compounded by the fact that my attempt would have to begin in the late evening. But since my choices were limited to one, I decided that I must proceed with plan A and hope for the best. With this determination of what I had to do, I went back to the station master.

I knocked gently on his door and went in.

'Yes, Sahib,' he said.

'Can you telephone or telegraph the station master at Ambala?'

'It is best if I am doing that to make a telegraph to him. Then I am thinking he will be more certain to contain the message.'

'Would you telegraph him? Please say to unload the baskets and to put them somewhere the most cool as possible and that I will arrive on the 1945.'

'And you will be claiming the baskets sir?'

'Yes, I will be claiming the baskets.'

'I will be needing the consignment information sir, if you kindly have them. Then I can make a most sensible message to my friend at Ambala for him to be knowing.'

I went back to the waiting room and my luggage, found the consignment paperwork and returned to the station master. After we had together composed the message, he said,

'We will be seeing a happy outcome after all Sahib, we are working very efficiently for your service to find these baskets. Do not sleep again and miss the train at noon sir, it will not be being a good thing!' He smiled a broad smile and waved his hand in the air as if to confirm his kindly goodwill.

There are many interesting towns and villages in India, but with every respect to its kindly inhabitants, Pathankot is not one of them. It is a drab and featureless place and overwhelmingly dominated by soldiers. By the time I had finished at the station, I had more than three hours to kill before the noon train. The heat turned from pleasant to unbearable. Such was the mix of anxiety and boredom that I explored most streets of Pathankot so thoroughly that I was creating interest. I re-encountered groups of soldiers or villagers I had walked past on a previous circuit of streets, and after getting some food, tea and cigarettes, I went back to the station to get my ticket to Ambala and to sit it out until noon.

I sat, I slouched, I paced, I wandered, I studied maps and timetables and counted the tiles of the waiting room floor; there were an odd 89 of them.

In my anxious state, I had bought a ticket that would place me in an air conditioned carriage, and at 10 minutes to noon I was the first passenger to board the train for Ambala.

The train was not an express; it was slow and stopped frequently. My impatience was as extreme as my agitation and as the engine puffed and wheezed slowly southwards, the heat grew mightily. Despite remembering the advice offered to me in Bombay by Madelaine, I bought drinks and fruit and food at frequent stops of the train, and by late afternoon I was suffering the consequences. The train arrived at Ambala – not at 7:45 as stated in the timetable, but just after 9:00 in the pitch dark, this because the Nagal Dam connection was an hour late. After the small rush of disembarked passengers had left, the station was eerily quiet and deserted of people. I was so tired and weak that I gave serious thought to walking away from the whole abominable situation; I would find a phone, place a call to home, 'Hi Dad, it's Mike, I want to come home, right now.' But I found the chickens.

The baskets had not been stacked neatly on top of each other as they had been at Pathankot; they had been thrown together in a piled heap such that many baskets had spewed their contents in a slithering of naked, almost obscene, bare chicken carcasses. This grand heap was at the centre of a large puddle of greyish water which extended around it in a circumference of about 12 feet. After the visual shock came the nausea of the smell, which caught one's throat when close to it. There seemed to be not one particle of ice left. At some point, a rough cloth tarpaulin had covered this heap, but it had slid forwards and lay in folds in the puddle.

With my bedding roll slung over my shoulder, I left this scene after only a two minute inspection and went to find somewhere to sit. On a bench from which I could see the mess of my disaster but 20 feet away, I buried my face in my hands and I sobbed until my hands and cheeks were wet with tears.

I must have sat on that bench for half an hour before I ventured back to the baskets to take a closer look. They had been heaped at the far extremity of the platform of arrival, and behind them was a low brick wall that marked the boundary of both the platform and the station.

Though the light illuminating the heap of baskets was dim, I could just make out that behind this wall seemed to be open ground, where there were sheds and two isolated freight cars that I could just see.

I began to pull the baskets apart to inspect the condition of their contents and to try and establish some order. I moved every basket so that they were all upright and laid them out around me. As I began to pick out the individual chickens, I found that those at the base were still cool and that more ice had survived than I had at first thought. I set about separating those which were packed at the base of the baskets from those which had been at their tops. Some of the chickens were plainly going off – they had a discernibly darker, bilious green under-colour and they smelled bad, though not rotten. By this process, I was able to build two piles of baskets, one that contained fresh chickens on ice, and another which contained a filthy mess of slimy polythene bags, slippery giblets and rotting chickens, which were turning blotchy green.

Thank God the station was quiet. A few people drifted in to find secluded spots to lay out their bedding rolls to sleep and to await future trains. I knew I was occasionally being looked at with curiosity, but I ignored all thoughts except that which saw me deliver some fresh, chilled chickens to the Embassy.

It was around midnight when I completed my work. I had stacked the baskets of good chickens neatly in a pile against the low wall; to anyone looking at what I was doing it would seem that I was making one stack. Once I had got all the good chickens in place, I took the bad baskets and lifted them up as though to make another layer of baskets, but instead of placing them on top of the others, I actually lifted them over the top of the pile and let them drop over the wall. I'm very sorry to say that I dumped something like 100 rotten chickens into someone's yard and I do, now, most sincerely apologise.

Once this heinous act was finished, I covered my remaining baskets with the tarpaulin and laid out my bedding roll in a dark corner nearby, where I could watch over them. Having four times examined the timetable board, I was sure of my departure time to Delhi the next morning at 5:00. Hopefully I would be away before anyone would discover my crime. A headline came into my head; 'N.E. Man Arrested in India. Chickens Are Evidence.'

One thing that worried me was that I would again fall asleep and miss the next morning's train. To placate this fear, I employed that old trick that American Indians used to use to stay awake; you drink massive amounts of water so that you're constantly up needing a pee. There was a public tap by the station toilets that claimed by its label to be 'drinking water' and I drank and drank and drank and I pee'd and pee'd and pee'd.

Something in my labours, or perhaps in my rehydration, had revived my energies. I hardly slept and was up, full of beans, at dawn.In preparation for the train to Delhi, and to avoid anyone poking about near the baskets, I secured a big trolley that lay unattended near the station entrance and loaded the baskets onto it. I wheeled the trolley with the baskets and my luggage roll down to the opposite end of the platform, away from where they had been. I hoped this would further cover my tracks.

I left the trolley on the platform and went to the ticket office to get my ticket for Delhi and the consignment labels and papers for the chickens. I stuck the labels onto the baskets, and at 4:45 was on board the train with the baskets safely stowed in the end baggage car. There were plenty of porters to help with this and I tipped them more than I should have. Though some of them were likely involved in their offloading the previous day, none remarked on their lesser number. I was in good spirits and felt there was yet hope for the whole enterprise, albeit on a smaller scale.

I had worked out that if I delivered a smaller number of chickens to the Embassy than had left the camp, I had plenty room to create a scenario that would explain the difference and leave me in the clear. Some could have been stolen, and some could have been crushed by a fall of other luggage or freight in the baggage car. I was in no doubt that a small degree of inventive fiction would yield a disproportionate level of sympathy and forgiveness.

The train was due to leave Ambala at 5:00 in the morning; the air was still cool then, and I had the strong hope that I could get the chickens to the Embassy by late in the afternoon and still in a cool, if not icily chilled condition. When the station master blew his whistle and waved his green flag, the train gathered up its bulk and rattled forward into motion in a series of sharp jolts. Once we had momentum, we steamed through the hot countryside and I settled down to rest and doze as best I could.

Something happens on a long journey when the mind is at rest and the eyes just see the passing scenery through a dusty window without identifying anything in particular. Meditation can require one to incant a rhythmic mantra that occupies the front of the mind so that the subconscious can rest and wander around those spaces it has not recently visited – a long railway journey can have the same effect. Once you have been politely chatty with those to whom some conversation is proper to the etiquettes of travelling, the mind becomes free to meander into those corners which it has not had the power to deal with in its usual active way. In this mode, the mind can approach the big questions quietly and without someone, or the self, interrupting with arguments. In this mode, instincts are fortified or whittled down a notch. In this mode, personal choices and preferences act as the truer reflection of the real self rather than those modified and twisted by considerations qualified by the immediacy of one's surroundings.

I was allowing my mind to consider the big picture that deals with the future, and considering what it was that I wanted to do in India. I had a letter from my father in which he raised the question of what it was that I proposed to do on my return from India.

There was no urging or hint to suggest a time limit on my stay, but he rightly identified that some expression of a precise ambition would be worth formulating. He had added that he fancied seeing me in a lawyer's wig, that I was certainly argumentative and that though he was not seeking to influence my own decision, some decision would be a good thing. I was thinking about what I was doing with the Tibetans and realising how much I liked them; I had thought that I ought to become a doctor, perhaps to return someday. But I also realised that I didn't have a brain capable of storing the information needed to become a doctor, and as my mind moved forward one small increment, I realised too that the train had been stopped, in open countryside, for longer than seemed normal.

I got up, wandered down the corridor to the carriage door and poked my head out of the window. I saw that a number of other people were doing the same thing and that some others were getting down from the train to stretch their legs. It was 3:00 in the afternoon and the heat was the most oppressing I had ever experienced. I went back to my compartment, which I shared with a family: a man and his very fat wife and two children. The air conditioning was working but it was not making a great deal of difference. The children were agitated and the woman fanned herself listlessly with a plastic fan.

'Oh, what is it now,' she exclaimed, 'why are we stopping for so long?' Her husband murmured some consolation that she didn't hear then he got up, wiped his neck with a handkerchief and left the compartment. I followed him and we both climbed down the steps of the carriage.

'Indian trains, you know,' he said, 'sometimes they are very very good and sometimes they are very very bad.' He squatted on the ground and lit a cigarette. 'Now,' he went on, pointing to the front of the train, 'now I think this is a very very bad one.'

I took a few steps here and there but was beaten by the heat and so returned to the compartment. As I sat down, the humming and slight clatter of the air conditioning unit slowed and then stopped.

'Oh my God,' said the woman, gesticulating at the air conditioning unit 'what next? Oh my God, my children are so hot.'

The train remained motionless. When it became apparent that we were to be stopped for more than just a temporary halt, I ventured outside again and made my way to the end of the train, to the baggage car. Its door was open and three men were sitting on the door's ledge. Behind them, I could see my stack of baskets, and beside those I could see a spreading wet patch which was, I knew, water from the ice melting in the baskets. Had the chickens been placed in a moderate oven, it would have been no less hot. One of the men sitting down made a gesture of holding his nose as I looked at the baskets. The others laughed and said something I did not understand. I motioned that I wanted to climb up and they shifted reluctantly. The whole floor of the baggage car was wet and a strong meaty smell of chicken hung in the still air. I was going to have a look under the tarpaulin, but I didn't and instead jumped back down onto the ground. The optimism that had coloured my day evaporated in the shimmering of hot air rising from a dusty, empty landscape. After an hour, the train driver, a magnificent Sikh in an equally magnificent turban, sauntered along the length of the train informing us that the engine had suffered a major failure and that a replacement engine was on its way.

'How long? How long?' we all asked.

'Maybe one hour maximum, maybe two,' said the driver, 'it is depending on the drivers at Narwana.' Like the ticket collector in Pathankot, he waggled his head in the same wobbly way as one of those dogs you see on the back shelves of cars. The sun heated the carriages to such a temperature that it was difficult to know whether to stay motionless or to stroll and make the effort to find a slight waft of wind.

At 5:00 in the evening, with the descending sun a great dusty fireball the colour of a tangerine, the replacement engine arrived at the back of the train and shunted us slowly to Barapur, a tiny spot of a station in a flat arid landscape. There, we stopped in anticipation of changing the engine to complete our trip to Delhi and, to a man, the whole train descended in a frantic heaving mass onto the platform and mobbed the two drink sellers in a shouting, pushing rabble of chaos.

I was in such a hopeless and dismal mood that I had not thought out what to do in Delhi. I knew the chickens would be a wretched mess, but I had not contrived a plan of action to deal with my predicament other than to get to Delhi and assess my options there. The passengers embarked back onto their various carriages bearing every conceivable fruit and drink and waited in newly animated spirits for the train to start again. I sat back in my seat pondering my fate. From the adjacent carriages, I heard the conductor calling an announcement and was heartened that we would surely be on our way.

'All change!' called the conductor when he entered our carriage, 'all change! We must be changing to another train, please be getting your luggage!' A loud groan like the moaning at a funeral rose from the throats and mouths of the passengers; it could have been for me.

I pulled my bedding roll from under my seat and made my way up the platform to the baggage car. There, porters were offloading luggage, boxes and bundles; I waited, watching, until there was nothing left to shift except my baskets. The moment came when there was nobody about and I climbed into the car. With the shunting and jolting of the train, some baskets had fallen and had spilled their contents, and the dark back corner of the car was strewn with a heap of chickens, giblets and slimy plastic bags. I felt accused by the carcasses. The train that was to continue the journey to Delhi lay on the opposite platform. I could see one guard with a flag looking at his watch and another who was shouting and closing the carriage doors. I had to make a decision. I could just get to the new train to finish my journey, but it looked as though it was leaving too quickly to get the chickens on board – the baggage and freight carriage of the replacement train that was at the extreme end of the other platform. If I abandoned the chickens, that would be the end of it.

I ran towards the other train, to the guard with the flag.

'Please, when is the next train to Delhi?' He shook his head angrily and turned his back on me to face the engine of the departing train. He raised his flag, blew his whistle and the train set in motion. He watched the departing train for a few seconds then turned to me.

'One hour, 1900, 7:00,' he said, pointing towards the platform clock. The time was just after 6:00. I thanked the guard and retraced my steps back to the motionless and deserted baggage car of the original train. I did not want to draw attention to myself, so I sat on my bedding roll just by the baggage car and awaited my moment. When I thought no-one was looking, I threw my roll up into the car, jumped up, and pulled the sliding door mostly closed so as to allow some light into the interior. My first action was to probe the base of some of the baskets to see if any of the ice had survived. Some had. It had formed itself into a few amorphous lumps. I reckoned that enough chickens looked fresh enough that it was worth repeating the sorting exercise I had under-taken the previous evening. I thought back to home, to a chicken in the fridge, and I'm sure I could hear my Mum's voice saying, 'oh, that'll be all right for a couple of days yet.' I didn't know how long a chicken remains 'fresh', but I sniffed a few close up and they seemed, sort of, maybe, okay. Having now had experience of how to separate out the baskets, it took me but 40 minutes to sort and repack the good chickens into a stack, which I constructed right at the edge of the door. The baskets containing the bad carcasses, which were now in the majority, I stacked in one high layer right up against the side of the carriage along which the door was located. This meant that anyone glancing into the car would not see the stack unless they peered right inside. When I was ready, I peeked outside. There was no-one nearby, so I pushed out my bedding roll and leapt down from the car. I decided it would be better to be bold in my next move.

I found a porter and led him to the car and before he had a chance to, I slid the door half open to reveal the baskets and jumped up so that he got the notion that I would hand the baskets down to him. He was confused that the Sahib should be touching or lifting anything and protested, but I shook my head vigourously, tapped my watch and pointed to the platform clock. There was a moment when he sniffed the air and turned up his nose, but at my urging he just shrugged his shoulders and in but five or 10 minutes the baskets were on the trolley and partially disguised by the soggy brown tarpaulin. There were now only five baskets so there was not that much to do. Ever the conscientious and responsible traveller, I closed the sliding door of the baggage car behind me and fixed the lever locks firmly closed. Somebody, sometime, would discover an awful mess.

The 7:00 train to Delhi arrived on time and the same porter and I loaded the five baskets into that train's freight car. An hour and a half later, I arrived into the hubbub and bustle of Delhi's New Station.

I considered myself lucky that I had hitherto found stations and places that enabled me to remove the bad chickens from the good and to re-establish my cargo into a functioning entity. But I knew that at Delhi I would likely not have such an opportunity; it is a great national railway station, teeming with crowds 24 hours a day, and it would be unlikely to offer a private spot where chickens could be inspected and sorted. I had decided I would have to stay with my baskets overnight at the station, but this caused me no hesitation or caution. It is a normal sight in all of India's railway stations to see individuals and families unroll their bedding and camp out for the night. The other circumstance that was in my favour was that the five remaining baskets did not smell except for the odd whiff.

Once the train had stopped at its platform, I summoned a porter with a trolley and led him to the baggage car. I helped him load the baskets and added my bedding to the pile. As I led him towards the ticket gate, I could see on my left a holding area for freight. There was a great mix of goods, but immediately to my left were stacks of wooden boxes piled to a height of about 10 feet. It somehow suggested a hiding place, and I directed the porter to wheel the trolley just past them. I looked behind the boxes and there was a space ideal for my purposes. We offloaded the baskets in a few minutes, I paid him, he left, and I sat on my bedding roll to think.

It was by then after 9:00 in the evening. I had decided to stay at the station overnight for the obvious reason that the British Embassy would certainly not be open at that time of night. Also, I did not want to be separated from the baskets. It might have been possible to find a cold store somewhere, but at that time of night such a find would be unlikely. The other factor in the equation was that I was thoroughly and utterly exhausted and I did not have the energy or motivation to do anything but get something to eat and get some sleep. I do not share most of humanity's distrust of other people, so I left my bedding roll and baskets in search of some food. I showed my ticket at the barrier and explained that I had to stay with some freight and would be returning. Just half an hour later, I was asleep by my baskets.

There is something of a tide to events that accompanies and taints each action right to the conclusion of the final chapter. Some people believe that an enterprise begun on a descending moon is destined to failure, and that no interim success will deflect the outcome from what was preordained – and so it was with my chickens.

I had woken early and had been able to re-sort my baskets one last time in the early hours, and after this cull my shipment comprised of but three baskets containing 29 chickens. I had no problems at the station getting my small cargo on board a small scooter-based truck. The driver, who allowed me to sit next to him in his tiny cab, went to the Embassy directly. When he helped me unload the baskets at the Embassy entrance, it was he who thanked me for helping him rather than the other way around. The baskets were at the British Embassy gates by 8:30. I was prepared to wait for the Embassy to open and sat on the pavement with my baskets at my side. By 9:00, when I thought the gates would be open, I pressed the buzzer on a speaker phone to one side of the gates. Through the tinny little speaker grill, an indistinct and distant voice said, 'Yes?'

I leaned forward to speak. 'I have a delivery of chickens for Mr. McKillop?'

The voice crackled back, 'We are not taking deliveries on a Saturday.'

I had no awareness of what day of the week it was. The explanation for the closed gates was immediately obvious.

'But they're for Mr. McKillop!'

'Mr. McKillop is not here and we are not taking the deliveries. Perhaps you can be coming back on Monday.'

'But I've come all the way from the Himalayas…'

'We don't take deliveries on a Saturday,' concluded the voice in the box. It clicked and went dead.

I abandoned the baskets of chickens on the pavement by the closed gates of the Embassy. I abandoned them there for good and forever, and at whatever consequence might ensue by their abandonment. I had had enough.

Without any further hesitation or deliberation as to what I should do, I got myself to the YMCA, checked in, dumped my bedding roll, had a shower and slept until dusk. I then went out to find some beer, and having bought these I smuggled them into the YMCA and, a rare thing for me then, I got steaming drunk.

6

The major arrives,
the author loses 200 chickens and plans to leave

I N JUNE, SIX WEEKS AFTER I HAD ENDURED THE IGNOMINY OF THE Rimpoche's silent anger, I had the growing feeling that my time with the Tibetans was due soon to end. This was not because of the Rimpoche; his chill towards me thawed back to warm friendliness. Indeed, anyone had only to refer indirectly to poultry, birds or any flying thing and he would smile and wag his finger at me, 'Embassy chickens good bad,' he would say forgivingly. It was more the fact that specialist volunteers were due at the camp and this would surely reveal that I had no distinct skills to offer. Despite my best intentions, I could not pretend that that wasn't weighing against me.

These feelings were brought to a head by the arrival not long afterwards of the major. He arrived by taxi and I happened to be near the Rimpoche's house when he arrived. I was witness to him getting out of the car and within his hearing when, opening the boot of the car to retrieve his considerable luggage, he turned to Tenzin and said, 'Just put my things over there would you?'

Tenzin jumped to it, of course, but the moment, and its implied assumptions, made their mark on me.

Major Adrian Allingham bore himself straight and erect at all times and there was a way in which he moved that conveyed the impression of preciousness. Apart from this posture, there was little to say. He was of average build and bald except for two thin drifts of hair which were neatly shaven and slicked back above the ears. His face was neither round nor square, nor oval, nor any shape, really – it was just a face with two milky brown eyes which seemed occupied elsewhere and a nose which terminated in a little ski jump. His age was difficult to determine; he could have been in his late 30s, but he could also have been in his late 40s. Apart from a red anorak, he was clothed in colours that yearned for the uniform – beige twill trousers, brown shoes, a mud green sweater and a light khaki shirt. I noticed that all his clothes were new and clean and that his trousers bore a crisp, sharp crease – a rare phenomenon in the Himalayas. My feelings of redundancy were reinforced by his arrival because the major had an aura of efficiency and sharpness – quite the reverse of my haphazard ways.

When he was introduced to the Rimpoche, he did not bow like everybody else, but as his best mark of respect, he did at least take off his tweedy peaked cap.

After the pleasantries and a quick tour of the camp, the major busied himself with setting up his quarters in the tea factory, an old storeroom next to Hazel's that we had cleared and washed in preparation for his arrival. Hazel had not been keen on having anyone else living close to her, though she did not explain why – I suspected it was because of the very thin walls.

For the first few days, the major kept mostly to himself, setting up his room and, as I had done, wandering and walking around the camp. Although it had taken some time to evolve, Ross, Jay, Hazel and I had established a corner in the hallway of the tea factory that was 'our' corner. After Hazel arrived, Tenzin was hard pressed to cook and look after three establishments of volunteers, so we set up a table and some stools to form a communal eating and cooking area; the availability of chickens to cook and eat had spurred this innovation, as well as the acquisition of two kerosene stoves. Tenzin was the one who liked the new arrangement the best because Ross and I would compete to find the most novel way to cook chicken, thus freeing him of some of his voluntary domestic duties.

It was here that we congregated in the evenings before departing to our individual quarters at night and it was here that the major eventually joined us. There were two things the major usually had about his person – a notebook and pencil, and a pair of brown leather gloves. The gloves were always carried like a baton and accompanied him on any walk; the notebook and pencil were with him, and in active use, at every moment.

'And how many people are in the camp?' he would ask, pencil poised to make an entry.

'Oh, dunno really,' answered Ross, 'sometimes 600, sometimes maybe as much as 750.'

'You mean nobody knows *exactly*?'

'Well no, people come and go.'

'Good Lord!' said the major, apparently unable to grasp the notion of an uncertainty, 'that's incredible.'

After the first two weeks, when the major had settled in and had wandered into every corner of the camp and had asked for every conceivable statistic, measurement, and the quantity of every known thing, he disappeared from view. Apart from awkward and uncommunicative sojourns with us in the evenings, he would stay in his room. Hazel said she could hear great rustlings of paper coming from the walls between them, but other than this clue, we had no idea of what he was up to.

The major's arrival had caused an upset to the old order that had evolved between Ross, myself, Jay and Hazel. The four of us were close in age and temperament, and though it was not an expressed thing, we shared an admiration for the Tibetans that made us feel very protective of them. The major had yet to reveal his worth, but he was a difficult man for us to deal with and, without cause, triggered those protective feelings. Ross, Jay, Hazel and I were at the instant of first meeting on first-name terms. But with the major, there was a natural inclination to address him formally, as though he had an authority which demanded it. There was a good deal about him that reminded me of school. To his credit, of course, the major in his dealings with us had put us at our ease; he had taken an early interest in the dispensary, and particularly in Hazel's new record keeping system.

'Now, just call me Ade,' he had said on his first visit, but one still felt the inclination to call him Major Allingham, sir.

It was now late June, and I had resolved to two things – to help in the camp as long as there were things for me to do and to resist any plan, scheme, venture or suggestion that involved me travelling to Delhi again. I returned to the dispensary and helped Hazel as much as I could. There was much to do there, as Hazel and Dr Mittle had introduced a clever new scheme whereby each patient had prepared for them a small notebook. This contained a summary of their ailment and the corresponding treatments. The system was advantageous in several respects; it speeded up each consultation, it recorded any courses of drugs without recourse to laborious translation or memory, and it laid the foundation upon which a true picture of the whole health of the camp could be created. The scheme required each patient themselves to keep the notebook and to present it at any visit to the dispensary.

Paperwork was not an activity I liked, but I saw the value of the exercise and I saw that Hazel needed help with it, so I was genuinely happy with the task. I felt more useful and I had always liked being involved in the dispensary.

The days were getting longer and warmer; life was settled, comfortable and happily occupied. I had by then been in the camp for over five months and I was familiar to the Tibetans to enough of a degree that I was at last getting to know some of them. Relationships usually began with the children. The children were beautiful, cheerful, brave and curious. Unlike their parents, they had no hesitation in watching me or Ross do something. They would stand very nearby any activity that we were undertaking, and sooner or later, an involvement or interaction would take place. We would hand them a spade, or get them to fetch something, or draw them a picture – whatever it was, it always involved laughter at some point. So Ross and I and Hazel and Jay usually had gaggles of children round about us, sometimes a pest but never a burden. It was not unusual to see Ross chasing a group of children round the camp to the sound of his, and their, high laughter.

As the children made relationships with us, so the parents became less shy and more willing to view us as ordinary human beings rather than as exotics. Their behaviour towards us was the exemplary of exquisite manners. It may seem a contradiction that people who are rough and filthy in appearance and who live in squalid insanitary conditions can respond to their surroundings by being polite to a degree that would flatter a diplomat, but that is the case. That they were also quick tempered, volatile and argumentative among themselves does not negate the significance of their attitude to 'outsiders'. It struck me then that the Tibetans are in character very similar to the Scottish Highlander. He (if it be a he) is someone who will offer every hospitality to the stranger and accord him a high status, but he is the same man who will happily stick a knife into the back of his neighbour if he suspects the vestige of a sleight. Like the Scots, and perhaps all the British, they are very good at giving, but not good at sharing.

As our familiarity with the Tibetans grew, we began to understand a little of the hierarchies and relationships within the camp. It always revolved around the Rimpoche in some way or another. There was a feudal organisation in full demonstration of that order in just about every aspect of camp life.

There was Kesang, a magnificent, unusually tall man distinguished by a hat that he wore at all times. The hat was of yak skin, reversed, brought to a high peak and with two ear flaps which hung hugely outwards because they were tethered like sails to the peak by a silk ribbon. The edges of the ear flaps were bordered with a rich red silk brocade, as was the slight peak at its front. I never saw him without his hat. When the Tibetans fled Tibet for India, they did so in family and clan groups; it's the same for all refugees – you stick with those you know and you re-settle as the same group. The Palabir camp was a camp peopled by the Khambas, the warrior, fighter class of Tibetans. The Khambas were the ones who took up arms, the Khambas were the ones called upon to determine any military response, and the Khambas were the ones first to resist, with arms, their Chinese invaders. It had been whispered to me one night by a camp fire within the camp that if I wished to go over the mountains to 'shoot up a few Chinese for some fun' then it could be arranged. I had suspected this was going on because one particular group of men would disappear for weeks at a time and I treated one man's wounds that I was sure had been caused by a bullet.

Kesang was always at the Rimpoche's side; he was aide-de-camp, he was the Rimpoche's lieutenant, and he was the Rimpoche's strong arm if needed. He wore a grand if threadbare tsuba, and its silk belt was adorned with knives, small shrines and reliquaries all made of silver inlaid with turquoise and coral. He was very distant and cold to us to begin with and had no English, but with Tenzin's intervention I managed some communication with him. I admired a knife that hung from his belt and after he had shown me it with great pride, he signalled me to follow him. His tent was by far the biggest in the camp proper and comprised of four tents placed together to make one; inside, the space was considerable and surprising. He went into the tent and a gaggle of children and women immediately left. He signalled me to a dark corner and pulled back a small rug. He revealed a saddle and pulled it effortlessly to the tent's door so that it was in the light. It was a magnificent, huge thing and made with silver over leather. The silver covered every inch of the saddle except the seat itself and was finely, minutely carved and chased with fighting dragons.

'Fighting!' he said in English and to my great surprise, 'horse fighting!' He clenched both his fists and shook them up and down as though he was beating something, or someone.

As June's early warmth bared the lower two-thirds of the mighty Himalayas behind the camp, Ross began hinting of his departure back to England. Although he could not bring himself to speak of it directly, I knew that he would be leaving and that I would be left with Jay, Hazel and the major.

Hazel had become entirely dedicated to the work of the dispensary and showed a missionary selflessness that made me feel ashamed of my own ill-disciplined and random efforts in the camp. Jay had successfully brought about the creation of the chicken rearing, and despite my disastrous intervention, the camp was making money by selling the chickens locally. Jay had never managed to persuade any of the Tibetans to help in any other capacity other than in the rearing of the chicks and had had to hire local Indian help for the killing and slaughtering of the mature chickens. He seemed happy and settled and had voiced no intention to leave.

Which left the major.

It was about three weeks after his arrival, and two after his self imposed purdah, that he announced one evening when we were all gathered for our evening meal that he had worked out 'a plan'.

'You see,' he began, 'this place has no organisation, and we need to help these people by putting an infrastructure in place.' He scuttled to his room and returned bearing three large rolls of paper and a thin baton.

'Now these...' he said, unrolling the rolls and pinning them to the walls by our table, 'are our objectives.' Truly the military man, he prodded the first sheet with his baton like the RAF Group Captain before a bombing raid.

'Number one, we need to mark the boundaries of the camp; number two, we need to divide the camp into zones. There will be four zones: Blue, Green, Yellow and Red. Follow me?'

A chicken leg which had been on its way to Ross's mouth halted in mid-air.

'Now, once we have the zones,' continued the major to an audience that I suspected was something other than us, 'it becomes easy to implement stage two, which is to issue identity cards to everyone in the camp. I can't see a future for this place unless we have identity cards. It'll be very simple, just a bit of card with their name and a corresponding number – that way, we can file 'em.

'Now, in order for all this to make sense, we have to have a central office. I'm sure the Rimpoche would much prefer not having people traipsing up to his house every hour of the day and night, so here...' and the major waived his baton around the general space of the hallway, 'will be the central office.'

'But what about the tea?' asked Jay.

'Ah!' said the major with great enthusiasm, 'I've thought of that! The tea moves up to the annex of the Woollen Mill. Plenty of room there, cleaner too.' Jay frowned but did not reply.

'Now, once we have zones and identity cards, we need to organise squads. The camp is untidy, dirty and littered with mess and the Tibetans need to be organised into squads, just volunteers from each zone you understand, to start cleaning the place up.'

The major spent about half an hour outlining his plans and concluded with the air of someone who awaits applause. It was not forthcoming.

'So, what do you think?' he said, tucking the baton under his arm.

'Only one thing,' ventured Ross, 'what does the Rimpoche think of all this? He's the boss.'

'Oh well, I've had several meetings with him, and we've gone over what we think are the main problems. And, I had extensive discussions in Delhi with Mr Starling before I came up here. He agrees with me too that the camp must have some modern management.'

'Yes, but the Rimpoche – have you told him what you propose – showed him your… your plans?'

'Well not exactly, not yet, thought I'd sweep these ideas past you first…'

If Ross, Hazel, Jay and I had had an outspoken representative to speak for us, he or she would have told the major that both his thinking and his proposals were bunkum. But because the three of us were junior to his years, and because we were anxious not to offend a newcomer volunteer, we compromised ourselves miserably by our half-hearted, equivocal half agreement. We agreed that, yes, the place was disorganised, and yes, a bit dirty and haphazard, but none of us had the courage to point out that what was being proposed was antithetical to every fibre in the Tibetan body… and that any twit with half a brain would have understood that.

The evening ended awkwardly and the major was clearly wounded by the consecutive points which we put up to confound his plans. I heard Jay humming 'The Dam Busters' to himself as we departed to our individual billets.

Jay, Ross and I left the tea factory in the warm dusk and wandered along the track, they to their tent, I to my shed further on and nearer to the camp proper.

'So what do you think, Ross?' asked Jay. Ross stopped and he looked around him – at the foothills before us where a thin crescent of a moon was peeping and behind which the snows of the peaks were tinged with a dark apricot glow. Beyond us, from fires of the camp, smoke slowly twisted into the air and seemed to hold the singing that was coming from below. The song was one of my favourites and one which usually accompanied a dance by the women. They would form a circle as they sang and rotate back and fore and, at the chorus, stamp their feet inwards into the ring with a great whoop and a shout. The song ended with a great peel of laughter then silence filled the air.

'Maybe we're the ones who have got it wrong,' said Ross reflectively, 'maybe we should be preparing the Tibetans for the realities of the big bad world instead of insulating them. You see what we have, is…' Ross could not find his exact meaning and paused. Jay spoke.

'What we have is a major fucking headache,' he said. And that seemed to sum it up.

In late June, I had a letter from my father. Unusually, it was not an aerogramme, that self-folding blue tissue envelope that I had been accustomed to receiving. It was a proper envelope and, on taking it into my hand and before opening it in the privacy of my own space and time, it felt thick and bulky.

When I opened it, I found three Bank of England 10 pound notes carefully placed between a folded page of the Aberdeen 'Press and Journal'. The letter explained that 'the overdraught is not too bad' and said that the money should be 'kept in reserve' should I wish to come home at any time, 'whenever that might be'. My father again raised the issue of what I wished to do on my return.

The money was a great blessing and I knew I could convert it into much more than its official rupee value by changing it through the black market street changers in Delhi. Before the arrival of this heavenly gift, my financial position had been causing me great concern. I had only a reserve that constituted the train fare to Delhi; all the rest had gone on medicines to treat chronic diarrhoea. Latterly, Hazel had managed to get a supply of Entrovioform that kept us all going, but my past expenditures had left me all but broke. I had been receiving my food from the Rimpoche, but apart from refunding costs on my trips for him, and occasionally knobbling some change from those, he was not giving me cash and I had absolutely no income.

In the first week of June, Ross confirmed that he was going home. He and I were trying to fix a pump in the yard of the tea factory; we had taken the thing to bits and were sitting on the ground, looking at its innards.

'I've decided I'm going, Mike,' Ross said.

'I kind of knew,' I said.

'Oh?'

'Yes. You've been away for a few weeks now really.'

'I suppose. Has it been obvious?'

'Not to others. But I sensed it.' Ross scraped a gouge in the mud with his heel.

'Ah, well. I shall miss this place you know. I worry about them! I sometimes wonder if I can ever stop worrying about them. I just wish I could wave a magic wand.'

'And what? Get them back to Tibet?'

'No, not that.'

'They'll never go back,' I said, 'not this generation anyway. They'll have to wait for China to collapse and by that time it will be generations away and the memory will have gone.'

'Maybe,' said Ross, 'and I have to get on with my life.'

'To do what?'

'I thought it would be so clear. Ever since I was a boy I wanted to go into the ministry, I thought that before I came here. It was one of the reasons I came. But now, I'm less certain. Isn't that strange?'

'But maybe that's what you have found out, that maybe the ministry isn't for you.'

'But that's the problem Mike, I came here thinking it would help me solidify my ambitions, but it's had the reverse effect. Now I don't know whether to go to Uni, find a job… whatever. I just don't know anymore. But one thing I do know is that time is passing; I'll be 21 next year and I need to get back.'

'Maybe when you smell that London smog again, you'll have a flash of inspiration,' I said.

'I doubt it. But I know I have to start all over again.'

Although this conversation was about Ross, it had an effect on me and I decided it was time I moved on too – a final decision, a certain decision. I knew that the Rimpoche would seek volunteers with specialist rather than general skills, and I could not see how I could usefully assist in any of the projects in the camp. I was getting increasingly bored, so I wrote to Kim and Patrice at 'BroMed' in Delhi to see whether there might be a place for me in Bihar. With the money I had received from home, I had the means to make a change. When Ross left three weeks later, the major had gone too.

The major had not fared well in his ambitions to introduce modern management to the Tibetans. The Rimpoche dismissed all of his plans, and the major had not taken this well. He had gone to Delhi to seek the support of Reggie Starling, but Reggie told him that the running of the camp was at the Rimpoche's entire discretion. Tenzin would report the various goings-on in the Rimpoche's bungalow, and the word from there was that the major had been wrong to try and insist that the Rimpoche take the major's view on what was right or wrong for the camp. After his Delhi trip, the major tried to help each of us with our tasks, but in that, too, he failed. Being his close neighbour, Hazel told us that from his room were audible odd noises and we noticed that the major was behaving in an erratic way.

When he tried to help Jay in the chicken shed, he couldn't stop himself from insisting that he knew how to rear chickens better than Jay and that Jay needed a system of modern management for the efficient rearing of chickens. In addition, he killed a number of chicks by stepping on them. Hazel was very gentle with him when he tried to help at the dispensary, but she had to insist that he stop trying to change everything that she and Dr Mittle had set up – she found 42 reasons that she didn't need his help. The major, knowing that Ross was to be leaving, attempted to create squads of Tibetan men to help on the building site, but this led to the first squad throwing their spades and picks into a trench and walking off. They objected to the whistle that the major used and the way he looked at his watch when he blew it to start work.

I was in my shed one evening when Ross knocked at my door. Jay and Hazel were behind him and looked anxious.

'Mike, you had better come, we've got a problem. It's the major...'

We went to the chicken shed and went in. The chicks wander around the extent of the shed under repeating rows of wide-shaded lamps, which, as a source of heat, are suspended about two feet above floor level. The batch of chicks was about six weeks old and had mostly grown their white feathers. The shed was therefore a sea of white pecking chickens. In the midst of this sea, like a giant plucked chicken, was a male human form dressed only in its underpants, on its hands and knees. Alas, the major had gone mad. We got him back to his room and into bed with some hot sweet tea and I had never seen such tenderness extended to another human being as was displayed towards the major throughout the whole of that night. Frantic driving to Dharamsala fetched Dr Mittle the next day, and a heavily sedated Major Allingham was taken away and never seen again.

As these developments unfolded, and Ross prepared to leave, the

Rimpoche summoned the four of us to his presence. Tenzin was in attendance, so we knew the Rimpoche was going to be saying more than his usual hello goodbye how are you. It was a moving little event. The Rimpoche spoke a few sincere and grand words of thanks to Ross and presented him with a small parcel wrapped in linen. Ross refused to open it saying that he would only do so when he was back in England.

'Otherwise,' he added, 'I will surely cry.' After this, the Rimpoche presented Ross with the traditional white scarf, or Kata, which is given as a sign of great honour. The Rimpoche had prepared a small table with glasses, beer, chung and arrak, and after his presentation he and his wife toasted our health and happiness. After an emotional Ross left for his tent, the Rimpoche wagged his finger at me and summoned Tenzin to translate.

'New volunteers coming. New people, good people. You will see. I have letter from Mr Reggie. Aggeraculturral expert number one, very good to make land good again. The other one is nurse again, very good help Hazel I think and soon maybe, maybe we get own doctor.'

'That's really excellent Rimpoche. Truly I am pleased.'

'This camp, this place' said the Rimpoche waving his arm around the perceived boundaries of his empire, 'is going to be very very good for Tibetans. I think people Swizzerland giving money for clinic here'

'Rimpoche, you are a wise man,' I said, 'but you are also a clever man I think, yes?'

'Not, no clever. Use carculator.' He giggled to himself and waddled serenely back inside his house.

Ross left the camp in June, but when the day came that I drove him to Baijnath for the train, our farewell was not the final goodbye. Ross had decided he would base himself in Delhi for a few weeks to see the city and its sights and to have a break before returning to England. We agreed that if my timetable could allow it, that we would meet to make a joint trip to Agra, something we both wanted to do.

In the interim, I had a letter from the odd-sounding 'Brogandanish Rural and Brotherhood Society' in Bihar saying that they would indeed be pleased to accommodate me, that they would give me my food and keep – and did I know anything about Land Rovers?

With this opportunity confirmed, I spent a day on my own walking in the hills behind the camp mulling over my options. My mind kept returning to the fact that I had no specialist skill by which I could be useful in the camp. When I got back in the late afternoon, I got hold of Tenzin and went with him to see the Rimpoche to tell him that I was going to leave. When I got back to my hut to write to the B.R.B.S. in Bihar that I would be coming sometime in the next few weeks, I had difficulty writing it because my hands were trembling.

I had been six months at the camp, and in preparing to leave I realised I had accumulated more goods and chattels than I had arrived with. I had been given or had traded some of my possessions for a good mix of Tibetan objects, ranging from shrines and knives to cooking imple-ments and water colours of the Yeti; my prize was a purple brocade jacket, which one of the monks had given me. I had to get a metal trunk to accommodate all this stuff, and full though it was I'd given away such things as I could.

My last days and weeks at the camp were spent alone and without the company of Hazel or Jay. Hazel had gone to Delhi to meet up with her parents and Jay had taken some time to himself to go camping in the surrounding hills and valleys. I was even without the company of Tenzin and the Rimpoche, who were in Dharamsala, so for a brief time I was completely on my own. It was then that I fell ill. I awoke one morning in a state of complete weakness, with the vague sense that I was lying in a pool of wet slime. My sight was fogged, my mouth dry and my guts and head were confused as to which was which and were connected to each other only by pain. My strength had completely gone, as though my inner self had left its host body – leaving only a small vulnerable thing to exist.

I was so weak I was unable to move, and the slime that was soaking and stinking up my bed oozed from me uncontrolled and uncontrol-lable. My stomach and bowels were racked with such an intense pain that each inward breath caused me to wince. Time slowed to a fuzzed inhabitation of gloomy spaces that lacked definition by sense or light, by time or experience. Stomach upsets and virtually permanent diar-rhoea had been a feature of life in India that I had had to get used to. All we Western volunteers suffered from it chronically, and it stalked our lives no matter how carefully we selected what we ate and drank. Having suffered various bouts of upsets, I knew that something entirely more serious was going on, but there was little I could do but stay in bed. One day became two, maybe three, but time was losing its meaning.

In some anonymous zone of the dark, some deep seated alarm bells must have awakened me to the seriousness of my predicament. Although I was so weak that any movement exhausted me immediately, I rolled off the charpoi and onto the ground. I dragged the sodden mess of bedclothes behind me, and then managed to get myself standing to switch on the light. I went to the door of my shed in the hope of being able to attract the attention of someone that might get help, but the inky darkness yielded up neither sounds nor any sign of life. It must have been deep in the night. I stumbled back to my charpoi and got on my stomach to search under it for any clothes or coverings that would make dry bedding. I dragged my rucksack and case forward to the floor and delved into them. Having emptied my bedding roll of any suitable stuff and thrown it onto the bed, I turned my attention to my rucksack and at its bottommost recess felt two heavy objects. The first was the tin of peaches which Dr Calder had given me and the second was the asparagus from Madelaine.

I had regarded these offerings with a slightly cynical amusement, as though both Madelaine and Dr Calder had odd, ill-judged ideas as to what a young man in India might appreciate. But their discovery was that of treasure. I really had forgotten all about them.

I held the tins, one in each hand, unable to decide whether to have the peaches or the asparagus first. My thirst and dry mouth were such that the peaches seemed the more urgently desirable. Then the vague, vegetable saltiness of the asparagus seemed more sensibly satisfying, and somehow more grown up. I set the tins before me on the edge of the bed and, after an intense panic that I couldn't open the tins, found a knife with which to stab their tops. I began with the asparagus – drinking the juices, then sucking the spears. Heaven they were. But the greatest joy was in the sweet syrupiness of the peaches and, somehow, the warmth and sunshine I sensed in their flesh and juices. I blessed both Dr Calder and Madelaine and crawled back to bed, feeling bloated as if I had had a great five course dinner. The next morning I awoke feeling weak but nevertheless whole and human again and able to walk and get about.

It wasn't long before Hazel was back, and she moved heaven and earth to obtain food for me to satiate a raging hunger which afflicted me for a week.

Despite the distraction of my illness, the big event of my departure from the camp loomed nearer and nearer and finally arrived without the option of me being able to avoid it. My strengths had returned and I was ready to leave.

When that day dawned, I was up very early. The sun was peering over the rims of the foothills and the very tops of the Himalayan peaks were glistening white with snow crystals. The air was warm, the grass soft and lush, the sounds of the camp happy and domestic. I had declined the offer of a lift in the jeep to Baijnath and chose instead to take the bus back – the way I had arrived. Tenzin organised a cart and muscled help to take my trunk to the end of the camp road, and walked with me as I waited for the bus to take me to Baijnath.

It was only at that poignant moment that I realised who it was that had meant the most to me in those six months. It was not Ross, though he had become a good friend; it was not Hazel, nor Hugh, nor Dr Mittle, all of whom I liked and admired; nor was it even the Rimpoche, for whom I had developed the greatest respect. It was Tenzin that was my friend above all others – there was not a more likeable young man in all the world. As he waved goodbye to me on the bus, his outline and his smile receded into the distance behind me; I left the camp, never to return.

After installing myself at the Brothers to Medicine Centre in Delhi, I met Ross a week later and we headed off late one afternoon to the train station for our trip to Agra, overnight because it was cheaper. We piled our luggage into our carriage, and with some time to wait, we wandered up and down the length of the train. Ross had that very English passion for steam trains, and as we came to the great black engine, he surveyed it with knowledgeable eyes. The engine was fired up, steam was hissing from valves and pipes, and it seemed like some great sultry beast waiting impatiently to pound out its might into the day and the night.

Ross began chatting to the driver, a cheerful Anglo-Indian.

'The Sahib likes the trains... no?' he shouted.

'Yes!' shouted Ross. I stood back and watched the two of them talk trains and steam.

I left them for a few minutes to saunter the length of the train, and when I came back, Ross said, 'How do you fancy riding the footplate to Agra?'

I knew by the very wide smile on his face and by the tilt of his head that he desperately wanted to.

'What, here? On the engine?' I asked.

'Yes.'

'What do we have to do? Shovel coal?'

'If you want to. I'll do it. Honest!'

'Okay.'

So we clambered up the rough steel steps into the cab of the engine, Ross with the ease of experience, me with a grab and a slip.

The guards on the platform began to wave their arms and flags, their whistles blasted through the cacophony of noise and imperceptibly brought the engine to the centre of everyone's attention, as though some race were to begin. As if sensing this attention, there arose from the engine a sense of drawing in a long breath as if it were oxygenating itself for an almighty high leap. The sound of air being sucked in was followed by the hissing of gurgling steam, which became the first crescendo from the engine's whistle. It began as toothy, hesitant spluttering – and then, as if it had cleared some irritant in its breathings, it emitted a piercing shriek that made us wince. I had the funny feeling that the engine had turned its attention to us now and was saying 'Hey, just watch this!'

A minor earthquake rumbled beneath my feet as the driver pushed a huge lever away from him; the engine uttered a deep grunt and shuddered forward, then stopped. The driver jiggled at the lever again, pulled it backwards a bit, then forwards fully, and we moved very slowly ahead. Once in settled motion, the engine took ever deeper breaths and we gathered pace as it clattered over the rails and points. Within a minute we'd left the lights of the station and were in sudden darkness and shrouded in thick, choking smoke.

We moved slowly through the darkness, picking our way through the sidings and southwards, away from Delhi and into the night at a steady, even pace. Once we were clear of the city and into the countryside, the driver winked at Ross and began to increase our speed. The engine found a rhythm, and as it picked up speed it began to become more and more an animal.

Smoke belched from the stack, sparks showered into the dark like fireworks, and Ross shovelled coal into the furnace with an energy that astonished me. When he was done, he flicked the furnace door closed with his shovel as if he had been a driver all his life. The driver laughed and laughed and pulled the whistle as we thundered into the hot night.

I took my turn at feeding the furnace with coals, heap after heap, sweating, feeling the blisters arise on my hands. Then the journey settled and we stuck our heads out of the sides of the engine to feel the hot air sweep across our faces and we whooped and hi-ed and took the schoolboy enjoyment for all it was worth. Ross took a handkerchief and wrapped it round his brow, the driver made tea with boiling water from a steam-hissing valve in the engine, and we settled into the journey, roaring through the quiet, dark night. It was like riding a great greasy beast, a thunderous skeleton. When we left Delhi it was searingly hot, but as the night lengthened it got colder and colder and I retreated into a corner, out of the rushing wind and the smoke and the sparks and the rattling and shaking and incessant clatter of the engine. It was so noisy, we learned the sign language for when it was time to re-stoke the boiler or blow the whistle as we approached our stops.

Although we stopped a few times on the way, we rode the footplate right to Agra and staggered from it exhausted, deaf and frozen very early the next morning. Ross and I had arranged this trip only by the days that we could manage, and were lucky to have come to Agra on a night of the full moon. Like much of travelling humanity, we marvelled at India's favourite building and returned to Delhi the next day ready to write postcards.

7

Bihar and four Land Rovers,
the Buddha Tree and minor enlightenment

B IHAR SITS TUCKED UP INTO THE TOP RIGHT-HAND CORNER OF India, bordered by the mountains of Nepal to its north, by hot arid plains to its south and by (what was then) West Bengal to its east. In 1967 it was suffering a full blown catastrophe of drought and starvation. Some 52 million people were roasting in a landscape that had turned to dust and was blowing away before their eyes.

The events that produced this disaster were both climatic and political. Appendix 2 provides a background to one of India's most serious modern disasters.

Of the many agencies that came to the aid of the Biharis, some were international and famous – Oxfam, CARE and Unicef. And there were many others not so well known, one of which was 'The Brogandanish Rural and Brotherhood Centre'. The 'B.R.B.C.' played its part too.

Based in the town of Brogandanish in the south of Bihar, it was a quasi-religious charity funded from Canada and England by a small religious order whose brethren and sisters devoted their incomes to supporting the Centre in Brogandanish. Members of the order periodically changed lives from working in Canada or England to working in India, where they would normally stay for a period of five years.

The B.R.B.C. was founded before Indian Independence in 1947, and in the 25 years since its inception it had grown to be an important feature in the town of their adoption.

It was to this organisation and at this place that I arrived, very hot and tired at the beginning of July 1967. I had no understanding then of the background to events, and at the railway station I was puzzled by the presence of armed soldiers who lazed on the dusty ground around the water tower used to replenish the trains' boilers.

The heat was nothing I had ever experienced before; it had a merciless, vice-like, squeezing effect that made it difficult to breathe as I left the air conditioned carriage into its surrounding, suffocating oppression. The sun was a blazing chromium dazzle whose staring malignancy in the sky provoked a searing blindness, which instantly narrowed the eyes into a painful squint. Any metal that one touched accidently, on the elbow or thigh, burnt the skin and left a smarting heated sensation.

As soon as I left the station's overhanging shade I was assailed by a group of women, some with babies wrapped in the rags of their saris; their hair was matted and filthy, all visible limbs were smeared and caked with dust and mud – their strong, acrid smell was that of concentrated skin.

'Piasa Sahib! Piasa!' they wailed. In their voices was not the bored monotony of the accomplished city beggar, nor the irony in that of the practised street working boy – theirs was the voice of unmistakable desperation, and on their faces were expressions of breathless fear and urgent distress. A few of the women did not even speak, but twisted a bony, gnarled hand in an upward circular motion to their mouths that conveyed their hunger better than any words. The women followed me to the taxi rank, some touching and pulling at my shirt.

I ignored them in the way I had come to practice effortlessly – by avoiding any eye contact; if that happens, you're sunk and the reaction to some deep instinct is triggered and pity bursts its containment. In that event some mysterious pneumatic force acts upon the hand and makes it extend into the pocket. But I had learned to resist this.

The taxi took me to the outskirts of the town of Brogandanish, where the driver paused at the end of a curved dirt track leading up to the Centre, a jumbled collection of buildings set back from the road by about a hundred yards. The land was flat as far as the eye could see. From the taxi I could see that there were many people congregated at the front and to the side of the Centre – a dark quivering mass that from a distance had the air of a swarm of brown, dusty bees. A woman approached the halted taxi, tapped on my window and looked at me with a mix of accusation and contempt – her thumb pressed into her bunched four fingers, her hand outstretched.

'Here?' asked the driver uncomfortably.

'Yes, this is the place,' I said, seeing the large blue painted sign at the roadside. As we bumped slowly up the driveway, the driver had to sound his horn to clear the way of people standing aimlessly on the track and assembled nearby in small, squatting groups – these were same dusty people, emaciated and filthy, their limbs flabby with slackened folds of wrinkled skin.

The crowd was gathered at the right hand side of the track, which ended at two wooden slatted gates, one of which was open. At the open gate an elderly Indian man sat in a chair. I got out of the car, and as I did the man approached me.

'You are maybe Mr Hendry Sahib?' he said. I got my roll from the taxi and paid the driver, who left with much unnecessary hooting of his horn as he picked his way through the people on the driveway. I was led inside the gates to a shaded planked veranda, which fronted a neat whitewashed two-storey building. The man pointed me towards a door at its end before he returned to his seat.

As I approached the door it opened from within, and standing before me was a tiny, rotund woman with a hooked nose and a perfect pixie face; a light grey linen scarf covered her hair and framed her rotund prominent cheeks and tiny pointed chin. Her head seemed to be permanently bowed and she looked up at me from eyes raised as if she was straining to see the top of a tall building.

'You must be Michael,' she said, 'please do come in.' She raised a hand in a motion like half a Papal benediction and urged me in.

'We've been keeping an eye out for you these last few days,' she said, opening the door. I followed her into a cool tiled hallway that felt fresh and airy. 'I'm sister Wisely,' she continued, 'you must be so hot from your journey. Just leave your things here for the moment.'

She shuffled her way before me and led me from the hallway through a winding corridor towards the back of the building to a kitchen.

'Now, I must get you some lemonade,' she said. She kicked a stool that she climbed onto to reach a cupboard above her to get a glass – she was a great deal shorter than five feet.

The kitchen was a big spacious open room, plain and white, with a long table covered in a cream oil cloth set at its middle; around the table were about 12 plain wooden chairs with rush seats of the sort used in catholic churches. There were three windows to the outside wall of the kitchen; these let in a muted, shaded light through bundles of twigs, which formed a thick screen between the open windows and the outdoors.

Sister Wisely set a glass before me at the table and bade me to be seated.

'Now tell me all about yourself!' she said and hoisted herself up onto a chair opposite me. She listened to me with her head canted to one side and with her hands clasped together in front of her on the table. I had the growing feeling that I was in the presence of someone holy.

When I had explained how it was that I came to be at Brogandanish, she gently and thoroughly interrogated me and had the important elements of my life sorted and catalogued in a few minutes flat.

'I can see you're going to fit in just fine,' she said, 'you'll meet the rest this evening. They're all out, but everyone should be back by about six. Sister Margaret may be a bit later because she's had to go to Bhopal. Now, perhaps you would like to get unpacked and have a wander round. You do know about Land Rovers, don't you? I do so hope so.' She looked at me with enquiring eyes and paused for a moment as though she was about to say something but changed her mind. 'You're in room 14 on the first floor; I hope you don't mind if I don't come up, I do find the stairs difficult. I shall leave you to it because I must get on with tonight's service.' Sister Wisley slid herself back to ground level and with a sweet smile left me on my own.

Once I had unpacked my things in a tiny room on the first floor, I went back to the kitchen and out the exterior door into the shade of a bamboo roofed verandah; before me was a large courtyard bounded on three sides by outbuildings. At the centre of the yard was a circular well contained within a raised brick wall about two feet high. The open part of the courtyard looked onto flat, open scrubland and a track ran from the end outbuilding out past the furthermost buildings. I stepped from the shade into the scorching sun and heat and peered into the doors and windows that faced the courtyard.

The Land Rovers were in a shed at the extreme right of the courtyard and behind two green arched doors, which swung easily open. Once my eyes had adjusted to the darker light, I could see the British stalwarts – there were three of them. One had its bonnet up and had dismantled engine parts and spanners strewn about its wings and on the ground nearby; one was jacked up and had its front wheels off, and the third was covered in such a thick layer of dust that it was evident that it had not run for a long time. I ran my hands over them like a doctor diagnosing a patient.

The shed was bigger than its frontage suggested – at its rear it continued out to a right angled extension, which formed an 'L' shape; this rear part was about 25 feet square and was filled with light from a span of dirty windows that looked out over the empty scrubland and the outside back wall of the main courtyard. This area was filled with discarded furniture, old oil drums and the junk that is too good to throw away but not valued enough to be worth fixing. The room had the air of an artist's studio or workshop, and set into the wall adjacent to the windows was a deep fireplace that suggested it might have been a forge; I peered up the chimney but it was dark and blocked. There was a charpoi in one corner next to a long workbench equipped with a vice and a tower drill and upon which were a scattering of spanners, tools, oils and fluids and an ancient monster of a battery charger. I flicked on a light switch on the wall and a ceiling bulb lit up, then went pop and smashed to the ground.

I went back to the Land Rovers.

When I had first got in touch with the B.R.B.C., their reply had asked if I was familiar with Land Rovers. Although they had not been more specific on the point, I now realised that my anticipated purpose at Brogandanish was to fix and maintain these vehicles. When I was 16 and 17 I had played about with cars and had worked on engines with my brothers and friends, but I was not an experienced mechanic. Most of what we did to cars was to alter their appearance to make them look as though they could go faster than they actually could. Fixing cars is mostly common sense, plus a little knowledge. For the common sense I hoped for the best, and for the guidance I searched the Land Rovers, the shed and the rear workshop for a workshop manual. I found exactly what I needed lying in the dust of the shed floor. On inspection it seemed complete and concurrent with at least one of the vehicles I was to work on. I brushed it off and blew the nestling bugs from the inside covers, relieved that I would likely manage a fair attempt at the task in hand.

As the afternoon wore on, the sun spread the intensity of its white hot glare over a wider, blurred circumference of the sky and softened in the hovering mask of dark blue dust that filtered the light of the early evening.

Sister Wisely was drawing water from the well when I returned after a long walk around the environs of the centre; despite the fantastic heat I had needed to be in open space after my long train journey.

'Let me help,' I said.

'Oh thank you,' she said, 'you are so kind.' I took the rope from her hand and pulled up a bucket of water.

'If you splash the twig bundles tied to the front of the windows, it'll keep us a bit cooler,' she said, 'make sure you wet them thoroughly – the more the water evaporates, the cooler it is inside… it's like, oh, how would you say it, D-I-Y air conditioning…' She laughed to herself like a child who has used an adult word she was not quite sure of the meaning of and left me, giggling as her stooped frame shuffled away.

In the evening, by the time everyone was seated around the big table in the kitchen, I had met most but not all of the staff of the centre. Neil and Maureen were a husband and wife team from Canada, both doctors. The sisters were six in number – Sisters Margaret, Wellbeloved, Wisely, Truman, Campbell and Plumb. The sisters all wore identical plain grey head scarves, except for Sister Margaret, whose scarf bore a single dark blue stripe at the crown over her forehead; I assumed this was a sign of some superiority. Also in the kitchen but seated at a separate small table were Sadar, the man who had been at the gate when I had arrived, and his grandson, called Batuk. One member of staff was still to arrive when food was served.

I had been introduced to each as they had arrived at the centre from their various jobs and found it difficult to remember names, so I bowed my head low when Sister Margaret began the very lengthy grace.

'…and as we welcome a new member to our community, oh Lord,

may Your blessings be on Michael and may you keep him safe and bless him.' I bowed my head even lower.

After our meal, the group began to show its nature. Sister Margaret was clearly the Alpha; she had a snippy, curt manner that she disguised with an invariable, narrow smile at the end of each statement.

'Now, Michael,' she said, 'we all help with the clearing up, don't we?' She turned on her smile, then she turned it off again.

Once the kitchen tasks had ended and I had been instructed in a kindly but firm way as to which cupboard kept the glasses, and which drawer contained the dishcloths, I sat for a while with Neil because he seemed the most comfortable to be with. He was a handsome, dark-haired man in his early 40s with an easy manner.

'So, have you had a wander round?' he asked.

'Oh yes. I went for a wee walk and I've seen the Land Rovers. But the heat...'

'Ah yes, the heat. So what do you think? About the Land Rovers?'

'Well, I haven't but really looked at them in any detail. I'll take a close look tomorrow – but as far as I can see, they don't seem to be beyond repair. I mean they haven't been crashed or anything.'

'Well there are two more we have; they're going okay, but Sister Margaret's one's brakes are squealing. And John should be back with the long wheel base any minute. It's running okay, but it needs a service badly, John tends to...'

'John?' I interjected.

'John Winkles, South African chap, he's our drilling man – he helps make the tube wells we've been developing here.'

At this cue, I heard the screech of brakes outside in the courtyard, the hard slamming of doors, the barking of orders and the pounding of running feet.

'That'll be him,' said Neil. One of the sisters dropped an enamel basin onto the floor with an almighty clatter and my radar discerned the brief-est, fleetest freezing of the postures and movements of all those in the room.

The kitchen door flung open and in stepped a short gorilla of a man dressed in dusty, oil smeared khaki bush gear – shorts, multi pocketed shirt, knee length socks, scuffed, clumpy boots and a wide brimmed leather hat with the word 'BOSS' stitched crudely on its front. In one hand he held a pair of leather gauntlets and in the other a massive, cruel-looking sheath knife – and both these items, and his hat, he threw roughly onto the kitchen table. He looked like a man who would snack on broken glass and carpet tacks.

'Evenin,' he said to the company at large, then at me, 'you the Land Rover man?'

I stood up, hand outstretched.

'Yes, Mike Hendry.'

'Good to see you man.' He grabbed my hand and squelched it shapeless. 'Oh,' he said, 'I forgot.' He went back to the kitchen door, opened it and yelled out 'Sanjee! Get back here will you! Get those jerry cans onto the generator trolley on the double! No, no, the blue ones... the petrol ones you silly shafter – juldee-juldee you ape! Now where was I? Oh yeah, Mike...'

In the brief minutes since he was heard to arrive in the courtyard, a setting had been laid out on the kitchen table and a great deal of food was spread out around it – noticeably more than the rest of us had had. All the sisters melted away from the kitchen, leaving Neil and Maureen and myself to chat as John gnashed and munched his noisy way through an Everest of popadums and chutney.

I was very tired from my day and took my leave before John had finished his meal. I went upstairs to my little room and opened its window to let some vestige of air in, and I looked out into the dusk and wondered what the hell I had got myself into. The lights of the town of Brogandanish were before me in the near distance, and directly below me I could just see the edges of the small encampment that had established itself on one side of the centre. The smell of the smoke from the few fires there, mixed with the faint wailing of Indian pop music, wafted into my room and triggered a desperate homesickness.

I closed my eyes and imagined the cool wet grass of Aberdeenshire fields and hills and the coldness of the River Don tumbling over itself into pools of amber glassiness. I willed to my mind the chilling winds that blew around the valleys of the burns I had walked since a boy – all of which I was coming to love and miss mightily. I imagined what my family at home was doing: in our sitting room, the dog sleeping, shamelessly belly up in front of the fire, my brother and sister doing their studies upstairs in their bedrooms, my Mum laying out the breakfast things in the kitchen, my father nestling and teasing a tumbler of whisky, pretending to read. And I summoned up the image of the house getting to bed and becoming silent – apart from the slow tick-tock of the grandfather clock at the bottom of the stairs. And I thought of my brother David in Calcutta and I yearned to see him.

Without the preamble of a knock, the door to my room opened and John came in.

'Okay man?' he asked.

'Yeah, fine. Want to come in?'

'Nah, going to my pit, have to be up early – crack of dawn I am. What do you make of them then?' John cocked his head signifying the downstairs.

'Oh, don't know yet. Seem nice enough.'

'Yea, well. Neil's okay I suppose. Then there's the sisters, eh? There's not a one of them I'd poke. Well, g'night man.'

'Yeah, goodnight.'

I settled in to the centre and my routine established itself very quickly. All staff members had their own breakfast and then departed to their various tasks. Neil and Maureen, Sister Plumb and Sister Campbell went to the leprosy hospice, which the centre ran as part of their mission. The hospice was about a mile away and was attached to the local hospital. Sister Margaret was the one who dealt with all things administrative and spent much of her time in her office. John Winkle was away from the centre most of the time, drilling tube wells. He would be loudly present for a few days servicing the small drilling rig, its generators and a mass of paraphernalia, then would leave with his two assistants and be away for a week or 10 days at a time. When he left, there was a tangible relaxing of the atmosphere. Sisters Wisely, Truman and Wellbeloved stayed at the centre and were responsible for the actual feeding of people who came for assistance. They were helped in the physical humping and heaving of the huge cauldrons and the sacks by Sadar and Batuk. I helped first thing in the morning to mix up the great vats of powdered milk with water, and I would check the stock levels of grain, rice and the few tinned items, which were kept strictly under lock and key.

At the centre, the rations, the grain and the milk were laid out on a series of long tables and at 10:00 every morning, the gates were opened. Before this moment, Sadar would organise the crowd from a pushing mass into the semblance of a queue at the gate, and he carried a stick that he would raise threateningly to make sure this happened.

When the gates opened, the people surged forward and took a bowl if they did not have one. They worked down the line, receiving ladles of milk and cupfuls of grain and, sometimes, rice. What was given was never enough and it was always less than the person preceding had received. Sadar had an eagle eye for those who tried to join the queue for a second time. Women with children received more than women on their own, and it was a good week before I noticed, consciously, that there were virtually no men in the queues.

'The men will not come here,' explained Sister Wellbeloved, 'they would rather die of hunger or thirst than admit to the world that they had been reduced to this.'

The first session of feeding took about two hours, and I would be in the background mixing up more milk or fetching more grains as the demand grew. We were supposed to have a set ration of all the commodities in order to keep a regular outflow, but we were permitted small variations if it was thought it appropriate. After the feed, the gates were closed and padlocked and all the containers and implements had to be washed. At first I volunteered to help with this, but my offers were rejected, so I would get to work on the Land Rovers. I would work on these until mid-afternoon, and then I would help prepare the second feed session, which took place at 4:00. This second event was usually a smaller affair because many of the recipients of the morning session would return to their homes. Some of the women would walk five or six miles to the centre to get their rations, then return with them to their families. If the afternoon sessions were the smaller affair, they were also the much more ill tempered. This was because it was peopled by those who had virtually settled into the camp adjacent to the centre, and it was these desperates who were at the furthest extreme of destitution; they depended almost entirely on what the centre gave out. The camp's inhabitants had had time to establish both the familiarities and contempt that generate from mutual habitation, and the camp was the scene of many bitter shouting matches between one group or another – always over perceived unfairness, true or otherwise, measured in tiny fractions of advantage or disadvantage. When I once or twice took a hand at ladling out the grain, Sister Truman gave me stern instruction that the ladle must be filled to its level top – and not heaped over that, nor depleted below it, and that each ladle should be levelled with a flat stick to achieve this. The volume of milk or grain handed out was observed with acute intensity.

Thus, the afternoon sessions, though shorter, were fraught with tension and punctuated with squabbles. It burdens the Western mind with a great effort to realise fully that there are many people who really are so close to death by starvation. It's a notion so far removed from (my) personal experience that there are no terms of reference by which to create the scenario; dammit, if you're hungry you go to the fridge – and the only problem is in the choosing of what to eat. Shall I have the pork pie with chutney, or will the cold chicken and a dash of cranberry sauce hit the spot better?

As to my routine, at about 3:00 or 3:30, I would wash, then help with the afternoon feeding. I called these events 'feeds', but the sisters called them 'services'. Inside the centre, the evening meal was generally at 6:00, after which, rather than join the society of the kitchen, I would return to the Land Rovers.

I decided I would concentrate on one vehicle at a time to establish what was wrong with them – at the end of this process I would know the sum total of spares that would be needed to get all the vehicles going; since spare parts had to come from Delhi, I wanted there to be just one order that would see all of them fixed. In this strategy, I was confounded when the first Land Rover burst into life once I had only put back together those bits that had been disassembled. I didn't know what had been wrong with it and I earned heavy gold stars for getting it mobile within a week of my arrival. I was duplicitous and underhanded in the manner in which I presented my accomplishment for judgement.

In anticipation of completing the assembly of the dispersed bits of Land Rover number one, I had charged up its battery, ready at least to get the engine turning over so that I could begin the diagnoses of why it would not start. But start it did. With the shed doors closed, I managed to get it into motion and found it went forwards and backwards, and, with a very hefty heave on the brakes, it could be stopped. This achievement was clocked up just after the morning feed. Rather than take it for a trial drive there and then, I waited until the evening when I knew everyone would be in the kitchen, and therefore in hearing of the courtyard.

After the evening meal, I said to no-one in particular that I was going back to work on the Land Rovers. I opened the shed's doors, started up the engine, and with an unnecessarily loud revving chugged around the courtyard and around the well, making sure I passed near the kitchen windows and door with the engine at full tilt.

Neil came outside in response, as did Sister Wellbeloved and Sister Margaret. With feelings of guilt not apparent to my small audience, I basked in their praise and shrugged off the matter as if, oh, really, it was nothing less or more than was expected. Sister Margaret smiled for the first time in response to a happy feeling rather than a stressed one, and she became, at that instant, quite another person.

As the weeks slid by and the Land Rovers were awaiting the arrival of their various parts from Delhi, I began to clear the back, studio part of 'my' shed. I had decided I would live there rather than in the main building, where the smallness of my room was becoming oppressive to me.

In the course of working on the Land Rovers I made great friends with Batuk, Sadar's grandson, who spent much of his time with me. As he handed me a spanner, or held a cable, I would teach him the English words of each part, and he delighted in this enterprise. He was about 10 or 11 and we became firm friends – he was always waiting for me at the shed whenever I turned up in the late morning to start work. It was perhaps wrong of me, but I gave him a penknife I had never used and he took to carving odd bits of wood, which he found among the sheds.

In my move to 'the studio' as it became known, Batuk helped me wash the place until it was clean as a whistle; the windows were washed and light streamed in onto the newly whitewashed walls, I got some material from Sister Wisely for curtains, and in late July I spent my first night there. It was cooler than the house, quieter, and the place had a benign, friendly atmosphere.

In the matter of the Land Rovers, I had decided that it would be sensible to do more than get them going. They had suffered badly from neglect and practically every aspect of their workings had been affected by dust. Filters were clogged, seals were crusted and damaged, and every nook and cranny was packed with years of dirt.

Batuk and I set about taking off and cleaning all the possible components that we could reasonably take to bits. Batuk proved a quick learner; I would show him how to take apart the brake cylinders to check and clean their seals and, with very little guidance, he would manage to execute exactly the same procedure to another wheel. When I needed help to bleed the brakes, I explained how the system worked. He was slow to understand, but once he did understand, he knew how to do it thoroughly and understood the whole picture.

Life at Brogandanish was not all work. Most Saturdays, we would pile into Sister Margaret's big Land Rover and drive to a cool rock pool where we would picnic and swim. An overhang of rock butted the pool, and diving from there into the deep cool water was unforgettable. The pool was a 20 minute drive from the centre and lay down a steep long path. I came to look forward to these little expeditions because I loved swimming and the relief of the cool water was so intense that the memory of the sensation seemed to last two or three days. I enjoyed them too because they were happy affairs when the sisters became people other than sisters; they came equipped with a canvas beach screen and changed into swimming costumes and splashed and swam with delight and fun.

At the centre they addressed each other as sister this or sister that – but at the pool, they called each other by their first names, and though I could not attach any logic to my surprise at this, I was both surprised and touched.

The only drawback of the pool was that it was populated with monkeys that inhabited the rocks and bushes which surrounded the pool, and these were so bold they would steal any scrap of food or clothing that was within their reach. I have always loathed monkeys and watched them warily.

The pool became my solitary destination too. The first Land Rover I had fixed was not entirely safe to drive, but it could be driven with care,

and I would often sneak off on a hot afternoon and plunge into the water
to cool off. The first time I went on my own, I was in such a hurry to get
into the water that I left the Land Rover door open and the monkeys
made off with every stitch of clothing I had. I had to drive back in just
my trunks and bare feet.

After the parts for the Land Rovers arrived from Delhi, I was a month
bringing the three vehicles up to a usable standard, and by that time
it was August and the old feelings of redundancy began to creep back.
There remained Sister Margaret's and John's Land Rovers to service, but
I had had a look at them and was sure they needed nothing more than
maintenance.

It was decided that John would keep his vehicle for a week's trip that
he had to make and that, following this, he would have the use of one
of the ones I had repaired while I serviced his vehicle, and the same
general scheme applied to Sister Margaret's Land Rover. This having
been decided, I could see that the end of my usefulness to the centre
would lie but a month away, maybe six weeks at the most, and I began to
fret about what I should do once that time was reached.

I had given myself a year to spend in India and had had always aimed
to be back in Scotland by November or December at the latest. I had had
a letter from Ross, who had arrived back in England, and he extolled
the benefits of flying back – but I had decided I would like to see more
of the world and had thus decided that I would get back overland. I had
worked out that the trip would likely take two to three weeks, which
meant that in order to get home by November I would need to be planning my departure for sometime in late October. If my timetable was
correct in assuming I would be finished at Brogandanish by the end
of September, then that gave me only a month of leeway before taking
steps to make my way home. Suddenly, I felt the strictures of a timetable
and my other limitation – money.

I told Neil of my general thinking: with the Land Rovers in good heart
and with a stock of spares neatly stacked in my shed for future use, my
time at Brogandanish must surely be coming to a close.

'Have you thought of staying?' he asked. 'I don't think John will be
here much longer; he has talked to me about going back to South Africa,
but not with any precise date. When he goes, maybe you could take over

the rig. Don't forget Sanjee can show you the ropes – he's more qualified and experienced than John is…'

'But I thought John –'

'That's what John would like you to think. But Sanjee's the one to show you how to drill wells.'

'I'll have a think about it, Neil,' I said.

'In any case, even if you don't want to go drilling wells, you're welcome to stay on here and help the sisters, I'm sure they'll find plenty for you to do. And besides, I'm a director of the Canadian base organisation, and if you wanted to stay for more time, I know I have just to give them the say so, and you'd be very welcome here. We just can't pay you any money though. I still think it would be a good idea to go with John on his next trip and at least see how to dig a well. And Muzzrah has a fine temple.'

The next day was calm and quiet and I found a diary. On blank A4 sheets I copied out the days and weeks in a grid that spanned August to December. I had wanted to have a couple of weeks to myself – maybe to travel a bit, maybe on my own or with Kim, who had suggested a trip to Nepal. I marked out the time I would need to get home and worked out what leeway of time I had. There were some four weeks that seemed available for everything I wanted to do, and I decided that I would go with John on his next drilling trip. It was well away from Brogandanish and I felt it would feel like a working holiday in new surroundings.

On the day I was to speak to John about accompanying him on the next drilling trip, he was later back from his toils than usual.

I was in my own studio and heard him arrive in the courtyard to the usual shouting and banging, and waited an hour or so to be sure he had eaten and was in his room. I went through the courtyard, into the kitchen and upstairs to his room. Since he did not have the habit of knocking on people's doors before entering, I just opened his door and stepped in.

He was sitting on his bed and he was surrounded by wads of money, one fistful of which he threw hurriedly into a tiny suitcase at his immediate side. His face clouded with instant anger and he jumped to his feet, half covering the sight of the cash, which he knew I'd seen.

'Wha'd ya want, man?' he growled.

'Oh, sorry John...' it was an awkward moment – he didn't have any hope of disguising or covering the cash strewn about his bed, 'I spoke to Neil, I was wondering if I could go with you to Muzzrah to the new well?'

'Huh, after the rig are you? Neil's been blabbing has he?'

'No, not at all, just wanted a trip, that's all.'

'I'll see.'

'Yeah, well okay. Thanks, see you later.'

'Yeah.'

I turned and closed the door behind me.

A few days later in the kitchen, after the evening meal, John came to see me in my shed.

'Look man, I'm okay with you coming – okay? But I need to set the rig up on my own with Sanjee, 'cos only I can do it, on my own, see. I'm like that, okay?'

'Yeah, fine, fine,' I said.

'I'll come back here the weekend after it's all set up then I'll take you to see the second stage. I'll show you, you'll see everything. Okay man?'

Awkwardly, he held out his hand and he squelched me again, best buddies.

'It's a hard, hard graft,' he said, 'drilling's hard graft.' I nodded as if I knew.

'See ya,' he mumbled.

At the end of the following week John, Sanjee and a third man I had only seen briefly before, Parfitt, loaded up the big Land Rover and its trailers in preparation of establishing a new well. I tried to assist, but the three of them were so practised that I just got in the way. John had a delight in showing his physical strength. I had helped Sanjee carry one of the drill bits from the store –the two of us barely managed it and were left with sagging knees and hurting backs after the work – but John could pick up one of these solid steel lumps of metal with apparent ease and toss it into its rack as if it had been a feather. He liked being watched and would let out puffs and grunts to accentuate his effort so that everyone was made fully aware of his presence – not that that was ever unnoticed. He was gigantically strong. His calf muscles were like the overhangs of rocky cliffs, his arm muscles bulged like carnal, sinewy balloons, and his shoulders had somehow the quality of dinosaur bones.

The Brogandanish Rural and Brotherhood Centre had been pioneers in post-war India in developing tube wells – these being a practical way to alleviate periodic drought and to ensure a water supply to settlements where old wells had dried up. The centre had developed its well operations to a highly sophisticated degree and, though I never saw it, there was a cement works near the centre where the rings lining the wells were made, and at the centre, one of the biggest of the outbuildings around the courtyard stored a wealth of drilling equipment. Because the centre had been in operation for many years, the immediate vicinity around Brogandanish had many wells. As a consequence, new wells that were being dug tended to be further afield. This was true of the Muzzrah well.

The new site was some 50 miles south of Brogandanish; being so distant, the crew were to stay at a guest house nearby rather than commute daily back to the centre. Once the rig had been set up and the bore started, John would come back for the necessary supplies and would return with me to the new site to begin my education in drilling.

Exactly according to plan, John wheeled back to the centre on his own on a Saturday evening, the Land Rover towing only a generator that had developed a fault and needed fixing. The generator powered the arc welder and was essential to the operation; it would go back with us, hopefully fixed. On Sunday, John toiled over the generator on his own. By the afternoon it was running again and pouring fumes around the courtyard.

Very early on Monday morning, we left the centre and went to the road that ran directly south from Brogandanish; John was a scary, over-speeding driver who relied upon the power of the horn to clear the road ahead. I'm an easy-going passenger and have the view that it's best not to complain of excessive speed, since this makes the driver more prone to show off his competence – illusory or not. But with John, I had to speak up.

'Jesus, that was close!' I squealed as he swerved around a bullock pulled cart.

John only muttered to himself, 'Stupid apes. Stupid, stupid, stupid, can't these people see...'

I looked frequently to the rear of the Land Rover, where the trailer carrying the generator swayed dangerously in the dust stream of our slip. When we stopped for petrol, I excused myself from the front passenger seat and moved to the back on the pretext of wanting to read the maps.

'Suit yourself,' said John, 'we're almost there anyway – 'bout another 10 minutes.'

As John accelerated faster and faster down a long, descending straight, I sensed the architecture of my existence shift imperceptibly but definitely. As this curious sensation grew in certainty, I noticed simultaneously that the Land Rover was pitched with a slight downward and sideways list and that a wheel was overtaking us.

'Oh, look,' I said entirely in innocence, 'there's a wheel!' I pointed to the thing that was streaking past us on our immediate right.

Then, I yelled out, 'what the...'

'Fuck!' John shouted, 'the trailer...' As he spoke, the Land Rover's nose swung sharply to the right towards the opposite ditch; John yanked the steering to the extreme left – in the midst of this manoeuvre there erupted from behind us a screeching, sckrriching noise. I turned to the back and saw the generator slowly falling over onto its side; there was a shattering crack as the hitch between the Land Rover and the trailer burst apart. As the Land Rover too was beginning to cant alarmingly onto its right side into the ditch, I saw, on a helter skelter speeding descent, the trailer jerk violently back and swerve away from us on one wheel to disappear in a sudden explosion of dust. I saw, too, the black-and-white painted road pole come rapidly towards me at a very unexpected angle of attack, and then I blacked out.

A mysterious, floating time passed. There was a headline and there was a song. The headline was:

'N.E. Man Unwell on Way to Well – City Anxious', and the song was a French one that came from someplace far away, deep down in my mind. It's on a scratchy '78 record, the label is yellow and at its centre is the trademark of a cockerall. The gramophone it's being played on is an old wind-up one and the needle is blunt. The record begins with the kish-kish-kish of the needle being set on the record, there's a jolly introduction by a small string band, and then a man begins to sing. It's

Ray Ventura, I think. The words go: *Oh I'm sorry to say, your mule is dead and so is your dog but really, there's no need to worry, everything is "si bon, si bon". I'm afraid your wife has died and so has your son the castle has been burnt to the ground but really, there's no need to worry, everything is 'si bon, si bon'.*

Three inches from my face, and so close I could see the faint fur of hair on her cheeks, was an Indian woman with a bright red cast mark on her forehead, peering into the pupils of my eyes.

'Please, just keep still,' she breathed, 'I'm a doctor.'

'John?' I said.

'The other one? He'll be alright… look up – down.'

My right eye was swollen and black, I could feel a handsome lump on the side of my head, I had an aching shoulder, and my head was throbbing and singing. I got uneasily back on my feet to find John, who was sitting on the grass verge, his face streaked in blood. He was rocking backwards and forwards and had an expression of pain visible around his eyes, and he was gripping his testicles; the doctor was saying something to him but I couldn't hear clearly what she was saying from where I was tottering on shaky legs.

'No way!' I heard John say to the doctor, 'no way!' I came within earshot and I heard the doctor say 'Don't be silly, I'm a doctor, I need to check you over.' She held out her hand in a gesture of appeal, but he drew back.

'Don't touch me!' he squealed, 'I'm alright see? Alright? Ooooh!'

The doctor turned to me and said 'This man is being very silly and juvenile – I need to take a look at him, I'm a doctor.' I shrugged my shoulders.

She stood for a some seconds with a look of sad resignation on her face, then said to me, 'Where are you from?'

'Brogandanish,' I said.

'From the centre?'

'Yes,' I answered.

'I know Doctor Neil there. You must get him to examine… him, as soon as you can. How are you feeling?'

'I'm alright, really I am, just a bit woozy.'

She stayed for another 10 minutes, checked me over again then drove off towards Muzzrah. A small crowd had gathered and, as we recovered in the next hour, a tractor came by.

The Land Rover was in one ditch and the generator was in another on the opposite side of the road – amazingly, still vaguely attached to its chassis, though with its securing bolts twisted and mostly shorn. John was up on his feet and ordered around the man with the tractor in such an intimidating way that he meekly did as he was told. We dragged the Land Rover from its ditch first, then got the generator vaguely back onto the road, at which point the tractor and its driver made a hasty escape from any further demands.

One side of the Land Rover was covered in gouges and scrapes, an abstract impression of a metal pole ran from behind the front wing up to the roof, and the rear windows were smashed. The offside front wing was gloriously dented in towards the wheel and the rear door refused to close. But it started and would drive. John left me at the scene and drove to Muzzrah, and in half an hour came back with Sanjee and Parfitt. While I was waiting, I looked for the wheel, which had come off the trailer, and found it about quarter of a mile down the road, wedged into the branches of a viciously prickled bush.

In the heat of the midday sun, the four of us struggled with ropes, chains, poles and sledge hammers and managed to get ourselves into a mobile state. The liberated wheel of the generator trailer was gloriously fixed by a wooden pole, which acted as a temporary axle. If John had driven at 70 miles an hour for most of the journey to Muzzrah, the last few miles were achieved at a walking pace only. The heat was intense, burning and draining.

We stopped briefly at the well site, where Sanjee picked up his things, and then we went to our guest house to shower, rest and eat. John asked me if I would like to go into Muzzrah to send a telegram to Neil at the Brogandanish to convey the news of the accident, but I declined his invitation.

'Oh well, suit yourself man,' he said.

The 'accident' came to have more of an effect on the centre than simply the sum parts of damage caused to us, the vehicle and the equipment.

Just a week after we had been picked up from Muzzrah by Neil and Maureen in two Land Rovers, John left the centre. One evening he was saying 'g'night' and the next morning, he was gone. A week after this strange twist, which had everyone at the centre mystified and anxious, a Mr Jupta came to the centre and, in an irate voice, demanded to see some one 'in charge'. Neil was out and Mr Jupta waited most of the day, pacing up and down the driveway.

The story that Mr Jupta told Neil explained two things: John's immense stash of cash and John's midnight flight. John had charged Mr Jupta 500 rupees for drilling the well, in contradiction to the avowed intent of the centre to provide these wells as gifts of aid. It turned out that Mr Jupta was not the only person to have 'paid' to have a well dug on his ground either.

As this sad story began to unfold into a saga of duplicity and intrigue, Neil very kindly gave me some money and let me have one of the Land Rovers to take a week off to recuperate from the accident. I jumped at his offer. The very next day I was away and on the road to Bodghaya, the birthplace of Buddhism. I knew exactly where I wanted to go.

I had had no thoughts about becoming a Buddhist, but the Rimpoche had told me that I should go and see the Buddha tree in Bodghaya if I ever had the chance. Unknowingly, I wanted to re-experience the friendly and peaceful Buddhist feelings I had experienced with the Tibetans – perhaps it would be like going to see an old friend.

As I drove through Bihar, I realised I was having a holiday – and the pleasure of having my own vehicle, a little money and the freedom to go just where I pleased was intoxicating. I sang, I shouted, I whoopee'd and I waved to anyone that passed a glance at me. It was the first time since leaving home that I felt that I was doing something that my contemporaries and friends would never do – and the feeling gave me a rare sense of pride. I remembered the story my Rimpoche had told me.

It was in Bodghaya, 2,500 years ago, that Siddhartha Gautama Buddha sought enlightenment. With five friends he had lived a life of extreme austerity for six years, believing that this was the route to, well, whatever they were seeking. But Siddartha came to the conclusion that self denial in itself was not the answer. He announced to his friends that he would no longer live that life and they were so disgusted with him that they left him. How the Buddha broke the habit of his austerity seems to have been with the indulgence of some rice milk; having received this, he was offered a gift of grass so that he could make himself a mat. Thus endowed with these sudden gifts, he rested under a peepal tree and, facing himself East, he resolved he would not move from that spot until he had attained enlightenment.

'Here on this seat my body may shrivel up,
My skin, my bones, my flesh may dissolve
But my body will not move from this seat
until I have attained Enlightenment...'

Siddhartha called upon the Gods to witness his life of selfless denials and asceticism, and he forced all his body and soul to become one with the ground – and the ground shook. The God Mara was the God of Illusion, whose forces had blinded Siddhartha – Siddhartha's determination to find enlightenment defeated the forces of Mara, and the Buddha found his beliefs and his faith.

In Bodghaya, the tree beneath which the Buddha is said to have achieved his enlightenment is still there – though the tree has its own story too.

Two and half centuries later, the Emporer Ashoka, in dedication to the Buddha, built a temple near the tree and spent so much time there that his wife became angry; she sent men to cut the tree down while he was away for a time. But the Emporer managed to save some saplings that grew at its base; these he replanted at Bodghaya and in Sri Lanka at another temple to the Buddha that he was building. The second tree at Bodghaya died and a sapling from the Sri Lanka tree was brought back to Bodghaya, and that is the tree which has survived. Like the Buddha's enlightenment, the tree too, had its testing times.

Because the Rimpoche had told me the story of the tree, I held it with something more than affection; I felt I knew it somehow, personally and like a friend, and that I had an insight that was deeper than the story a guidebook might tell. Once I had reached Bodghaya in the mid-afternoon, the day had become cloudy and overcast, heavy with a sultry heat.

Near the towering Mahomat temple, the tree is to be found beside a wall inset with fabulous carved panels and bounded on its other three sides by a tall sandstone fence of wide bars. Set into one of the side fences is an elaborate wire and metal gate secured by a huge brass padlock; access to the tree is only for the privileged few. There is a paved walkway that surrounds the tree's 'compound', and this in turn is defined by another barred wall that shapes the walkway and gives it the feeling of being a sensible maze. The tree has an immense but short base, which splits into some five or six rising trunks that arch like stubby giraffe's necks, and from these, protrude very long, snaking, tubular boughs that hang over the walkway and are so long that they have to be supported by long metal poles. The bark is a light, flaky grey colour and the waxy leaves are shaped like a flat, very pointed heart at whose end hangs a small but sensual, pulpy green spike. The peepal tree is a species of fig, so it casts its leaves in autumn, and these are eagerly seized as mementos and relics. At the base of the tree, within its protected little compound and between the high walls of the temple, is the Diamond Throne – once as magnificent as its name implies, but now just a construction that looks like a four poster bed with its legs cut off, this covered in fabrics of red and gold, hung with garlands of marigolds.

I wandered among the crowds, enjoying being the tourist, and sauntered among the great number of temples that have been built over a period of centuries in celebration of the Buddha. Bodghaya is a site of pilgrimage for all Buddhists – Japanese, Thai, Burmese, Indian, Tibetan, and there were European faces there too. When I go to see a place, I prefer my own company and I prefer to be alone; I find it a better way to get to the feeling of a place rather than its tourist technicolour. Since I was to stay the night in the city, I resolved to return in the evening when the tree and I might be alone together. I walked and walked, stopped for tea, sat and thought of nothing and looked at the zillion Buddhas on sale at stalls and tents scattered throughout the main complex of temples and walkways.

I came upon a small stall attended by a thin, wizened old man who stood behind a table upon which were a line of small carved stone Buddhas – there were only about a dozen of them and they were all approximately the same: about four inches tall, quite well carved but crudely so from a dark green stone, just the usual tourist tat. That was all he had for sale. I don't know why, but there was one which, in an intangible but important sense, seemed to be mine, almost as if I had previously owned it. I hadn't looked and judged each one in comparison to its neighbour as if in preparation of buying one – I hardly ever buy such things at any time. But this one little statue was absolutely determined that he and I should be united. I'm not sure how this came about – by an invisible movement? By an aura? By the radiance of some attracting force? I bought it; the man wrapped it in a used and wrinkled shred of brown paper and took my money.

I went to find a room for the night, strolled among the streets of the city proper and drank in the colours of saffron, rose and plum green, the smells of incense, roasted nuts and cardamom, and the lights of the tilly lamps and candles and the brown and black glittering in the lowered eyes of the beautiful young women.

I went back to the Buddha tree a few hours later; the sky was that deep blue sapphire before the final dark and the stars drew the eye to their millions of sparkling pinpricks above. A slight breeze rustled the leaves and a single wall-light dimly lit one profile of the tree and cast deep shadows among its canopy and on the walkway surrounding it. The air was warm and comfortable, and apart from far distant voices, quiet and peaceful. I paced around the tree, back and forth; I looked up through its branches, I stretched upwards and managed to hold a leaf between my fingers.

I loafed and lounged in its close vicinity, I walked away from it to turn and see it in my backward glance, I sat on the paving stones around it and gazed at it, I crouched on my haunches and let its feelings spread over me, I lay on my back and imagined the tree's roots below me. In my reverie, I endowed the tree with a memory that I was asking it to recollect and communicate to me; I was urging it to tell me something that would help me to be at one with it – please, even for an instant. In my imagining, time swept away the layers of years that separated its beginnings to its present, like sand gathered and blown away to reveal the fresh greenness that it once had, perhaps on the very day when Siddhartha received something that was to affect millions of lives. What happens to those very few humans in whom there is a waiting potential, the realisation of which enters the core of all humans? What is created when their desires collide with their mental and social surroundings at a particular moment? Or is it, more cynically, that it is not what is in these beings, but some great need in the people who surround them – they satisfy those needs by utterances and actions that make them only seem godlike, emperors, kings and rulers, and in the seeming to be, they thus become the real thing by accident? Because that is the process by which all things are created: they have to be imagined first.

I did not approach the Buddha tree with a request or a need – I did not go to it to seek enlightenment and therefore it was not received – in this I avoided both success and failure. I have never understood what enlightenment is, or what above wisdom characterises its possession. I did not visit it with either humility or arrogance, I went to see it because I was curious and I went just as the young man I was. And yet, something did happen to me. Perhaps oddly, what I felt was gratitude, though to whom or to what, I could not define. I think I felt grateful to be alive – and in the interpretation of that, just plain bursting happy.

I felt in my pocket and drew out my little stone effigy of the Buddha and unwrapped it from its shred of tatty paper and felt its stony density in my hand. I was seized by an urgent need to touch and to get close to the tree. I slipped the Buddha back into my inside jacket pocket, looked carefully around me to see that I was not being watched, and climbed to the top of the protective fence; I had a moment's hesitation, then jumped down and landed on my feet on the hard earth that formed a narrow circumference around the base of the tree.

I was just four or five feet from it, inside its protective barriers; I stepped forward with my left hand outstretched and gently laid the palm of my hand flat against the bark. Although the first sensation was the bark's crisp roughness, I was aware that my hand was sensing a temperature that was both cool and warm at the same time. I then placed my right hand on the tree close to my left hand, and pressed lightly so that, again, the palm of my hand was flat to the tree. Again, the first sensation was of a temperature rather than a texture. I breathed in and out slowly; I was not thinking of anything. I brought my body forward and pressed it wholly to the trunk then opened my arms to embrace such girth of the tree as the stretch of my arms would encompass. I became aware that I was a little breathless, so my breathing increased in speed and depth – I was thinking of nothing but the tree. A period of time elapsed, the duration of which was unknown to me – perhaps it was a few seconds, perhaps a few minutes.

I relaxed and let my arms drop and I raised my head to look up through the branches; I took my Buddha from my pocket and held it against the trunk with both hands. In this position, I did say a prayer. I had the sensation that the feeling behind my words was recognised by something nearby. I felt that my effigy was now filled with something, or had a protective coating or had been touched by something whose effect was to change, invisibly, the atoms of its constituent parts.

After this, I sat at the foot of the tree, leaning my back against its benign bulk – just as if I was in the woods at home by the River Don, sitting for a moment of pleasant relaxation on a summer's day.

Where once the air had been warm and embracing, it became cool and signalled that it was time to go. In waking up, I returned from somewhere unknown with the need to return to the familiar and, checking my surroundings to make sure that there was still no-one nearby, I climbed out over the fence and quickly left the tree. I walked back to the Land Rover, found my guest house and went to bed. I sat the little stone Buddha on the table next to my pillow so that it would be close to me, and it has remained in that proximity to me ever since.

The next morning, I knew with a fresh and strong certainty that it was time to go home – not in urgency, but as a consideration that had to be factored in to everything I was to do in the near future. I spent just three days driving north towards Nepal and the north of Bihar, and then made my way easily back to the centre at Brogandanish feeling refreshed and confident.

Batuk was waiting with his grandfather at the gate of the centre when I got back. He ran up and helped me unload my few things back into my quarters in the shed. I would find it difficult to say goodbye to my little friend when the time came.

I had only been away from Brogandanish for four days, but on my return, I felt I inhabited a different space from that which I had occupied before I left – somehow more free, somehow more able to do with my time what I wanted rather than what I felt I ought to do.

The afternoon feed was in progress and I helped Sisters Wisely and Wellbeloved serve out the milk and grains, and I was in a happy mood.

Afterwards, as I helped Sister Wisely wash the urns and bowls, she turned her tiny form to me and said, 'I think you had a good holiday Michael.'

'Yes. I feel a lot better... somehow changed. It was a nice trip.'

'Ah,' she said, her pixie cheeks crinkled in a smile, 'that's because India has worked some of its magic on you.'

'Yes, perhaps it's that.'

'Oh undoubtedly it is,' she replied. She was scrubbing one of the big aluminium milk bowls with a bundle of short stubby sticks; the bowl was only a little less in height than she was. 'You know,' she went on, 'you are a young man, but even young men benefit from knowing where they stand in relationship to God, or any god really. Oh, don't worry, I'm not getting religious on you!' She giggled as she sensed the response in me that shied away from these 'deep' conversations. 'But if you look around at the people you know and meet, you'll find that what they believe about good and evil, about the existence of God, or the faith in the afterlife, really determines what they do in life and whether they have embarked upon a course of action that will make them happy. That is really what we want isn't it? To be happy?'

'Yes, we all want to be happy,' I answered, less than certain of what she was coming to.

'It's all about certainty, you see.' Her voice was full of the need to be understood. 'If we're not sure why we are doing something, time slips around us, at a distance, as though it is a place we might get to join one day when we find what makes us passionate, but in the meantime is reserved only for those who are doing real things. But if you are passionate about what you do, then time becomes something close and consuming, a partner. Yes, that's it, a partner.'

I ventured a question that I regretted as soon as I had uttered the words:

'Are you happy?'

'It's taken me a long time,' she said, unbending from her scrubbing, 'the mistake I made was in not realising soon enough what made me happy. I've only been here five years. Don't you make that mistake.'

'Will you go back to Canada?'

She laughed and rolled the bowl expertly on its rim.

'Right,' she said, 'that's that one done, two to go. Lift that one over for me will you?' She beamed her magical smile at me and began humming the tune of 'Onward Christian Soldiers'. As she leaned forward, almost into the bowl to clean its base, the bowl acted as an amplifier of her humming and rang out, intermittently, like a siren to the faithful.

In the last week of September, I said my goodbyes at Brogandanish and prepared to leave for Delhi. I had written to Patrice at 'BroMed' and asked him if I could just stay there for a while and perhaps help out until my plans for heading home had become more solid; he had written straight back saying that I could stay for a long as I liked and that there was plenty to do. On my last day in Bihar, clouds covered the sky as the precursor to the monsoon, and the air became cooler and more tolerable. For the first time in my stay, the evening meal was held outside in the courtyard. After this, I went for a walk in the dull evening light, around the centre and into the scrubland around it. I checked my things to make sure that I would be ready to leave calmly after an early breakfast. I went to bed in my shed and lay awake unable to sleep, thinking about what I might do with the few weeks left to me in India.

Brogandanish held one last sweet surprise that night. I had just drifted to sleep when I was awakened in the darkness by a great kerfuffle near my bed. In alarm, I switched on the light to see a great pile of soot and branches had fallen down the chimney – among the dust and debris were two adult and two baby owls looking very embarrassed and flustered. I had heard fluttering in the chimney over the weeks I had been in my shed, but I had never managed to identify the precise cause. Brogandanish was a place full of surprises and discoveries.

8

Nepal with a revolver and bats

THE MONSOON IN INDIA IS A PHENOMENON THAT EXCITES GREAT speculation. One of the reasons that Bihar suffered such a devastating famine in 1967 was because the monsoon had failed in both 1965 and 1966. Such rains as had fallen on Bihar in 1967 happened much earlier than the usual beginning of the season in June, having fallen, very heavily, in late April and May.

The monsoon in India has two thrusts from the south east of the country – one arcs to the north east around the eastern Ghats, and the other heads straight for Bombay in the north west. Because the time and intensity of the monsoon determines whether millions of people will have enough food to eat, it is a central topic of conversation – as to whether there are any portents for its arrival, what so and so's mother has predicted, and so on. As my train headed west, toward Delhi and away from the gathering clouds in Bihar, the countryside became greener, indicating that the monsoon had come and gone. It seemed no less hot, but the heat was more humid.

By now quite familiar with getting around Delhi, I took buses to get to the 'BroMed' centre rather than a taxi, and I arrived, hot, sweaty and dusty in the late evening. I noticed a familiar Land Rover parked at the door.

The house was full of music and Patrice was full of welcoming; there were guests and the house was full of noise coming from the lounge.

To my great delight, one source of this noise was Kim Fairweather, whom I had met before and had taken a great liking to. I had been at Brogandanish for just over three months and had been in the constant company of fine, noble and virtuous people whom I liked, whom I found it easy to be with and in whose company I felt relaxed and unthreatened. But as I joined Kim and the raucous crowd in the lounge, I realised I was greatly relieved to hear the word 'fuck' again and that there seemed an urgently felt need by everyone in the house to get wildly drunk and to party. One of the guests disappeared for half an hour and returned with crates of beer just as we had drained the kitchen of any trace of alcohol. We had eyed the bottles of sterilising alcohol in the drugs store, wondering how it might be with mango juice, so the beer arrived just in time. There was a record player and a friend of Kim's newly arrived from England put on the Beatles 'Sergeant Pepper', which he had taken out with him. This was magic, this formed the perfect background to my life, and I played it again and again until people were shouting at me, begging me to put on something else.

The next morning, the house rose late, quietly and slowly. Voiceless bodies made their way to the kitchen to seek any surviving water and juices left between the empty bottles, glasses and full ashtrays of our party. I crept up to the roof terrace and found Patrice, Kim and some of the other guests lounging in the deck chairs nursing hangovers. There was no conversation other than an occasional grunt and the murmured enquiry for aspirin.

I had two days to myself in Delhi. My hair had grown long and uncomfortable, my clothes were getting threadbare, I had run out of film for my camera and I had to get my photograph taken to put into my passport in preparation for my trip home, so I had plenty to do. After the rural isolation of Brogandanish, the cityscape of Delhi was as exciting as ever. With some time on my hands, I had the chance to visit forts and museums, take tea on Connaught Square, and be a relaxed tourist again. By my third day, I had achieved all my tasks and was in that state again that hovers between empty boredom and indecision. Kim too was itching to do something.

On the morning of my fourth day, Kim and I were sitting on the roof feeling hot and lazy; we were watching a man at a house behind BroMed.

He was filling a bucket from a tap on the outside wall of the house. He would then take the full bucket of water up a ladder to a tank on first floor and empty the bucket into the tank; there was another identical tank immediately next to the one he was filling. He came down the ladder and repeated the process. We watched him for a good two hours. It was Kim who noticed.

'You see those pipes?' he said.

'Mmm.'

'Well, he's draining the water from the tank on the right, back into the same tank. I'll bet he's supposed to be emptying the water from one tank into the other – see the two sets of pipes? They cross over.'

'Oh yes, you're right. You going over to tell him?'

'Nope.'

'Bastard.'

'No, just too hot. Why don't you go over if you're being the paragon?'

'Nope. Too hot.'

'Bastard.'

We watched the man on and off until lunchtime, still climbing up and down the ladder with his bucket, in the baking heat.

'I'm bored,' said Kim.

'So am I,' I replied.

'Why don't we do something?'

'Like what? Go into town?'

'Nah, better than that, something more exciting.'

We sat for another hour, casually, cruelly watching the man with the bucket, knowing he was tired, hot, and sweating.

'How about Nepal?' said Kim.

'How do you mean?'

'Let's go to Nepal.'

'Great. But I think it takes ages to get a visa.'

'Got your passport back from the embassy?'

'Yup, brand new photo, the new me.'

'Go get it.'

'Eh?'

'Go and get it.' I hobbled down stairs to my room. Kim came in.

'I'm going over to the Embassy,' he said, brandishing his own.

'The British?'

'No no, Nepalese. Know a girl there.' He bounded down the stairs and slammed the front door on his way out. He was back in less than three hours, beaming. Holding our passports aloft, he said, 'I've got them – look!' Sure enough, my passport bore the magnificent stamp of a Nepalese visa, good for two weeks from that day's date.

'Come on, let's go,' said Kim, waving his arms in impatience.

'Now?'

'Yes, right now.'

'What, right now?' I said, disbelieving that we could just leave on such a trip on the instant.

'Yes, yes, come on, we can be at Maradabad in a few hours.'

I rushed to my room, rolled up my bedding roll, said a goodbye and apologised to Patrice, and heaved my stuff into Kim's Land Rover. By mid-afternoon, we were speeding along the main highway to Maradabad, and by nightfall we were in a tiny village accommodated in the 'Lucky Star' guest house – 'lucky' only for the fleas, which recognised us as welcome hosts.

We set off early the next morning, east and north through Rampur, Khatrina and Mahendraga, ascending the lower foothills and leaving behind everything of the hot plains, their stifling heat and their intense cerulean skies. By the beginning of the afternoon, the clouds were thick and dark and the air was moist with a cool, shivery edge.

'Looks like the monsoon is about to happen,' said Kim. The rain began with a few spatters on the windscreen, then the heavens opened and torrential, beating, hammering globules of water fell just as if there had been a solid bulk of water dropped on us. The wipers whined rapidly at full speed, but we had to stop.

'Bloody hell,' said Kim.

'Bloody hell.'

We waited an hour, the rain eased to a steady English pour, and we drove through washed-out roads and decided to cut the day short at Hirnavah. The next day dawned bright and hot and sunny, as if no trace of rain had occurred – only the smell of dampness from the earth rising to our nostrils was evidence of the previous day's downpour. We shared the driving, a few hours at a turn; the day got back to its old baking heat and we sped through towns and villages. We could see we were weaving a path through the cloudy weather front that bore the rains – sometimes we were driving through showers that would suddenly become angry, urgent downpours which, a second later, cleared, and we were back into the sun glaring heat.

I was driving when we hit a goat. The village was just like a hundred others – an approach of a few scattered homes and farms, and then a narrow main street crowded with people and stalls and carts and trucks, then an exit similar to its approach. I had slowed to a crawl to negotiate the main street; I had stopped to let a roaming bullock take the road. As we left the busyness of the main street, I accelerated. The goat ran in front of the Land Rover and fell with a loud croak and a ghastly, bony crunching under the front nearside wheel. The impact slowed us nearly to a stop; the remains of the poor creature were caught around the wheel and the Land Rover would not accelerate except with a heavy drag to its power.

'Oh Jesus,' I thought. What happened to my brother came flashing into my mind, and a very frightening moving picture played just behind my eyes – we were surrounded by a mob bearing clubs and sticks, the windows of the Land Rover would be smashed, we'd be dragged out, kicked to the ground and beaten to a pulp.

I stopped and reversed, hoping the manoeuvre would free the carcass from the wheel.

'Mike, get the fuck out of here,' Kim said, quietly, menacingly.

There was a commotion gathering towards us, I could hear people shouting, I looked and people were pointing at us.

I reversed again, steering the Land Rover tightly to the right, I sensed something freeing up, I braked – someone was hammering at the Land Rover's rear window, his shouting angry and close.

I got into first gear and put my foot to the floor; the Land Rover surged forward, lurched over a bump, and then gathered speed. I noticed Kim crouched in the passenger's seat, his arm reaching up under the dash board.

'Drive on, drive on!' he shouted, turning to look behind us, 'fast as you can!'

'Jesus that was close,' I said. My left foot was shaking so violently with fear that the engine was revving unevenly. I drove like a madman for five minutes.

'Okay, we're far enough now, let's stop,' said Kim.

We had driven helter skelter some three miles from the village, so we were safe. I pulled onto a flat patch by the roadside and stopped. We got out to see whether the car was damaged – it bore not a dent or scratch and only a dusty spattering of blood under the wheel arch told any story.

'You okay?' asked Kim.

'I'm fine.'

'Best you drive again, so you don't lose your nerve. Thank God and hey ho.'

We got back into the cab, and before I had started the engine again, Kim said, 'Oh, one thing. I didn't tell you. Look here…' Kim put his hand under the dashboard again, fiddled with something for a few seconds and a hinged metal plate fell down. On the plate was a revolver, secured by two spring clips.

'This,' he said, 'is if we ever get into a real scrape – I mean, life or death. My Pa insisted.' He unclipped the pistol.

'It's loaded, cock the hammer like this… safety catch off here… kaboom. See?' He passed the gun to me.

'That's it… hammer, catch off, bang bang. Think you could use it?'

'I don't know – could you?'

'Life or death? Yes, I think so. But you don't shoot to kill, you just want to stop them – if possible get them in the leg or thigh. Got to be calm enough to think clearly though.'

'That'd be my problem,' I answered, 'let's hope we never need to.'

'Aye aye to that… on we go?'

The presence of the revolver had a curious, but temporary effect; quite unreasonably, it made me feel more grown up, more worldly in some way, as though we were on a real adventure instead of just a touristy jaunt. The feeling wore off, but I have to admit it was comforting to know what was hidden under the dashboard.

We drove in silence, privately reliving our narrow escape.

The day was baking hot and dusty – monsoon clouds were scattered here and there in the sky, but the sun bore down on us relentlessly. We would stop from time to time to change drivers, to have a pee, to drink, to stretch our legs and to check the map. It was about three in the afternoon when we pulled in to a shaded layby. Nearby we saw a small huddle of people surrounding what looked like a tall gallows. We wandered over to take a closer look.

India is full of holy men – fantastical human beings of weird and inexplicable appearance that often disturbs and perplexes Western eyes: they wore garish, almost macabre head decorations, bright yellow and ash, skin daubed with white and scarlet red, faces gaunt and ghostly. I had seen many of them and could not conceive of lives more different to mine, but what we saw was the most bizarre sight I had ever seen.

There was a hand cart, on high, spindly wheels, its rough wooden platform about six or seven feet long by about four wide. Secured to the cart was a metal construction similar to a child's swing – triangular with its base broad, and at its top, a single bar. Looped over the top bar were two 'S' shaped meat hooks and suspended from the bottom part of the hooks was a thin, wiry, holy man. The hooks penetrated deep into his flesh near his shoulder blades and their bottom points protruded through his skin – his weight was entirely borne by the hooks and his flesh was what held him above the level of the cart's platform by at least three feet. There was no doubt as to the reality of this man's predicament – the hooks were genuinely running through his shoulders and they were plainly a permanent implantation into his person. He hung, motionless, his legs straight, his hands folded in prayer against his bony, malnourished ribs. I circled the cart slowly, in disbelief – my cynical, Western eyes were looking for the trick that would explain what surely, surely was an illusion. But there were no wires, invisible supports or unseen mechanics – the man was suspended from the top bar by two meat hooks.

I gazed at the man's face, some seven or eight feet above me – his lips moved in silent incantation, his eyes blinked now and again, and when his eyes were open they looked only at some point vaguely above and far away.

Along his forehead were smeared three thick horizontal white-grey lines and his nose was similarly decorated with a single vertical line of white ash. He wore only a loin cloth of thin gauze, and around his wrists were bracelets of string and hair. Around one ankle was a strip of rag.

The cart was accompanied by three men similar in appearance to the holy man – these were his helpers and, perhaps, disciples. They were the ones who wheeled the cart from village to village, begging for money and food; a few other people were gathered around, standing, crouching in the 'presence'. The watchers were silent and gave nothing, except one who offered a gourd-shaped aluminium container of water. One of the disciples produced a long stick that had a tube shaped cup, bound at an angle to its end; he poured some of the water into the cup and hoisted it to the holy man's lips and twisted it slightly so that some water trickled out. Other than accepting the water, the holy man did not react in any way – he did only what his life had led him to, to hang by his shoulders. I went back to the Land Rover to get some coins and gave them to one of the holy man's helpers. He bowed in thanks and I felt somehow dirty – that such a sight had provoked me into giving virtually nothing in exchange for a sight which haunted me, and has done ever since.

Kim and I got back on the road, heading for Bareilly. There we got petrol, had some food and continued on our way to Sitapur. The countryside became cooler and greener. The day, which had begun hot and sweltering, became cloudy and dim. In the mid-afternoon of our second day, north of Barabanki, the clouds darkened and the rains came down. Although we had run into the rain, we had come to an area where the monsoon had been battering the landscape for days – the rivers surged with flood waters, the verges and ditches were awash, and the roofs and verandahs still dripped and streamed with water. We were on a busy road full of buses and trucks and cars – as we passed them, their wash and spray splattered over us. Kim was driving and more and more frequently we were encountering streams of water flooding across the road. We had to stop when we saw other vehicles coming our way, flashing their lights to demand right of way and picking their path slowly through the flood water, going from one side of the road to the other to find the shallows, guided by the rickety poles that marked the road's path near the rivers. The Land Rover is a heavy vehicle and managed the waters well and without problems, but as we forged ahead, there were times when we would feel the flood catch the side of the sills and pull us sideways in an alarming way. But Kim was a skilled and determined driver and I felt safe in his hands.

We came to a very long bend that led to our right, overflowing with an angry deep flood that swept over the road at right angles – to such an extent and depth that we could only just make out the road's continuation as dry land some quarter of a mile ahead of us. On our right was undulating ground that rose gently away from us and from whence the flood poured, and on the left hand side of the road there was just a swirling lake.

'That looks deep,' said Kim as we stopped.

We got out and made our way forward on foot to try and sense the depth of the flood ahead.

'Well look, there are a couple of stretches where you can make out the surface – there, and there,' said Kim, pointing. 'It's the middle bit that looks tricky, bloody fast flowing I'd say. What d'ye think?'

'Dunno, Kim, depends on how deep it is… if it comes over the sills, the water could catch us and pull us clean away.'

'Well, at least there are poles to show where the road is… can you see them?' I tried to judge the depth of the water surging round the poles; some of them looked pretty short to me.

We had to decide whether to risk the flood or turn back to Barabanki, some 20 miles away, and being two foolhardy young men, we decided to risk it.

'I just hope there's nothing coming the other way,' I said as Kim revved up the engine and edged into the waters.

About a hundred yards into the flood, Kim said, 'Easy. No problem,' and as he uttered the word 'problem' there came into view a Mercedes truck heading towards us. At this same moment, the Land Rover dipped into deeper water, the momentum of which caught our wheels on the right side. Kim strained at the steering wheel to compensate – I peered forwards to see the front bumper create a bow wave.

'Kim, there's a truck coming…' I said.

'I know, I know, I can see.'

The truck edged closer and closer, straight towards us, and my calculation of where we would likely meet was right in the middle of the strongest maelstrom of the flood. The truck came closer and closer, so that I could see the garlands of flowers decking its radiator, and closer still so that I could see the image of Vishnu decorating the roof rack.

'Put your lights on Kim! Full beam!'

'You do it!'

I found the switch and turned on the lights. The truck did the same thing, full beam, demanding right of way. Kim was keeping to the right hand side of the route indicated by the poles, edging forward, straining.

As the truck bore down and its details became clearer and clearer, I knew there was going to be a collision because there was not room for the two vehicles to pass by. When the truck was so close to us that I could see the driver was a Sikh wearing a green turban, I could see the look of fear on his face and then, in lethargic slow motion, just 10 or so yards in front of us, the truck began to keel over away from us. It jolted downwards as if the ground on its outside edge had vanished, then it fell away completely. It rolled over out of our way, like a wave, and as we passed it; I could see the underside of the truck as it fell and fell and disappeared – it sank entirely under the water, got caught by the current of water and rolled again so that it half-floated at a crazy canted angle.

'Oh Jesus!' I shouted, staring behind me.

'What's happened!'

'The truck, it's completely disappeared under the water… no, no, there it is. The driver!'

'I can't stop, I can't!' yelled Kim. The engine of the Land Rover was howling as he slipped the clutch, trying to keep a motion straight ahead through the water and towards the visible roadway.

I looked back at the hulk of the truck wallowing in the water – it had landed up on its side, motionless, about a hundred yards below us. A few seconds later I saw the driver urgently hoisting himself up out of his cab, looking towards us. Just before I lost sight of him I could see him standing up, waving a fist at us.

'Drive on, he's okay, I can see him!' We reached solid, un-flooded road and stopped immediately. We got out and looked back towards the scene of the accident, but we had gone so far round the curve, we could see nothing.

'God I hope he's okay,' I said.

'Well, I wasn't going to stop – I couldn't. I think discretion here might be the better part of valour don't you think? Best we scarper.'

The smaller (and better) part of me wanted to go back and make quite sure that the driver of the truck was alright; it was a morally criminal act to depart from another human being's desperate predicament. But the greater and worse part of me convinced itself that since the driver had had the spare capacity to raise a fist in anger, he was likely okay. At least that was the way I justified myself, and Kim's urgent appeal to depart the scene.

'And anyway,' concluded Kim, 'do you really think we could have got into that swell of water and out again?'

I had my doubts and a residing guilt, but we left nevertheless.

We got to Basti late in the evening and collapsed into our beds, exhausted and drained.

Nepal was in our sights and we hoped our third day would see us there safe and sound. We were up early the next morning and wove our way through Gorakphur towards our entry point to Nepal at Raxaul, hardly stopping except for petrol. After Grakphur, the road narrowed and became more precipitous as it wound its way through twisting gorges, gaining altitude with every mile. The mountain scenery felt familiar because it reminded me of the surroundings of my camp in Himachel Pradesh, and on our last stint I felt relaxed and as though I was in familiar territory. We reached Raxaul and the Nepalese border in the afternoon and we were waved through, though I had prepared myself for another headline – 'N.E. Man Nepal Gun Arrest Drama' – had the Land Rover been thoroughly searched.

We arrived in Kathmandu in the early evening, and Kim had an address of a cafe where he was to make contact with a friend who was to be putting us up. We found the place easily, parked the Land Rover and clambered out, our backs sore from a hard day's driving. There was an immediate feeling that we were in a place different from India. The air was lighter, the city atmosphere was more intimate and it was quieter too. The buildings, despite being exotic, were more homely and domestic, and prompted the feeling that this was just an old mountain village with a few big mansions and temples lazily scattered among narrow streets and squares.

The cafe we entered had, vaguely, the reminiscence of an English tea room from the 1930s – net curtains, a few small tables covered in oil cloth covers and table mats for the pots of tea. Untypical of the English tea room, though, was the display of cans of Scottish lager – something which would never be seen in India. The dozen or so cans of Tennant's were arrayed along the length of a high narrow shelf that ran the full length of the wall behind the serving counter. The sight and desire for these caught me off guard. From the time I had been at the Buddha tree, I knew with certainty that it was time to get home, and in my thirst for a glass of lager, I came up against a truth that I found uncomfortable – I was missing my home comforts.

Kim and I had tea, and then Kim left to seek out the British Embassy where his friend worked. I decided, since I was tired and travel weary, that I would just stay at the cafe on my own. I sat in a mood of doubting myself as I eyed the cans of lager. Kim was away for an hour or so before he returned with his friend Fiona; quite how it was that Kim seemed to have a wide circle of female friends who worked in embassies, I never knew.

Fiona Toffington was one of those country English girls of the sort who are big and hearty, who wear pearls and whose life in rural England is centred around the horse. She was in her mid- to late-20s with coarse gold hair and a healthy, ruddy complexion.

'Jolly glad to meet you,' she said, shaking hands with me.

We left the cafe and piled back into the Land Rover and made our way to the Embassy. A grand, 20th century building, the embassy proper sits behind a high wall that encircles a small wooded park. Some 400 meters beyond the grand front entrance and the big brass plate was a smaller, plain-painted double gate; we stopped by this, Fiona got out and unlocked these and we drove into the grounds to be faced with a small cottage – this was where we were to be Fiona's guests. The cottage had the air of a gateman's or gamekeeper's cottage. It had a tiled roof, french windows overlooking a small patch of neatly trimmed lawn, and overhanging the whole scene was a tall and immense sycamore tree. There was a great fluttering from the branches of this tree as we disturbed the peace of several hundred bats.

'Well, home sweet home,' said Fiona, showing us in. The house was a surprise in that, being an Embassy residence occupied by an employee of the Embassy, it had been furnished entirely as an English house. Chintz curtains, neat, antique mahogany furniture here and there, a brass warming pan in the hall, a Wilton carpet – an English cottage transported in its completeness from the Home Counties to the Himalayas. Though the cottage was small, Kim and I had each a small bedroom and the comfort of the bed and the surroundings was a wonderful gift in every respect.

We settled in, and then went back to the cafe and after food; Fiona showed us around Kathmandu. It was early evening, warm and balmy, and the sky was dotted with puffy, pearly clouds. We walked and talked and I listened to Kim and Fiona chat of mutual friends, of Pony Club meetings and house parties, and I could see I was in the company of the Upper Crust.

On the outskirts of the city, we came to what looked vaguely like a park – an area of dusty, grass-patched ground shaded at its boundaries by low trees; at its furthest extent was a small tumbledown shelter from which streams of prayer flags were strung out to the trees around it. There, a group of Tibetan monks were sitting around a fire; they were young novices talking excitedly to each other and laughing loudly. We approached them and greeted them. They seemed very friendly so we all sat down and began to talk in our best pidgin English. A football appeared and Fiona organised everyone into two mixed teams and set up goals. The game began in high spirits and such was our noise that a small crowd gathered to watch – and from that crowd two Americans, a British couple, a Dane, a bunch of Canadians and a dog joined in the game. The dog was the hero and the villain of the match. He was a big white mongrel with a black splotch over one eye and managed the trick of getting the ball in his jaws so that everyone ended up chasing him around the park; he was villain too because the ball burst between his teeth and he ran off with it and disappeared.

We all went back to the shelter by the fire and introduced ourselves and talked of the world which seemed to be, all things considered, good and hopeful – except to the two Americans. Both were in their late 20s and they were of draft age.

One wanted to speak of nothing but the Vietnam war – his hostility towards the Lyndon Johnson government was vociferous, bitter and reasoned. The other listened silently, and then said he was from Chicago.

'You all talk of Vietnam,' he began, 'you think you heard of violence

and killin' and all that – well let me tell you 'bout Chicago – man, you
think you live in a shitty place? Englan' an' all? Well, you won't believe it,
but the po-lice in Chicago have been shootin' people there and no-one
goddamn knows diddlyshit 'bout it here nor any place else that matter…
plain shootin' – murder!' The man's bitterness silenced us all. Kim, Fiona
and I drifted off back to the Embassy.

To get to the Embassy we had to pass close to the city centre, and it was
there that we were approached with an offer of some cannabis, which we
bought – a great big lump of the stuff. There was nothing premeditated
about our decision, it was just that when we were asked, we looked at
each other. Kim shrugged his shoulders and said, 'why not?' and Fiona
said 'Well, maybe…' which Kim and I took to be her agreement.

None of us had ever taken any drugs of any sort before and it somehow seemed just the natural extension of a wonderful evening spent in
exotic surroundings.

We made our way back to the Embassy cottage as the evening light
was at that most beautiful shade of turquoise-blue between day and
night, when the first stars can be seen. Being very British, we had tea
before the evening's main event. I had seen other people make joints,
though I was uncertain as to the quantities to use. I heated the resin into
a crumbly powder and mixed it in with tobacco and rolled my first and
only spliff.

In Fiona's front room there was a small, three-seat couch which faced
the french windows, and we three sat there like passengers on a bus.
Because none of us had any idea of the effect of cannabis, we agreed that
it would be safer if one person was to try it with the other two 'keeping
watch' in case of any bad consequence, and I was elected to be the first.
To further ensure that no harm would come to me, Kim and Fiona sat
on either side of me and held my arms in a gentle lock – this in case I
went berserk.

I lit the cigarette and drew in the smoke.

'Well?' asked Kim immediately.

'Nothing,' I said, 'absolutely nothing.'

I took another draw, deeper and bigger, held it in my lungs then ex-
haled the smoke slowly.

'Oh come on,' said Fiona impatiently, 'there must be something!'

I shook my head. 'Nope.'

Then a lightness of perception crept around me and my head felt as though it was going for a swim while the rest of me stayed at the side of the pool.

Kim asked, 'Mike, anything? Buggeration, we got conned!'

'Conned? Conned?' I replied with an over-emphasised sincerity, 'oh, I don't think so.'

'How do you mean?'

'No, how do you mean, Kim, I mean exactly, Kim, how do you mean?'

'Are you alright Mike? Mike!'

'I'm bloody fine thank you. Very bloody fine.' I began to laugh and giggle like a child who has found something of profound amusement but who can't quite pin down what the funny thing exactly is. That bit of my mind that always remains observant of my vital surroundings knew that the rest of its functions were offshore in a numbered account, somewhere distant, but still attached to my mental landmass by some tether that remained *just* reachable. At one and the same moment I felt I could regain sobriety if I needed to, but I definitely didn't need to because I was in a lovely place and felt no desire to leave it.

As the effects went a little deeper, the connections I had struggled to formulate in my mind became more tenuous and the pleasure more pure. I am breathing, I am fed and drunk; I am safe and happy, strong and, temporarily, a small god. In such a state, I feel capable of seeing those things that caution and fear have always screened from my consideration and I am not afraid of them – in fact, I am bold, I am liked and I am quite sure that the as-yet-unformed ambition that is growing in definition will make me successful and fulfilled.

Those who have taken cannabis will be familiar with the first giggly experience and the high pitched glee that it induces, and those who have not taken cannabis would not know the effects except in terms of it being similar to drunkenness, though even that does not express it adequately.

Fiona went next, and though I was in quite another fantastic place and mood, I hooked my arm though her elbow in case she flew away.

'Oh bloody,' she gasped after a few minutes, 'oh bloody hell!'

Then Kim had a go and I rolled another one and that was that; three respectable citizens turned inside out. We left the cottage for the garden and the trees. It was not fully dark but the stars were prickling the sky in their multitudes and we gazed up at them, dizzy in both the physical and spiritual sense.

'Gaw!' said Kim his head bent back.

We had left the cottage for the open air of the trees and the sky, and we would laugh at the slightest oddity, real or contrived. We looked with an artificial intensity that persuaded us that we were suddenly and wholly converted into the person who sees the whole detail of a leaf or a bat's dropping. We staggered and we laughed, we jumped and whooped, and in a vaguely frightening way we realised that there was another person was in our midst. The new person had a torch and was waving its beam, catching each of us in its blinding glare, one by one, like criminals caught in the guards' searchlight.

Fiona's voice rang out, 'Tashi San! How bloody well are you?'

Kim and I were clinging to a tree trunk, engrossed in the 'meaning' of the bark, when the torchlight illuminated us – we darted behind the tree and dropped to our knees like schoolboys playing hide and seek when 'it' is nearby. We looked towards the cottage and the source of the torchlight. Tashi was a short, neat Japanese man, dressed in a suit and tie. In one hand he held a bow and in the other, a quiver of arrows.

'Ah, Miss Fiona,' he said bowing, 'how are you?'

'Just splendid,' said Jane, 'bloody splendid.'

'I was wondering, Miss Fiona… I was wondering…'

'Yes Tashi, what do you want?' Fiona placed her hands on hips and wavered gently from side to side like a guardian of the gates.

'I was wondering,' said Tashi bowing, 'if I might have a bat or two?'

'Don't see why not' said Fiona affably, 'what's it for?'

'Soup.' said Tashi. 'Bat and noodle soup… for the restaurant, you see.'

Fiona shouted over to Kim and I, and we came out from hiding.

'Oi! Boys! D'ye think it'd be okay for Tashi here to have a couple of bats? Courtesy of the Embassy of Her Majesty? For soup would you believe? Tashi has the only Japanese restaurant in Kathmandu… and Nepal for that matter. Actually, it's probably the best Japanese restaurant ever known to mankind. How d'ye get in Tashi?'

Tashi bowed again. 'The gate. As usual.'

'Thought it was locked.'

'No. It was open.'

'Oh bloody fuck, eh excuse me. Well, yes, fire away. You've got the noodles you say.'

'Yes,' said Tashi, 'but not the bats.'

Fiona considered this.

'Well,' she said finally, 'what the fuck, help yourself. But keep it quiet, we don't want the Ambassador poking his fuck-off plumed helmet into this. They are his bats, after all.' Fiona found something very funny in this and let out a roar of a laugh.

'And that's Kim and Mike by the tree,' she added, 'or up it, as the actress said to the bishop. Boys? Tashi's a friend, okay?'

Kim and I were still by our tree and we bowed as Tashi shone his torch at us.

'Aaaah soh,' we chorused.

The sober body and mind would find shooting bats from trees, with a bow and arrow, a difficult enough thing – stoned, it was chaotic.

I helped by pinpointing a bat in the beam of the torch. Tashi would shoot with his arrow and Kim and Fiona staggered about below the tree, hands outstretched in preparation for catching the falling bats. Kim crashed into Fiona and they fell down in a heap, choking in uncontrollable laughter. Kim, Fiona and I all tried the bow, and the final score for the night was three bats, all neatly skewered by Tashi's sharp shooting.

It cannot be that Tashi did not realise we were stoned. But he was a calm, good-natured man and he politely excused himself when we tried to persuade him at the end of the hunt to join us for cornflake munchies. When he left, we returned indoors to the cottage. We had our cornflakes and we talked and laughed a whole lot more. As it became late in the night, I began to get the vibe that Kim and Fiona were feeling amorous. I left them to it and went outside again and found a tree to lean against; I looked up at the stars, which were, in the full dark of night, glistening in the heavens above me. If you look at stars for long enough and keep your gaze at its widest angle of appreciation, you may see a satellite making its track like an orbiting star. And with a sudden gasp, I saw my moving star, moving north towards the mightiest peaks of the Himalayas. I made a promise to it, that I would remember that night.

As to whether drugs are a menace or a blessing, I have no doubt that, in moderation, they are a blessing. As long as homo sapiens has walked the earth, he and his wives and his mistresses have felt the need for wildness, escape and a glimpse at madness. Since the need is present, and since the answer to that need is also present, it is inevitable that the one will seek the other, as in all things.

Those who condemn their use outright should ask themselves why it is that the need for escape or wildness is generated in the first place. If they were to use their intellectual skills in understanding that, then their response might have to take into account the wider circumstances of those whom they seek to judge. The cynic would say that the very people who condemn any use of drugs are the same people who contribute most to creating the stresses of life that in turn generate the need for release from those stresses – usually to their own profit. The man in the pub might also hold aloft his glass of alcohol and ask what difference there might be between getting sozzled on booze and getting high on cannabis. The two stimulants cohabit side by side on the same cliff edge; yet one is encouraged, advertised and milked of tax income, and the other is vilified and condemned.

This experiment in my life left me feeling exhilarated and fulfilled and not the least bit guilty or ashamed. I think Kim was feeling less bullish than me and Fiona vowed she would never touch the stuff again. In her case, I think she was embarrassed that her vocabulary had found a fuller expression than her embassy work would normally permit.

Kim and I had a further two days exploring Nepal in the Land Rover and we both fell in love with the place. After tear-filled farewells, we left Fiona, the high airs of the Himalayas, and a country of mystery and charm. Just outside Kathmandu, I threw away the remaining lump of cannabis, hurling it out of the Land Rover window as the mountains sped past. We headed back for Delhi via a haphazard and leisurely route along the Ganges and arrived back at the 'BroMed' Centre three days later.

It was now late-October in 1967 and my return home was to begin in earnest. From speaking with all those I had met who had travelled unusually to or from India, I had decided on leaving from Bombay by ship to Iraq rather than overland via Pakistan and Afghanistan. Going through Pakistan did not seem to present problems, but I had heard too many stories of young Western men getting into trouble in Afghanistan, largely because they are assumed to be there because of drugs. I did not want to get hit over the head because somebody thought I was carrying either dope or cash, particularly as all my plans for my journey were on the assumption that I was to be travelling alone.

Other than getting to Iraq and the Persian Gulf, I decided that my route home should be decided by what travel arrangements were expedient rather than planned. Again, from other people who had been through the overland trek, I had heard of people planning detailed itineraries only to fall victim to cancellations and the vagaries of chance.

Kim and I got back to Delhi the very best of friends. We talked about going back to the UK together overland in the Land Rover, but Kim wanted first to take a trip to Kerala and the south and I felt this would impinge too much on my plan to be home in December, so reluctantly I declined the trip. Another reason was that I was not well off like Kim and I had very little money to get home with – I could not thus contribute to the costs of the journey.

As I wrote letters, investigated routes and means of transport in Delhi, Kim busied himself with helping Patrice before his next trip. In Delhi, I too had much to do. Since I had decided I would wander home rather than by a planned route, I realised I would need to carry information with me that would help in any of a variety of countries that I might find it expedient to travel through, so that I could find out quickly such basics as the currency, the main cites and highways, and so on. This meant getting hold of maps and, in some cases, visiting embassies.

Since I was so short of money, I had to sell my beloved Leica and take in exchange a cheap little Brownie camera that I hoped would serve to record my trip home. I was very sad as I left the photographic shop in Connaught Square, watching through the window as my camera was taken away to the back. It was like saying goodbye to a friend. I wrote to my father telling him of my plans and basic timetable and asked him to send 50 pounds to Madelaine in Bombay. I had spent most of my money with Kim in Nepal and, on a purely financial footing, had been irresponsible in going to Nepal at all. Once again, I was flat broke.

I was about 10 days in Delhi and said farewell to Kim when he drove off one morning, heading south for his last trip in India. I had swapped my bedding roll for an old rucksack of his and that was to be my luggage on the way home. We wished each the best of luck and, with just a trace of male embarrassment, I told him he was one of the finest men I had ever met.

As the time neared to leave Delhi for Bombay, I had one last day of ease and relaxation and decided I would try to find Mrs Mehta. I went to her house and was met again by her daughter.

'No, my mother is back in Derha Dun, you have just missed her. Shall I tell her any message?'

'Yes, just say thank you. I hope she will understand.'

'I'll do that. Are you going back to England?'

'Scotland... yes.'

'I hope you have a good flight,' she said. And that was the last chance I had of meeting the person who was responsible for me going to India. I never met her and I never heard from her later.

My last visit on that final day was to see Dr Calder. Although I had not seen him since the beginning of my stay in India, I had had thought of him frequently and had been comforted in the knowledge that he would have been a source of willing help if I had got into a scrape. I went to the seminary and was shown into the hall. In the distance, from the chapel, there came the echoing music of a choir singing the 23rd Pslam, one I have always loved. I listened intently. After the singing stopped, Dr Calder came down the arched corridor towards me. He was fully the minister, in a dog collar and black suit. We sat in the hall and I said that I had come to say goodbye.

'So, back home then?' he said.

'Yes.'

'Do you think you'll come back?' he asked.

'I don't think so,' I answered. 'I'm not sure I would have the commitment, and I've found out that I'm more wedded to my comforts than I realised before coming here. I know that sounds a bit sad, but it's the truth. And by the way, your peaches were a life saver!'

Dr Calder laughed and said, 'well, you know where I am.' There was a vestige of disappointment in his voice. I think perhaps he harboured the hope that I might 'see the light' in India.

We said our farewells and I headed back to Connaught Square for a last, loving wander round its colonnaded shade and life.

The next day I was on the train to Bombay, and once there I made my own way to Madelaine's flat. Sidir came to the door.

'Madame is expecting you,' he said. Madelaine appeared, her fine self draped in a magnificent chiffon cape of lemon yellow.

'Ah dear boy, how nice to see you,' she said, embracing me warmly. She kissed my cheeks, then gripped my arms, and holding me at that distance to regard me, said, 'you have not changed one bit, except that you are very thin, too thin. Now, tell me all. Sidir, two mammoth gins!'

We sat in her lounge, which overlooked the glittering sea. I told Madelaine about all things I had done, and lastly of my intention to head back overland.

'But you are completely mad,' she said, 'why don't you fly? You'll be home in 12 hours.'

'I don't know – because it's something I want to do.'

'But on your own?'

'Yes. Plenty of others have done it. I've met some of them.'

'Yes dear, but they're hippies. Not our sort at all. If it's money, I shall pay your fare myself. And just exactly how much money do you have?'

'Well, Dad's sending 50 pounds, which should be here in a few days, and I've got rupees worth about another 22 pounds, so I should have enough.'

Madame puffed in exasperation. 'Oh Lord,' she said.

My absolute determination to go home overland was just one thin percent stronger than Madelaine's absolute determination that I should fly, but once she saw that I was not to be moved from my intention, she accepted it and helped me as much as she could. Over the next few days she bought large quantities of medications and dragged me around shops where she attempted to reclothe me, tidy me up and somehow prepare me for a trip into outer space.

'Now, what about gloves,' she would say, 'by the time you get to Europe, it will be winter, probably snowing and I've always found that if one's feet and hands are uncomfortable in any way, life is miserable... try these leather ones, they're very good.'

In addition to equipping me for my trip, Madelaine wheeled me to her own doctor, who jabbed me frequently with a cocktail of injections. He indicated that he suspected something was wrong with me because my weight was so low. He wanted to start investigations, but I wanted no delay in my departure and I refused the days and weeks that would have been necessary.

'You are impossible,' said Madelaine.

Before I could leave India, I had to have my passport stamped by the Indian tax authorities; one is not allowed to leave until this formality is undertaken and the right stamp imprinted into the passport. I had been warned that the process could be tricky and this proved to be the case. I presented myself to the Tax Office, and after hours of waiting in the hot gloom of bureaucracy I finally came head-to-head with Mr Ahmed. Mr Ahmed would not accept my (truthful) version of how I had supported myself for a year. He said that it was not possible for me to have survived in India on the sum of money that had been my income. After an hour's interview, he remained unconvinced about my circumstances and refused to issue me with the appropriate certificate and stamp. He furthermore insisted that I re-present myself and voiced his hope that next time I would offer a more convincing story about how I had paid for my life.

I had booked myself onto the SS Sandmartin, which was due to sail from Bombay on the 14th of November, just a week from the day of my first tax inquisition. I re-presented myself twice after the first interview each day thereafter, and on the third succeeded in persuading the authorities as to the accuracy of my financial state. By that time, I had received 50 pounds in traveller's cheques from my father, along with a letter earnestly urging me not to travel overland. He wrote 'whilst I can see that you might wish the adventure, I think taking the risk of getting a knife in your back is not worth what you might get out of your journey. Since you are so far away, I cannot force you into this, but I ask you nevertheless to consider what I say.'

My father's letter gave me pause for thought, but no more than that; I didn't feel afraid, nor did I feel any regret at rejecting his advice. On the same day that I received his traveller's cheques, which he had managed to get unsigned from a bank manager friend, the Prime Minister Harold

Wilson was to have a direct effect on my life – this by devaluing sterling. My whole sum of money to get home comprised of just over 70 pounds – after devaluation, the worth of my money went down to less than 60. Mr Harold Wilson said at the time of devaluation that 'devaluation does not affect the pound in your pocket'. Nobody had told The Prime Minister I was in India about to head home and that he was not referring to my pocket.

In the few days before my planned sailing, Madelaine had me neatened up at the Willingdon Club barber. Regarding the result and brushing my shoulders, she said, 'well dear, when we go into the world, it's best to be honest about who we are. Others will recognise you as a clean cut, honourable man if you look neat and tidy. Your hair was far too long and might have given people entirely the wrong impression. Long hair is grand for girls but is an abomination on boys over the age of three.'

On the 12th of November, 1967, Madelaine took me by taxi to the docks and there we found the SS Sandmartin bound for Karachi, Oman, Qatar, Bahrain, Kuwait and Basra.

The terminal was just an old industrial shed peopled by a crush of mankind laden with bundles, cases, bicycles, trunks, bags and wailing children. The heat was stinking and leaden. No matter where or in what queue one waited, legs and lungs were jabbed by the sharp edges of suitcases, wooden boxes and umbrellas. There was pushing and shoving, shouting, sweat pouring and sweat soaking. Because it seemed imperative to edge towards such and such a counter or table, people would not leave their queue for any reason. Therefore, children would pee where they stood or crouched, which added wet smelly puddles to the unpleasantness.

With my passport stamped, with my rucksack on my back and my passage ticket between my teeth, the time came to say goodbye to both Madelaine and to India. At the wide shed doors and in the shade of the interior, close to the bow boarding ramp, Madelaine clasped me strongly to her.

'You must take very great care on this absurd adventure,' she said, dusting a non-existent speck from my jacket, 'just be yourself and trust to the good of people. BUT, don't ever be ashamed to run away if your instincts tell you to, and if this is the circumstance you find yourself in, you must run as fast as you possibly can. Good luck, dear boy.' She hugged me even tighter for an instant, kissed me, then turned and walked away.

Part Two

9

The Red Sea and one of the world's richest men

I HAD A DESK PASSAGE FROM BOMBAY TO BASRA, IN IRAQ, WHERE I was to disembark. The general scheme of my plan was to work my way via Baghdad and Mosul into the south of Turkey, then north to Istanbul.

The 'SS Sandmartin' was a British vessel of the British Oriental Steamship Line, which regularly plied the Bombay-Persian Gulf route – she was a freighter with minimal cabin accommodation, but its front deck was available to foot passengers. 'Deck passage' means literally what it says – you live and sleep on deck. On the main deck, just in front of the bridge superstructure and stretching across the whole width of the ship, was a barrier of black steel bars about 12 feet high, such as you would see at a zoo or prison. It was into this forward, fenced-off area of the deck that we headed. There was a vague feeling of being a refugee.

Deck class passengers embarked via a railed boarding ramp onto the front deck and the crew and posh passengers boarded by a second ramp midships. There was a gated section in this wall of bars that gave onto the deck behind it; this gate was locked with a chain and padlock. The front deck was filled with more than a hundred people who claimed deck space with their bedding rolls and effects. The scene was one of shouting and waving, pushing and screaming as people fought to create their own space. I was near the end of embarkees, so when I got to the deck and worked out what I had to do it was already crowded and there seemed little room for even one more individual. I wandered around, stepping over people and unable to see where I could settle with my rucksack.

I gave up and just leaned over the rail to watch the ship's final preparations for leaving. Soon, the horn gave a shrill blast, the boarding ramps were hauled back to the quay and the deck began to quiver as the engines churned the water to make stern way. As the ship slowly swung around, I gazed at Bombay – a high, bright sun gleamed in a blue hazy sky just like an English summer day. The Gateway to India became visible as we made way, and from this landmark my eye tried to find Madelaine's apartment, which was near to it and facing the sea. Madelaine could have seen the ship but I could not locate her building exactly. The city receded into the distance, and as it became smaller and smaller to my eye, I felt happy and excited to be going home.

By the time I watched the land horizon all but disappear, the deck seemed to have every one of its square inches occupied either by people or luggage. In looking around me, I realised I was the only white face among the deck passengers. I had to wheedle myself into a small gap right in the middle of the deck; an unpopular spot since it was exposed both to the sun of the day and the cold of the night. But I squeezed myself in and unrolled the sleeping bag Kim had given me; it was a very thin light one, but it served as the marker of my territory. I sat down for a while and started to study the fist of the papers and tickets I had been given when boarding. I couldn't make sense of the roll of green and yellow tickets which I had been handed at embarkation.

The day wore on and I found the coolness of the sea infinitely refreshing after the close heat and dustiness of Bombay (perhaps of India as a whole). I leaned over the rail, watching the bow wave splash through the gleaming green-blue water. The gulls reeled above, the ship's engines found their constant, and the air was wonderfully clean and fresh.

We had left Bombay in the early afternoon. A hooter on deck sounded at about 5:00; when this sounded, the greater proportion of the desk passengers got to their feet and ran to a stairhead at which a long queue formed.

Not knowing what was happening, I joined the queue and worked out the meaning of the roll of tickets I had been given. The queue worked its way slowly down a flight of steep iron steps on the Port side to the lower deck, where three tables were arranged in a line. Upon these tables were vats of food – curries, dhal and rice. Having watched those in front of me present their tickets, I retrieved mine from my pocket and at my turn presented one – in return for this I was handed a bowl of curry, rice and chapattis. Another stair on the opposite side of the deck led back up to the deck and there, under the open sky, one ate. It was easy to tell which people were regulars on the ship – they had the best spots under the rails and knew when food was served: they would be ready at the stairs before the hooter sounded. There has always been a tradition of Indian labourers working in the Gulf and most of the deck passengers were men returning to building sites.

After the evening meal, the deck settled down; the children were subdued, men took to the rails to talk and to smoke, and groups of men and women either consolidated their small territories or mingled with those they knew. By nightfall, the deck was abed. The night was hot so I lay on top of my sleeping bag, looking up at the stars, the deck vibrating beneath me, the ship pushing its way through the seas towards home. I was anxious about the trip; for all the assurances to myself that I would make it, I did doubt my decision to travel alone. There had been various opportunities to accompany other people, though they had not been to my timetable. But I was scared that night and I was restless and ill at ease.

The ship and its compliment awoke early the next morning under a glorious, clear blue sky, and the first hooter sounded just after seven when I was still asleep. I had a long wait in the queue to get tea and chappatits with my next meal ticket. After this I wandered round the rails and killed time, resting, snoozing and looking up at the sky. About mid-morning, at the barrier which separated the front deck from the rest of the ship, I saw one of the ship's stewards at the gate, undoing the padlock. He was dressed in a sparklingly clean white bar jacket that had a line of black buttons running across his right side. He was about 50 with short black and grey curled hair, a West Indian, I thought. I was standing at that moment, and it seemed as though he was signalling to me to come towards him. I didn't think anything of it to begin with and looked around me to see who might be the object of his attention. I turned to him again, and it became clearer that it was me he was trying to make contact with. I pointed a finger at my chest and he nodded and made a signal that I should come to him. By the time I had picked my way carefully over to him, he had opened the gate.

'The Captain would like to see you,' said the steward.

'Me?'

'Yes.'

'Is there something wrong?' I asked.

'No sir, not at all – please follow me.' I passed before him and he relocked the gate.

The steward led me to a bulkhead door, then down an internal corridor to a light and spacious room. The Captain was sitting at a finely polished oak table and motioned to a chair opposite him. He was about 40, with slightly balding thin, sandy-coloured hair, a weathered and tanned rectangular face, and kindly eyes.

'Take a pew – nothing to worry about,' he said, 'Fancy a cup of tea? Coffee?'

'Coffee would be lovely.'

'White or black? I'm the captain by the way, Richard Winston.' He held out his hand.

'I kind of gathered that – thank you, pleased to meet you. Black with a touch of milk is what I like.'

The captain nodded to the steward, who then melted away.

'So,' said the captain, 'what on earth are you doing on the deck of a ship going round the Persian Gulf?'

I told the captain my story. The steward came in with a tray of silver service and poured me a coffee.

'So, headed back home?' asked the captain.

'Yes.'

'Which is where?'

'Aberdeen.'

'Ah, the granite city. Six months of winter followed by six months of bad weather – froze nearly to death in a hotel there a long time ago. The… Hyperion?' he asked.

'The Imperial, by the harbour.'

'Yes, by God, that's the one. Still there?'

'Yes, as a matter of fact I know the owner's daughter, Rosemary.'

'How long you been away – since you left home?'

'Almost exactly a year now.'

'Your parents alive?'

'Yes, Mum and Dad.'

'That's good. Do they know where you are?'

'Sort of,' I said, and he laughed.

'Well, tell you what… there's a spare cabin if you'd like it; you'll be much more comfortable. There's no need for chaps like you to rough it on deck. Oh, don't worry, there's no charge. January, get Mr Hendry's things from the deck and put them in one of the starb'rd aft cabins would you?'

'Yes, sir,' said the steward, bending slightly to the captain, 'it is just the rucksack isn't it sir?' he added to me. I nodded and he left.

'I expect you'd like to shower and clean up,' said the captain getting up, 'just relax a while and I'll see you at lunch – about half twelve? I'll send January to fetch you, and if you need anything, just ask him. Okay, come with me and I'll show you your quarters.'

In considerable disbelief, I followed the captain up a deck to a short corridor with neatly varnished doors and in which hung a smell of wax polish.

'There, you'll be a lot more comfortable I think.' The captain showed me into a spacious cabin, spick and span, light, airy and with a porthole open to the breeze. 'I have to get back to the bridge – see you for lunch.' I was lost for words.

The captain closed the cabin door behind him. I looked around at my surroundings and felt the softness of the bed – its sheet turned down, its pillows puffed and starched. There was a gentle knock at the door and the Steward came in with my rucksack, which he set down at the foot of the bed.

'Oh, thank you,' I said, 'is your name… January?'

'Yes it is, sir. January. My father named his children after the months. In Trinidad this is quite common. Can I get you anything?'

'Oh no, no really, this is, this is just wonderful.'

'Then I'll come for you at about 12:20 to show you where the dining room is.'

'Thank you. Thank you very much.' He left and closed the door quietly behind him. I peeked into the small bathroom, which lay behind a plastic curtain, and spied the shower, the soap and the clean towels.

I lay on the bed, cautiously, as though it were forbidden territory. My mind analysed the situation to see what flaw might lie behind my good fortune. Lulled by a gang of slave traders? The fall guy for a drug deal? But the captain had a face that could not possible harbour such intrigues or falsity. I could only keep my wits about me and see what happened.

At 12:20 precisely, there was a discreet tap on the door and, having showered and cleaned myself, I was led by January to join the captain for lunch. At the table already seated were the first officer, a German, and three other officers, two British and one Indian. January served a beef and shallot stew, with smooth invisible efficiency.

Adapting easily to my new surroundings, I snoozed after lunch, took a stroll around the deck and regarded the vulgar masses on deck and behind bars with a mixture of relief and suspicion; relief as to my luck, suspicion that there would surely be some flaw in the flow of milk and honey.

Dinner came and was as congenial as lunch. After brandies, everyone left the dining room, and as January whisked away the dishes and glasses, I was left with the captain.

'So, what route are you taking?' he asked, 'I see you're due to disembark at Basra?'

'Yes, I thought I could get overland to Baghdad and from there to Istanbul…'

The captain drew a deep breath.

'No,' he said, 'I can tell you straight away that that will be impossible. You must have heard of the war? The Israelis? There's no way you'll get into Iraq, Iran, Saudi or Syria for that matter. The only place you might get in is Kuwait, and if you do get in, you'll be very unpopular.'

I had had little exposure to any media or news for many months; such information as I had gleaned about world affairs was minimal. I recalled I had heard something of the war, but I had not calculated that it would have any effect on my ability to travel; wars are always something at a distance and affect other people.

'You mean, I definitely wouldn't get through Iraq?' I asked.

'No way.'

'But I thought I could travel anywhere.'

'Absolutely not. There's been a full scale war and the British are seen as collaborators with Israel. Because of that the British are persona non grata – no Arab country will consider even a transit visa. But, I'll make some enquiries tomorrow on the ship-to-shore and I'll try and get clarification from our head office – they will know what the current status is. In the meantime, I suggest you just relax and enjoy the voyage. We'll be in Karachi in two days where we're picking up a very important passenger. He'll be on board from Karachi to Bahrain. Lovely man. Tomorrow I'll show you round the bridge if I've time. Anyway, glad to have you on board, have a good night and I'll see you in the morning.'

'Captain Winston, I really must thank you most sincerely for your kindness. You really have been…'

'Really, it's nothing,' said the captain, holding up his hand to stop me, 'I had a boy once, just like you and… anyway, goodnight.'

I said goodnight and the captain left me to my thoughts. In the quiet comfort of the empty dining saloon I nursed the balloon of brandy before me, deeply unsettled by the news that the route I had chosen for my way home was barred shut. Part of me could not accept that the Arab-Israel war was something that could affect me; it seemed so unfair.

The 'Sandmartin' steamed up India's west coast under fabulous skies and warm luxurious breezes and approached Karachi. At dinner the night before we arrived there, the captain asked the first officer: 'could Mike come ashore with us? When we meet the sheik?' The captain then turned to me and asked, 'your passport up to date?'

'Yes,' I said, 'new photo, new stamp from the embassy in Delhi, just a few weeks ago.' 'No, as a British citizen without a visa, he could not legally go ashore,' the first officer said.

'What about shore leave?' asked the Captain.

'He'd have to be a crew member.'

'We got a spare uniform to fit him?' asked the Captain.

'Yes, I think we could fit him out – as a junior officer.'

'Okay. Mike, how would you like to become a member of the crew for a day?'

'Great!'

'Hans, get this young man fitted out first thing tomorrow morning. We ETA at, what, 1000 hours?

Get him ready for nine.' The captain laughed out loud and left the dining room chuckling.

Good as his word, the first officer came to my cabin early the next morning with a uniform, black shoes and an officer's peaked cap; his manner was cold and he didn't seem at all keen at what was going on. Everything fit except the trousers and shoes, which were both a bit big, but it was perfect otherwise – I became Mike Hendry, Junior Officer on board the 'SS Sandmartin'.

I waited on deck, enduring the sniggers of some of the crew, and when the Captain arrived I gave my best salute.

'Okay Mike, you look fine. As far as the cap is concerned, just follow me. If I take off my cap, you take yours off and if it's off for anything more than a few seconds, tuck it under your arm. Stick close to me, and if I have to introduce you to anybody, I'll say you're a new trainee just out from England. Got it?'

'Aye Aye, Captain, training it is,' I answered.

'And if I need to go off somewhere, stick to Hans.'

'Okay, I'll stick to Hans.'

Before we disembarked, I gave my passport to the Purser for inspection and stamping by the Pakistani Port Authorities, who were due to come aboard just before the captain's party was due to leave.

By 11:00, there were four of us in a big American car being driven to the Karachi Hilton to meet the sheik – the captain, First Officer Hans, a young English officer called Keith I had spoken to only briefly, and myself. On the way to the hotel, the captain explained the purpose of our journey. 'Of course, we don't normally meet passengers before they embark, but the Emir is a sovereign ruler who frequently travels with us and it is vital that we accord him very special treatment. He has helped us in many ways and it had become a tradition that I meet him at his hotel before he comes on board.'

We arrived at the hotel and made our way through its palatial entrance. When the captain took off his cap, I did too. The hotel's atrium was filled with deep armchairs, potted plants and coffee tables. The rich, faintly perfumed air echoed in its glass and rich vastness. At its centre was an entourage of many Arabs standing, talking and sitting, and at epicentre of these men I could just see, seated in great splendour, a relatively short man dressed in magnificent robes of brown, white and gold. There was no mistaking who was the important person.

Our party approached the group and stopped at its periphery, saying nothing, our caps held easily under our arms. We stood quietly, talking now and then amongst ourselves until someone gave a signal. At this, the captain stepped forward and approached a man close to the sheik, who had stood up. They were out of earshot, but evidently there were friendly greetings and familiarities.

The captain talked to the sheik and his immediate staff for about 10 minutes, and then came back to us.

'Fine,' said the captain, 'all set. They should be on board in about an hour. Duty done.'

We drove back to the ship to await the sheik and as I boarded, the Purser handed me back my passport which had duly been stamped with a 'Shore Leave' stamp. In our absence, sheets of hessian had been stretched across one gangway to screen the stern boarding point and the mid deck from the vulgar gaze of the deck passengers.

Still dressed in my officer's uniform, I watched as the sheik arrived in a procession of seven brown-and-gold Cadillacs; the lead car stopped just ahead of the midships boarding ramp. From it stepped one male Arab passenger in a plain white tunic and sunglasses. He bounded up the gangway and greeted the waiting Captain. The sheik then got out of the second car and came immediately on board, at which moment there were more friendly greetings between the sheik, the captain and the first officer. The sheik's right-hand man stayed in the background. As the captain led the sheik into the ship, a caravan of luggage was carried onto the 'Sandmartin'. As well as the ordinary trunks and suitcases, which were disgorged from the Cadillacs, there came, from the back seats of the cars, about 12 baskets, each about the size of a lobster creel. In these baskets were pigeons. In four grander baskets borne gently on board as if they were explosive devices were the sheik's falcons, their heads covered with magnificent hoods decorated with gold and plumed feathers.I watched these comings and goings from the aft deck and from the cover of a winch casing, trying to seem invisible because I was still in uniform and felt awkward because of it. Once the Cadillacs had been emptied, they melted silently away in funeral procession. I made my way via the sea-side of the ship to the bulkhead, which led to my cabin, and there changed out of my uniform; it had been an enjoyable, if short, vocation.

The passenger accommodation on the 'Sandmartin' was centrally located one level beneath and behind the bridge. Internally, the cabins were laid out in four small blocks with the corridors forming the shape of a cross. My cabin was the most aft on the starboard side; the total number of cabins was about 12. From the noises coming from the corridor outside my door, I could hear the sheik and his small entourage settling into the cabins in the block diagonally forward of mine. I had wondered if I might be put back on deck because of the need for cabin space, but nothing had been said. Among a few other cabin passengers who embarked at Karachi were two young women whom I had seen coming on board – I heard them being shown into the cabin next to mine. The morning's excitement and bustle died down, and in the afternoon the only noise and activity was the loading and offloading of freight from the 'Sandmartin's' holds. I felt wary of wandering about the ship because I was nervous of bumping into the sheik, so I went to find January and with his help got some maps. He took me down a deck and showed me into a small lounge room in which there were some shelves of books. January left me and I found both a good atlas and a map that showed the whole Middle East and suited my purpose perfectly. I retreated back to my cabin to study it and to try and work out how I was to get out of the region and onwards to home.

In the late afternoon, the 'Sandmartin' blew its hooter and the decks began to shudder as she moved slowly astern and then out into the Arabian Sea. I went on deck and watched our departure. January came to find me and told me that the captain and the sheik would be dining alone later and that dinner would be early, at 6:00. Because I was at a loose end and because I had been unable to figure out my journey, I sloped off to the dining saloon early and sat quietly, just to savour its comfort. As 6:00 approached the dining room filled up. In addition to the ship's officers and two men whom I had not seen before, there arrived the two girls who were in the cabin next to me. The girls were startlingly pretty and when they hesitated, not knowing what table they might sit at, the ship's officers rose to their feet as one. January came in on the scene and set a table for them, much to the evident disappointment of the men in the room. After we had eaten and conversation had begun, the girls were drawn into the conversation and we learned that they were actresses heading for Abu Dhabi, where they were to be auditioning for a t.v. commercial.

I had been on board the 'Sandmartin' for three days and I was having no difficulty in adjusting to my comfortable circumstances – fighting for a bowl of dhal on deck seemed a long way away. If the state of my physical comfort was ideal, then my mental state was the complete opposite. The captain had suggested that I might be allowed entry to Kuwait, but my ticket was for a voyage to Basra, which meant there was no cost in getting off the ship early. Furthermore, Kuwait was bounded by Syria and Iraq, and if I was to get into Kuwait, I did not see how I could get out of it by land. I recalled being told by someone I met in Kathmandu who had been in Kuwait that it was essential for anyone trying to travel cheaply to keep any time there to a minimum, because everything is so mystifyingly expensive. I don't know why it stuck in my mind, but I remember him telling me that a cabbage in Kuwait costs about £1. Although I felt secure on the 'Sandmartin', I knew that in only a few days the ease and luxury would come to an end. With these troubled thoughts clouding my mind, I wandered on deck to watch the sun fall behind the sea. January appeared at my side.

'The captain asks if you would like to join him,' he said.

'Yes, I'd love to… now?'

'Yes,' said January, 'and his highness will be there too.'

I was taken aback at this.

'With the captain, or just there?'

'His highness is sitting with the captain.'

'What do I say… I mean how should I address him, as 'Your Highness'?'

January said, 'yes, 'your highness' is a suitable form of address, though strictly speaking at first introduction he should be addressed as 'your royal highness', he being of the blood royal.'

Armed with the confidence as to how to address the sheik, I went to the dining room and knocked at the door and there saw the captain and the sheik sitting together at the now-cleared dinner table. The sheik's man was sitting by himself at a smaller table nearby reading a paper, but there was no-one else in the room.

'Come in Mike,' said the captain, 'I've been telling his highness about you. Come and join us.'

'I'm honoured to meet your royal highness,' I said, slightly bowing and sitting down opposite the captain. The sheik nodded.

There followed a long evening of talk, punctuated by cigars brought by January. The first one made my head swim. The sheik listened to a brief recounting of my travels and occasionally would ask his man for the translation of a word here and there. The subject of my journey home did not come up and we talked mostly about the American War; the sheik seemed interested in my views.

'And do you think other young men from England think the same thing?' he asked.

'I think universally. I cannot think of a single time when someone has said the war in Vietnam is acceptable or justified.'

'But you do not wish to live in a communist world?' he asked.

'I have not experienced life in a communist state, nor is it certain that a British communist state would come out the same as a Russian or Chinese communist state – but in principle, I do not think I would like to live that way.'

'Then the war is worthwhile,' said the sheik.

'It depends on whether you think that's what it's really about and whether there are other ways of protecting a state from a communist threat,' I answered.

'Such as?'

'Such as education and literature. If a population understands the differences, then…' I said, but the sheik interrupted.

'You are a dreamer, I think!'

'Perhaps. But history has said that the pen is mightier than the sword.'

'Maybe, but it's wise to keep a sword hidden somewhere too.'

There came a point in our evening when the captain and the sheik talked of local and immediate things and I felt redundant. I sat awkwardly for a while but did not know well enough how to extricate myself and leave. The feeling was answered when the sheik himself got up.

'I will retire,' he said, 'I always sleep well on board the 'Sandmartin'. There are no telephones.'

The captain and I got up, and I bowed my head again as the sheik left the room.

'We'll be three days to Bahrain and tomorrow I promise I'll show you round the bridge,' the captain said.

I went back to my cabin and the ship ploughed its way towards the Gulf of Oman.

The next morning after breakfast, I went on deck. The sheik's baskets of pigeons were stacked against a bulkhead on the middeck, and by them was the man who was the sheik's attendant, though to call him just that underestimated his status, I think. He saw me and beckoned me over to his side.

'I am Hassan,' he said, and held out his hand.

'Pleased to meet you,' I said.

'If you come later this morning, his highness will be here, with his falcons. Would you like to see them?'

'Oh yes.'

'Then I shall ask him if you can.'

True to his word and but an hour later, the sheik came on deck, the rear part of which had been cleared of all crew and passengers. I was nearby and Hassan signalled me to come forward. The sheik gestured that he had seen me and I bowed my head again and waited and watched as the falcons were taken from their cages. How magnificent they were. After a few minutes, Hassan took a pigeon from one of the baskets and flung it into the air. It flew almost vertically upwards and then began to fly in a circle. The Sheik had a falcon on his arm and had already taken off its hood; he watched for a minute or so, then raised his arm and pushed the falcon airborne over the waves. The pigeon was by this moment quite far from the ship but the falcon gained height over it. The pigeon, circling to find its bearings, came near again to the ship and at that point the falcon plunged from its great height and thrust its talons into it. A puff of feathers scattered from the pigeon and the falcon came back to the deck and to the sheik. As the falcon landed on his arm, the sheik turned to me and beamed a great smile.

I watched this extraordinary event for about an hour; pigeon after pigeon flew out over the waves and each was knocked out of the skies by the falcons.

During the rest of that day, I did little but wander discontentedly from deck to deck, unable to settle to anything, worrying about how I would get beyond Basra. After paying for my passage from Bombay I had a bit less than 50 pounds left.

I didn't see the captain, as I had hoped, but in the lounge in the afternoon I made the acquaintance of the two girls from Lebanon – Azale and Leila. They were easy company, and asked a million questions about Britain.

At dinner that evening, the girls and I sat together at one of the smaller tables in the saloon as the crew sat at another, and I sensed a slight tension because of it. Later in the evening, after dinner, I had retreated to a tiny saloon bar, which formed a sort of lobby between the kitchen and the dining room. It was a tiny space with just two linen-covered bar tables, which were used at meal times as the collection point for cutlery and serving dishes. I was sitting in peaceful and happy solitude when Hassan came in. He greeted me, made small talk then asked the strangest question.

'Those two girls,' he said.

'From Lebanon?'

'Yes, those two girls. You have spoken to them?'

'Oh yes.'

'And they are friendly, yes?'

'Yes, I'd say so.'

'Do you think it might be possible, I mean, if you were to ask them… to come to your cabin?'

'What the girls? Into my cabin? I hadn't thought actually…'

'Yes, but if you asked, do you think they would go?'

'I don't know, I could try. Why?'

'His highness would like to talk to them. Alone.'

'I see,' I said.

'Yes,' said Hassan, 'his highness would be very pleased with this favour.'

It did click what was going on and I felt cornered – if I said no, it would somehow reflect badly on the captain, but if I said yes, I was nervous about what might happen to the girls. I reflected quickly that the girls looked pretty world-wise and could look after themselves. It was something in their legs that informed me.

'Okay, I'll try. But I'm no Gregory Peck.'

'Sorry?' said Hassan.

'Never mind.'

Azale and Leila were in the small lounge on the deck below. When I joined them, they were playing cards; they seemed happy enough for me to sit with them, and within a quarter of an hour I had taught them gin rummy and snap. They didn't take to the gin rummy, but they played snap with a fighting spirit. We had all had a bit to drink and the game became louder and more frantic. The time came when the moment was right for me to take the plunge and invite them to my cabin for one last drink. Leila was equivocal and Azale adamant that she would not.

'Oh come on,' I said, 'just one drink...'

'Well okay,' said Leila, 'just one, then I go.' Azale did not seem very happy about this and they spoke heatedly in a sort of French I could not understand.

'Of course, of course,' I said, 'honestly, just one drink.'

'I shouldn't really be here you know,' said Leila after I had closed the cabin door. She stroked a finger through her delicious black hair.

'Oh I know. I know. What can I get you to drink?'

'Just a little little Bacardi.'

'Coke?'

'Some. And Mikey...'

'Mmm?'

'Ice. I'm hot.'

'Ice and I'll be two minutes,' I croaked. As I left the cabin to go up to the saloon for drink, Azale was letting herself into the cabin next to mine; she scowled at me.

'Listen Azale, Leila is right next door,' I said in a low voice, 'we are just having one drink, okay?'

'Pah!' she said and pulled the door closed firmly in my face. I was feeling distinctly rotten about it all.

Hassan was waiting at the end of the corridor outside the sheik's cabin. As I passed him on my way back to the small saloon bar, I jerked a thumb to convey to him that Leila was in my cabin and that she wanted a Bacardi and coke. As I squeezed passed him in the narrow corridor, he smiled a rotten smile, saying 'Bacardi and coke?'

'Yes,' I replied, 'and ice. She says she's hot.'

'Ah,' said Hassan, like the evil schemer he undoubtedly was, 'this is excellent. His highness will bring her the drink and perhaps manage to cool her down.'

I went to the saloon bar and there spent a solitary hour and a bit. I had nothing to do but help myself to whisky, and this I did in an un-happy frame of mind. I was a little comforted in that I could not hear screams coming from the lower deck, not that I could have heard them anyway.

Hassan appeared after a couple of hours and too many whiskies and I was relieved to get back to my cabin; it was in a tidier state than when I had left it and someone had been in and given it the once over.

The day had left me tired, the whisky had left me quite drunk and I stripped off and got into bed, grateful that the day was over. Though I did not know what had happened between the sheik and Leila, I had not liked what had happened and felt regretful and ashamed. It was a hot night; I turned off the light and turned over to sleep.

I was awoken by a gentle knock at the door and the entry of someone into my cabin. As I opened my eyes in the half dark, I could make out a white human shape; it might have been a ghost but that its breathing was audible. In curiosity rather than fear, I flung off the sheet that had covered me and stood up – I was just in a tee shirt and nothing else.

The light went on and Hassan stood before me, smiling.

He came towards me and to my great surprise pushed me; I fell backwards onto the bed, and as I did so he lifted his tunic and revealed his erection. He clambered onto top of me, forced my legs apart and attempted to relieve me of that other kind of virginity. I was taken abso-lutely unawares. I awoke rapidly and fully and as I worked out what was happening, I pushed his shoulders with my hands and then drew back my legs, got one foot onto his chest and gave him an almighty shove. In this encounter I was saying and shouting, 'No! No!'

He fell onto the floor, onto his back. He scrambled onto his feet and once again tried to push me onto the bed.

'Come! Come!' he was groaning through his heavy breathing.

There was a very determined fight in which my agility beat his strength, and at the end I put a hand on his shoulder and said, in as strong voice as I could muster, 'no' to him. When it dawned on him that he would not have his way with me, he turned and went to the door. When he stood in the corridor, I put a hand on his shoulder to show goodwill and to cover his embarrassment, if indeed he was feeling any.

'Goodnight Hassan. Goodnight!'

As he turned to leave, I saw Hans, the first officer, at the end of the corridor. What he saw was me, naked and flushed, touching Hassan's shoulder, saying goodnight. He looked at me with undisguised disgust.

When I woke next morning, the ship was quiet and not in motion. I got up and peered out of the port hole. The sea was dead calm, the water a deep green-blue, its surface oily and glassy. I did not want to face the body politic in the dining room, and after a shower I went back to bed, my mind recalling with distaste the events of the night before. I dozed, and when I was sure that the dining room breakfast would be over, I dressed and stole to the kitchen and cadged just a cup of tea from the cook. I took my tea back to my cabin and looked over my map, still very anxious about how my journey home could be achieved. It was a miserable morning.

By about 11:00, I took the chance of going on deck, and as I emerged from the interior into the blazing hot sun and crossed the deck to the port side, I saw the ship's launch being lowered from its davits. Before me, I could see a group of tiny islands – dusty, rocky looking places. By the aft gangway was the sheik, Hassan, Leila and Azale, looking and behaving as though they were all the best of friends. As soon as I saw them, I withdrew behind a door to hide myself. They did not see me as they waited for the boat to be lowered into the water. Once the boat was ready, they made their way onto it down a steep gangplank, and one of the ship's crew followed with two basket hampers; once these were stowed and the crewman had returned on board, the launch cast off and puttered off towards the islands with Hassan at the helm. I could just make out Leila popping the cork from a champagne bottle.

The captain came up beside me.

'They're all going for a picnic on one of the islands,' he said, 'looks like fun.'

Straight away I told him of the events of the previous evening and he just shrugged his shoulders.

'Well, I'm glad you told me,' he said, 'I'll have a word with him when he gets back. That can't happen again. You sure you're okay?'

'Yes, I'm okay. Who'll you speak to?'

'The emir, of course.' We stood for a moment watching the launch as it changed course and steered towards one of the islands.

'Come on,' said the Captain, 'I'll show you the bridge'.

From that day, I kept myself to myself and the only company I sought was that of the captain when he had time. As soon as I could, I made my peace with the girls, who were both ostentatious in the new Cartier watches on their wrists.

'Nice watch,' I said to Leila.

'Yes, it is,' she said, touching it lovingly.

'And I see you got one as well,' I said to Azale. She lowered her head a little shamefacedly and said, 'yes, he gave me one too.' I did not bother to bring the double entendre to her attention, because I had lost my *joie de vivre*, but later, the remark delighted me into laughter. To my great surprise, they thanked me for 'introducing' them to the sheik, but the matter was no longer of interest to me because I was getting more scared with every mile the ship sailed.

The 'Sandmartin' had another surprise.

I was on deck, heading to my cabin one afternoon when a voice called out, 'Hey, you're from Aberdeen I'm told.' The voice was unmistakably Sauchiehall Street.

By a bulkhead door, holding a can of beer, was a great big man in filthy overalls. He was certainly in his late 50s, maybe a little older. He had a John Wayne face that was grimy and wrinkled, and he was almost bald except for a disorganised mess of grey-yellow hair that blew about in the breeze.

'Aye, that I am,' I said, answering his Glasgow with my Aberdeen.

'I'm frae Glasgow. Fancy a tin?' He held up the can he was drinking from.

'Why not. It's hot enough.'

'Come on then.' He motioned me to follow him and he led the way deep down into the bowels of the ship, to the engine room and to a tiny oven of a sound proofed office.

'I'm Dougie,' he said, closing the door from the din of the engines, 'chief engineer. And you're?'

'Mike Hendry.'

'Oh aye, I heard about you. Dickie mentioned you were on board.' I frowned, not understanding the remark.

'The captain, Dick Winston,' he said as he tossed his empty can expertly into a dustbin brim full of other empty cans. He immediately grabbed another from a crate below his chair and ripped it open.

'Oh, right,' I said.

'So, you're on your way home then?'

'Yes, though God knows how. The war.'

'Aye, they've fucked it up this time, no mistake. You might be alright into Kuwait though. And you've met our friend the sheik?'

'Yes, and not without its problems.'

'Aye, they say he's a shagger from hell. You know once he met a girl in Stockholm? He was at some oil conference or something. Took a fancy to her. Well he didn't get to lay her then, but when he got back home he sent his 747 back to Stockholm, fetched her in a car, flew her out to Bahrain and then to his Palace at Bar El Shu'aib, shagged her, then flew her on the 747 back to Stockholm. Imagine!'

'It can't be true!' I said.

'Sure as eggs is eggs. She must have been some kind of stuff, eh? Mind you, when you're worth £150 million from the oil, you can do what you like, eh? What a man! Sheik the Shagger. How's you're beer?'

'It's fine, thanks. You would need something to drink in this heat.'

'I manage 50 a day,' he said emptying his can, 'sometimes 60 if it's hot.'

'You don't call this hot?' I exclaimed.

'Naw, not today,' he said, mopping his brow with a filthy rag. It must have been more than a hundred degrees.

The 'Sandmartin' steamed sedately into the Persian Gulf from Oman through the Straits of Hormuz, around the islands of Abu Dhabi to Qatar and Bahrain, through islands and ports with the names of Ras al Kaima, Zarqa, Umm Said – sounding like a blend of sweetmeats and murmurings of love. At Bar El Shu'aib, the emir was met by another fleet of Cadillacs led by one golden Rolls Royce. The falcons were gently transported into the first three Cadillacs and a swarm of lackeys fussed the emir into the Rolls. There were no ceremonies and no goodbyes and he and his procession wafted away from the ship's side into the dusty heat. I had spoken to the him briefly a couple of times before he left the ship, and on our last meeting he kindly wished me good luck on my journey home.

Two days later, the 'Sandmartin' docked in Kuwait. I was both relieved and nervous. Before I left, the captain took me to his cabin.

'Well Mike, it has been a delight meeting you. I'm worried that you're going have problems getting through Iraq or Saudi. I can tell you now that his highness has said that if you get stuck or stranded, he will help you. He said if you wanted to fly home from Kuwait, he'd see to it. He took a liking to you, you know.'

'He said that?'

'Yes, he did. What I suggest is that you go ashore and see how the land lies. You can contact me by going to our office in Kuwait, and they can put you through to me on the ship to shore phone. You must promise me that your pig-headed stubbornness won't stop you doing the sensible thing. I mean that.' The captain gave me a card with the Kuwait office address of the British Oriental Steamship Line.

With my rucksack on my back, I felt again like the man I had been before I had stepped on board the 'Sandmartin' – very poor. I said my goodbyes to the captain and headed into Kuwait City.

10

Kuwait, blood and Beirut

KUWAIT WOULD SEEM A STRANGE PLACE TO MOST EUROPEANS; IT is big and sprawling, dusty, concrete and alien. My first task was to find somewhere to stay and I tramped the streets looking for a cheap hotel. I worked my way from the skyscraper hotels at the centre further outwards in an ever-increasing circumference. I walked for hours, and at about 3:00 in the afternoon checked into the misnamed Grand Hotel. Their doorway was a small double door situated down a narrow, filthy alley. The proprietor was a surly, curt-mannered man who displayed an immediate contempt for me. He showed me his cheapest room. Through a corridor that stretched the depth of the whole building, he took me out to a yard, to a shoddily built annex that seemed to have been abandoned and uninhabited for years. It reminded me of the coal sheds at the back of our house in Aberdeen. He unlocked the door of a room and I looked in. It was more of a lean-to than a room. It was about eight feet long by about five wide; the walls were unpainted breeze blocks and the floor was raw concrete. There was a slit of a window set along the top of one wall, and its light illuminated a metal bed frame with bare-metal criss-cross springs. There wasn't even a mattress on the bed.

'This?' I asked.

'Ten dinar,' he said, 'this.'

Because it was the cheapest I had seen and because it was getting late in the day, I took the room.

'Forty Dinar,' said the man.

'You said 10,' I answered.

'Deposit.'

'Deposit?'

'Deposit 30 dinar. I need see passport.'

'I have to go to bank to change more money,' I said, 'it is a long walk.'

'Taxi,' he said.

I hitched up my rucksack and walked more than a mile back to the centre, where I changed more of my depleting traveller's cheques, then tramped all the way back again. I was absolutely exhausted when I got back to the hotel. The man took my money, noted down my passport details and handed me the key to my room as if it had been a dead rat.

If I had ever felt alone and frightened in my travels, there was no worse extremity of those feelings than when I sat down dejectedly on my bed and pondered my plight. The immediate worry was, again, money. Kuwait is an expensive place and the reduction of 40 dinars left me with little more than 30 pounds to get home, even though some of that money would come back to me from the deposit. I thought back to the comforts of the 'Sandmartin'. Although the captain had promised me his help, I did not want to accept it. Nor did I wish to accept the offer from his highness the emir, though I cannot explain what logic underpinned that decision.

In a state of fear, I lay on my bed, grateful again that I had a sleeping bag. I waited until it was dusk before venturing out to try and find some food. I tramped back towards the city centre, where I had noticed a burger bar, and realised I was shaking as I handed over another 10 dinars for a meagre meal.

The next day was spent back in the city centre. I found the embassies of Iraq and Saudi Arabia, where I explained my planned travel. But at both these places I was assured that I would not be allowed entry. I was advised by both embassies that my only option was to fly out of Kuwait. I tried the Iranian Embassy, thinking I might get a cheap boat to somewhere in Iran and then onwards to Turkey and Istanbul. The Iraqi and Saudi embassies had been resolute in their refusal to allow me entry; the girl at the Iranian embassy was equally adamant.

'No,' she said, 'the border will not let you in – why don't you fly?' I kept being asked this question, but I could never reply that it was simply because I did not have the money for the fare. The effect of my enquiries made me realise that it was hopeless to consider any land route out of Kuwait. I had two options. One was to use my remaining funds to go back to Bombay, to Madelaine and to a flight all the way back to the UK, the end of my attempt. The other was to see if I had enough money for any sort of flight that would get me out of Kuwait.

At the end of my first day in Kuwait, I sat in my room, despairing and in a black mood. My money was disappearing with every cup of tea and every bite to eat; even though I walked everywhere, I could not avoid some expense draining my meagre resources. I had found a burger bar that was cheaper than the one I had visited on my first day, so I went there on my second evening. Kuwait City is not amenable to the walking visitor – everything is geared towards the car. And walking through the city, I was strongly aware of hostility towards me – men in cars passing near me would spit. I felt I was being watched in an atmosphere of suspicion, as if I were a spy or interloper. I arrived at my new eating place and there, there was a young man dressed in Western clothes more shabby and threadbare than mine. He was at the counter and I sidled up beside him.

'Hi,' I said.

'Good God!' he replied, 'where the hell did you spring from?'

We sat down together and he leaned close to me as if he did not want to be overheard – with good reason.

'I've been trying to get out of this dump for 10 days now,' he explained, 'what a shit place. And expensive or what? Do you know I paid two quid for a coke the other day? Two fucking quid!'

This was Wally, a stubble-chinned, baggy-panted Manchurian on his way to India. To do what, he wasn't sure: he just wanted to get there. He related his travelogue.

'Well, it hasn't been easy what with the war and all. Right from Turkey, it's still the bloody war. You can't go there, you can't go there. Bloody hell.'

It was a relief to meet a Brit in circumstances similar to mine. He went on: 'Finally managed to get enough money to get out. I'm getting a boat tomorrow, right down the Gulf.'

'How did you manage that?' I asked.

'The money? Selling blood,' he said, stashing ketchup sachets into his pocket.

'Blood?'

'Yeah, blood. If you go to the Kuwait General Hospital, you'll get 30 dinars a pint. I've done two so far. Know a bloke who's on his third; he's looking a touch pale, mind.' Wally pulled up his left sleeve and showed me his bruise.

I asked him for more information.

'It's easy enough. They'll take anyone. But you got to make sure you answer a couple of questions right, otherwise they turn you away. First, they ask if you've had… oh, a long list of diseases, syphilis, hepatitis, the clap, stuff like that. You gotta say no, never had any of those. Then they ask you where you've been. You mustn't say anywhere in the yellow fever zone – Vietnam, Burma, that sort of area. 'Part from that, you roll up your sleeve, pray to fuck the needle's clean, then you pick up 30 dinars at reception. The blood man hands over a slip, nursey at reception hands over an envelope. Cash lolly. Oh, and you have to go between 3:00 and 4:00 in the afternoon – it's a set time every day. M'on my way tomorrow. Thank fuck, can't stand this place. S'fucking spooky.'

We parted as beleaguered friends in a strange place and wished each other luck. When I got back to the Grand Hotel, I knew I had to act decisively the next day, and as part of that determination to face reality, I decided I would have to see if there could be some help via the captain.

On that, my third day, I was up early and walked directly to the B.O.S.L shipping office. I explained my story to the girl at the reception window, but before I had finished it, a pleasant, balding man who had overheard me came from a side door and towards me.

'You must be Michael Hendry,' he said, 'Captain Winston has left word that you might call in. I have an envelope for you.'

'For me?'

'Yes, he sent it from the 'Sandmartin' the day he sailed. I'll get it.' He disappeared for a minute and returned bearing a buff envelope which bore my name. I walked to the window and opened it. There was a letter and cash.

The note said 'Mike, I hope the enclosed will help you get home. If you receive this, it means that you have either seen sense or are in difficult circumstances. Either way, I'm glad you did it. Get in touch once you get home – I'd like to know you are safe. Richard.'

I bit my lip as I read it. I turned to the man who had brought the envelope; he was looking at me.

'Will you tell Captain Winston – thank you?' I said.

'I shall.'

I left the office and went to a quiet street corner, where I peered at the money and counted it without taking it out of the envelope. There was 20 pounds in English sterling notes. Without further procrastination, I went to three travel agents to find out what flights were available out of Kuwait at the cheapest cost. The only destinations that were suitable were Cyprus, Lebanon or Turkey, and after making a complete pest of myself at one very helpful travel agent, I decided that a flight to Beirut was the right choice. It took most of the day to get this organised and to get a visa from the Lebanese embassy, but by early afternoon I had a flight to Beirut booked and paid for.

The flight had cost just a little less than the sum Richard had given me. I realised that getting to Lebanon was but one more step on the way home, even though I would land there virtually penniless again. I was due to leave Kuwait on the afternoon of the next day, so I had time to find and to get to the Kuwait City Hospital to sell some blood.

The Kuwait City Hospital is one of those bland hospital buildings that are the same the world over: a canopied entrance, sprawling concrete and narrow, sealed windows. I went to the main reception desk, where I was directed to the blood donor department; the woman behind the desk had been very chirpy and cheerful when she asked if she could help, but her face and tone changed when I explained I wanted to sell some blood.

'Oh,' she said, 'one of those,' as if I had transmogrified from a respectable human into a tarantula.

In the waiting room of the blood donor department were seated, despondently, three Europeans: a couple and a man on his own. When I walked in, the male of the couple said 'well well, welcome to the den of Dracula.' The couple laughed. He was in his 20s, in a thick tartan shirt, shorts and with long hair in a pony tail. She was about the same age, dumpy, in jeans and a tee shirt that said 'Cio Baby' in pink sequins on the front. I noticed both had lumpy sticking plasters on their wrists.

I sat down.

'So, how are you coming here?' asked the man with the pony tail. His accent was Italian.

'On my way back to home from India,' I answered.

'Home?'

'Scotland.'

'Ah, bonnie Scotland,' said the man, 'and how did you hear of this place?'

'I met a guy last night… at a burger bar. He told me. Said it was 30 dinars.'

'Hey Camelia,' said the Italian to his girlfriend, 'that would be Wally…' Camelia said 'si, that would be Wally'.

'From Manchester, yes?'

'That's right.'

'Manchester,' repeated Camelia, 'Wally come from Manchester.'

The man asked me, 'So where you headed after this…'

'Flying to Beirut tomorrow,' I answered, holding out my arms like the wings of a plane, 'I wanted to go overland, but I couldn't get through… it's the war, I suppose.'

'It is the same for us, we feel like the spies, we are watched, watched, watched wherever we are going. They think we are the Americans.' He raised his hands in gesticulation and let them fall heavily on his thighs.

'Where are you from?' I asked.

'Paragiio. It is near Milano, we are going to Japan.' Camelia repeated that they were from Paragiio, on their way to Japan.

'If you are going to Beirut, go to L'Auberge du cercle de la Jeunesse,' said the man, 'it is cheap, and there will be others there. We stay there, we meet nice people there.'

Camelia said they had met nice people there, yes, it was a nice place.

A man, looking like a butcher in white rubber apron and matching rubber boots, came into the waiting room from behind a counter. He was holding a file and looking at the paper clipped to it. He was a young man, very tall with a just a hint of Boris Karloff, with a bolt through his neck. He said 'Balchante?' He spoke the pronunciation with difficulty.

The Italians stood up.

'Si, that is me.'

The man in the apron handed the Italian a slip of paper and briefly looked over at me. As the Italians gathered themselves together, they made for the door and said to me 'good luck, huh? And to you, too…' The last words they addressed to the man on his own beside me; he looked up and gave a little wave, but said nothing.

'So you,' said the hospital man to me, 'you do blood?' His voice was cold.

'Yes, I do blood,' I said.

'Come.'

I got up and followed him through a glass-topped door into a small anteroom, and he sat down at a small, beat-up desk. He opened a drawer and took out a form which he clipped to his board.

'American? You?'

'No, England, Scotland.'

'Diseases, yes? You have smallpox, hepatitis, syphilis, jaundice?'

'No,' I said.

'Anaemia? Aoemba dysentery?'

I paused because I had had dysentery, but was it amoebic?

'No,' I lied.

'You been any yellow fever country?' He read out a list of countries.

'No.'

He stopped reading from a printed list and looked up.

'Where you been?'

'Nepal most. Some India.'

'No China, Burma, Malaysia?'

'No China, Burma, Malaysia.'

'Group?'

'What?' I asked.

'You know group blood?' His voice was impatient.

'I think it is 'O'.'

'You think so?' he said.

'I'm not sure.'

'Okay. Your name here and passport.' He passed the file and a pen over to me. I filled in my name and address in Aberdeen and my passport number. I handed the file back to him. He didn't check it, just threw it on the desk and got up. There was a part of me that wanted to halt this episode, and I hesitated for a moment. I am not a happy liar, and I had not so much lied about the potential diseases I carried but had convinced myself that I was not the carrier of anything contagious or serious. Such doubts as I had then melted away when I thought of the consequences of not getting out of Kuwait; they were better off without me, and I was better off away from them.

'Come,' he said.

I followed him into an adjoining room. There was a chrome-and-black plastic arm chair, next to which was a metal trolley laid out with tubes and needles, tourniquets and dressings. Although we were in a hospital, the room did not feel like a hospital treatment room – it was more like a broom cupboard. The floor was cracked lino and the walls were pale yellow and bare.

'Sit,' he said, beginning to prepare the equipment. He pointed to my right arm and gestured that I should roll up my sleeve. I was unhappy. Quite suddenly – as soon as my wrist was rested on the arm of the chair – he applied the tourniquet and slammed the needle into my wrist. I winced with pain and he smiled very slightly. When he released the tourniquet, he handed me a spring clip hand exerciser.

'Push pull,' he said, 'I come back,' and he left the room. I was alone, praying that the needle was clean. As my blood pulsed out of my body, I made a mental note that I should work out how many miles my pint of blood represented. If 30 dinars paid for my travel from Lebanon to Turkey, my blood would be worth 500 miles per pint – a very efficient fuel.

When the man in the apron came back and withdrew the needle from my arm, he said: 'Your friend. You tell him, no more blood.' He didn't put any dressing on the spot of blood that seeped from the bruised wound on my arm.

'My friend?'

'Him…' he jerked his head in the direction of the waiting room.

'He is not my friend,' I answered.

'No more blood,' he said, 'come.' I got up, my head wheeling slightly with light-headedness. I followed him back to the waiting room, where I sat down.

'You wait,' I was told, and I was left in the waiting room alone with the solitary man who had been there when I arrived. He had a curious appearance – at least curious for Kuwait.

He was a man in his 20s, of pale face and neat, golden, public-schoolboy hair. He wore a grey English woollen overcoat, and by the look of his trousers, a grey suit with plain, brown, thin-soled shoes. He looked as though he had just stepped out of an office in some London suburb to get a sandwich. He wore round, horn-rimmed glasses that gave him the air of an academic. He was sitting on a chair, leaning forward, his head cupped miserably in his hands. By his side was a suitcase that attracted my attention for the bizarre reason that it was the exactly the same as one my mother had – printed grey with cream edge protectors and matching cream handle; the sort of suitcase used for a short trip or holiday – but unusual in the context of the Blood Donor Department of the Kuwait City Hospital.

'You okay?' asked the man with my Mum's suitcase.

'Oh yes, just a bit light-headed.'

'First time?'

'Yes. You?'

'Third.'

'You've given three times?'

'This week.'

'Jesus. Well, Prince Charming told me to tell you no more – he won't take any more.'

'He said that the last time.'

We waited in silence for about 15 minutes, and then the tall young man came back.

'Hendry?' he said to me, knowing perfectly well who I was. He handed me a slip of paper from his clip board – I looked at it, but it was entirely written in Arabic so I didn't know what it said.

'O,' he said to me, 'group 'O'. Cash at Reception.'

He turned to my companion and handed him his slip of paper.

'No more blood. Go now. Not come back.'

He turned and slammed the door to the ante room behind him.

I sat recovering for just a few minutes then said to my co-blood donor,

'Come on, let's cash in these slips and get some tea… isn't it a tradition that you get a cup of tea after giving blood?'

We collected our cash, left and went in search of tea.

His name was Malcolm. He had left the UK with 20 pounds and had arrived in Kuwait three weeks later with not one sous penny to his name. Malcolm was not going anywhere in particular, though he had the vague notion that he would land in India with the hope of then getting somehow to Australia. He told me a sad tale. His father had died and, to his great shock, his will had been complicated by the fact that his father had got married just 10 days before his death and Malcolm had not known about his marriage. The woman whom his father had married had been like a mother to him, but the terms of the will had made it quite clear that she and her grasping family had sought to fleece his father at the expense of Malcolm's relationship with his now stepmother. It was quite obvious that the step family had conspired to conceal the information of the marriage to him. His situation was doubly shocking because he had once been engaged to the daughter of the stepmother – and though that had ended, he had been shocked that he had so miscalculated her trust and her morality. The betrayals of his ex-fiancé and his stepmother had been so shocking to him that he felt the only solution to his annihilated feelings was suicide, but his sister had prevailed upon him and he decided that a long journey would assuage his feelings of anger and betrayal. I asked him if he thought his journey was helping.

'Not really. When I'm walking, I just think over some of the things that were said – they didn't make any sense at the time just before Dad's death, but when I saw his will, all the deceptions became clear. I just don't seem to be able to get it out of my mind. One thing I have decided, though, is that when I get to Australia, I'm going to write a book about that family. It's going to be a bestseller.' I pondered this for a moment, then said, 'And in the meantime, you're running the risk of endangering yourself by selling three pints of blood in a week… you don't suppose you're indulging your hurt feelings in self-flagellation?'

'No, not a bit, I need the money.' As he said this, he smiled for the first time since our meeting.

Malcom had been sleeping rough in a park, and between his loss of blood and his lack of food and sleep, he was a physical wreck. Near the hospital, we sat down on a grass bank. It was baking hot and Malcom finally took off his overcoat. I explained my plans.

'I'm off tomorrow to Lebanon, in the afternoon. Come back to the dump I'm staying in, leave your things there then we'll get some food at that burger place… don't worry, I'll pay. Then you come back with me and see if you can't get some rest, you look as though you need it. The room's quite revolting and uncomfortable, and you'll have to leave very early, but at least you'll get undisturbed sleep.'

And so it turned out. We tramped the hour to the hotel and I got him to wait out of sight while I took his case to leave in my room. Then we walked the mile back to near the city centre and the burger bar – by then it was early evening. I saw Malcom's hands were shaking as we ate. We stayed in the air-conditioned cool for as long as we could and used the toilet facilities to wash and clean ourselves, then left. I went to a bureau de change to change a couple of traveller's cheques, and then we wandered like a pair of tramps just to kill time. With sore and tired feet we trudged back to the hotel. The sky was a smoky blue by then. We darted up the alley at the side of the hotel like thieves and sneaked in to our little shed. I gave Malcolm the bed and I slept on the concrete floor to spend an intensely uncomfortable night, my last in Kuwait. Before finally settling, we pissed outside by the door. Somehow, the discomfort and squalor went naturally with everything I had experienced in Kuwait.

By some mysterious mutual recognition of time, we both awoke at the same moment in the very early morning, when the dawn was still dim. I wrote down some names and addresses, including that of 'BroMed' and Patrice in Delhi.

'If you get to Delhi,' I said, 'be sure to go to this address. Patrice is a good man and you can be sure of at least a couple of nights of free accommodation. And who knows, you might want to do some work for them and stay longer. It's up to you. I suggest you should get out of here as soon as you can or you'll become a basket case.'

'I know, I know,' he replied, but I didn't believe he spoke with any honesty. I asked him how he intended to get out of Kuwait and on his way to India but, he hummed and hawed and left me with the impression that he was a man in trouble.

With the cold dawn light brightening, I got him out of the room, down the alley and on his way. I watched him for a few moments, his suitcase in his hand, for all the world still looking as though he had slipped out of the office to get a sandwich.

I dozed for a while and waited for the morning proper to come. I rolled up my sleeping bag and stuffed it into my rucksack. In an exchange involving very few words, I got my deposit of 30 dinars back from the hotel and began the long hike to the airport.

11

Turkey. Istanbul to Trieste

THE FLIGHT TO BEIRUT WAS OVER THE DESOLATE SANDS OF SAUDI Arabia. Then, very suddenly, the land below was green and lush and I could see the ocean. An hour later I was in Beirut trying to find L'Auberge du Cercle de la Jeunesse.

Kuwait's hostility had left me stressed and I had left with a bad impression of the place. In fairness, there may have been parts of Kuwait that were beautiful, but I did not see them. Similarly, the few Kuwaitis I met were hostile to me, and though I did not know it at the time, they and other Arabs had very good cause to despise me as British. Although the Arab-Israeli war of 1967 had been over for more than a few months, the after-shocks of that event were still tangible around the Middle East. In the heat of the early days of that conflict in 1967, as a propaganda ploy, Radio Cairo broadcast that the Israelis had been assisted in their bombings by the Americans and the British. This was repeated by Syrian and Jordanian radio stations and taken up by influential Arab newspapers to the degree that the great majority of the Arab world were being told by their governments that the British had supported the Israelis. In truth, the motive behind this propaganda was an attempt to persuade the Soviet Union to assists the Arabs. This strategy failed because the Russians knew it was false, but in the minds of Arabs, the British were collusionists and therefore to be despised as much as the hated Israelis. British diplomatic relations with Egypt, Syria, Iraq,

Algeria, Sudan and Yemen were all broken. At the time, the only thing I knew about all this was that I was being spat at in Kuwait.

Although I knew nothing of it at the time, Beirut had suffered mightily during the six day war that had raged in the months before I had left India. Only five months before my arrival in Lebanon, all American citizens were evacuated from Beirut, such was the pressing danger to them from local attack and assassination. And though the political hostility to Americans and their perceived allies was as present in Beirut as it had been in Kuwait, it felt much less so as soon as I began my wanderings.

Kuwait in 1968 seemed to me to be an ugly, sterile wasteland of dusty concrete blocks, but Beirut was a city steeped in charm and beauty. Its warmth and conviviality radiated from the walls of finely proportioned buildings, pretty street corners, palm trees and squares. The city had a restrained, quirky grandeur that conveyed its distinguished and prosperous past. It felt at ease with itself and with the world, like an old man whose life has come right and who is relaxed and happy. I thought then it was the most beautiful city I had ever seen, and I still do. Its later destruction must rate as one of humanity's greatest blunders.

I arrived in Beirut on the sixth of December, three weeks and a few days from my departure from Bombay, and three weeks and a few days away from my target of getting to Aberdeen by Christmas. The plane arrived from Kuwait in the mid-afternoon and I had left my rucksack at L'Auberge du Cercle de la Jeunesse by five. I had found L'Auberge easily.

As always, I indulged my wandering nature in the fullness of its desires and walked the city until it was dark and late at night. With French spoken and printed throughout the city, its shops, restaurants and cafes, I felt connected to humanity again. I adored Beirut with a love that made the deepest impression of any place I had ever been. Whereas finding cheap food in Kuwait had been difficult and challenging, in Beirut it was easy and enjoyable. The hostility to me as a Westerner was there, but somehow more dispassionately expressed. *Well, yes, you are a British pig, but I think you will agree these croissants are the best you will ever taste.* I got back to L'Auberge very late, met no-one and went straight to a meagre but comfortable bed.

The next morning I determined that I should immediately head into the city to trail around the embassies to try and see what overland route

might be available to me. I was armed with my notebook and passport
and went to the lounge of the hostel to sit and organise my thoughts
before setting out. In repetition of so many of my arrivals and departures, I met there a mix of people, among whom were a British couple,
two French girls, a Frenchman, three Canadians and a Norwegian –
travellers all.

From speaking with them all as a group, I was made to understand that
there was no land route available to a British subject; I was beginning
finally to get an understanding of the consequences of the seven-day
war on my life. Israel to the west would be safe once I got in its territory, but getting through to that point was known to be very dangerous;
people were getting shot there. To the east and north was Syria and none
of those who had attempted to travel through it had been successful
in getting a visa. The only way out of Lebanon was either by sea, into
the Mediterranean, or by air – the shortest flights from Beirut being
to Adana in Turkey or to Cyprus. The Turks were not well disposed to
American or British citizens, but the Canadians told me that I would
likely get a short transit visa to get from Adana in the far south east
up to Istanbul. As to the situation in Cyprus, they had no information.
The Canadians had come from the Turkish coast and had sailed from
there to Beirut. They said they had no problems in Turkey except for the
intense cold.

The Frenchman declared that the best route would be via Israel, but in
this opinion he was alone.

I didn't want to believe the information I was being told because I
doubted whether I could afford the flight to Adana, and even if I did
manage to pay for it, I would land in Turkey penniless and unable to
get any further. I preferred to believe that I might find a ship heading
for the north Mediterranean. When I expressed this plan with the air of
one who has the answer no-one has thought of, I was disembarrassed of
the ambition by the Norwegian, who told me that he had tried exactly
that plan and had found such hostility and suspicion that he believed
the route to be out of the question. The Auberge was costing me about
£2 per night and food was cheap, but my resources were so lean I was
anxious to keep travelling as quickly as possible – I did not relish the
prospect of getting stuck in Beirut.

I left the L'Auberge, headed into the city, and found, respectively, the Syrian and Turkish embassies. At the Syrian Embassy I was told sharply that there were no relations with Britain and that travel through the country was not only impossible, but forbidden on penalty of prison. The Turkish Embassy proved to be frosty in manner but willing to issue a transit visa, valid only for travel. Next were travel agents, where I found out the cost of flights – to the Mediterranean, to mainland Europe and to Turkey: the cost of the flight to Adana was about £15; achievable, but risky. I asked too about passages on ships, but in answer to my questions they just shook their heads. One did offer me a luxury cruise to the Bahamas, though. I found out about trains and buses in Turkey in case I had to go that route, and learned that the bus from Adana to Istanbul would be about £8 – at least I might be able to get to Istanbul.

The city's charms enticed me once more, and I was led through its streets and alleys, squares and avenues in a reverie of delight until the day had passed and I had still not confirmed or committed to a definite travel plan.

In the evening I returned to L'Auberge and went to the lounge, where most of my new friends were gathered, though the Norwegian was not there.

'So?' asked the Canadian,

'Nothing,' I said, 'flight to Adana looks like the only thing.' No-one replied. Then the Frenchman spoke.

'Tomorrow we are going to Tyre in my car, shall you come with us? It is just a day of holiday, to see the coast – some say it the most beautiful in the whole world. John and Martha, they are coming.' The Canadians nodded.

I said I would think about it overnight and thanked him for the offer – I knew I was tempted.

I went to my room and in the privacy of my own space, laid out my money on the bed. Taking into account a further expenditure for one more day at the L'Auberge, plus some food, left me with about £20. If I had to fly to Adana, then take the bus to Istanbul, I would be left with just £6 – hardly enough to get me from Istanbul to Aberdeen.

The next day, I awoke in a state of indecision. I was tempted by the prospect of a day trip to the coast with the others but realised that this was my way of avoiding the decision I had to make – whether to risk all remaining funds to get to Istanbul or hang on to try and find another route home. I got up, had some breakfast and went for a walk. There was something in the greyness of the day and a sense of gathering clouds of two sorts that made my mind up. I went back to L'Auberge, packed, paid my bill and got myself to the airport by bus. It was a sudden decision but I felt much the better for the taking of it.

The flight to Turkey only took two hours. From Adana airport, I went straight to the bus station to get a ticket for Istanbul. I was lucky in that my bus was soon to depart, and I was on board and on my way by early afternoon.

Whereas I had felt a relaxing of tension when I entered Lebanon from Kuwait, that tension returned the instant I landed on Turkish soil. In Lebanon, there is familiar French written and spoken – so speech and signs, instructions and labels are familiar enough to be understood, and therefore not intimidating. In Turkey, there was no such comfort for me. The language was mysterious and the words were not a bit like their English or European equivalents. I could not read any signs, nor could I understand such basics as the label on the bus window, which, I supposed, explained how to open and close it. At the bus station I had taken a timetable and road map, and on its reverse side were listed the mileages between cities; between Adana and Istanbul was listed as being 850 kilometers, about 600 miles, Adana being to the far southwest of the country. With language difficulties and having been in a stressed state, I had not, in the Adana bus station, asked when the bus would arrive in Istanbul. It had not bothered me.

As the afternoon became the colder early evening, I checked the timetable and managed to work out that the journey was to take 24 hours. The bus was quite full, but not uncomfortably so. I realised that everyone had food and drink with them and that I had neither, not even water. I noticed, too, that most passengers had rugs and blankets.

Though Lebanon was a hot country, it felt lush and accommodating to human comfort; Beirut had the advantage of sea breezes and the shade of palm trees. Turkey, by comparison, seemed barren, sparse and alien to human comfort; the landscape was a colour that was neither green nor grey, dust nor earth. The spaces (for that was all it felt like) that the bus trundled through seemed flat and empty of character, people, vegetation, animation, colour or atmosphere – it seemed to be vacant and waiting for some act of God to fill it. I'm sure there were rivers, and hills, valleys and trees, flowers, birds and croaking frogs, but I do not think I ever saw such things. Turkey is one of the richest countries on the planet for archaeology, and anyone not appreciating its treasures could surely be accused of ignoring the best. But I just saw the film of dust by my window getting thicker and thicker.

Except for the rich, who miss out on such things, most people have experienced a nightmare bus journey – because of missed connections, cancelled flights or just bad luck. Such journeys are remembered both in their wholeness and as the conglomerate of a multiple of things – screaming babies, garlic breath, very large people crushing you, rucksacks falling on your head sharp edge first... the list is long and well documented. What is not sometimes recalled, and is difficult to colour in the telling, is the nothingness – a featureless, dull but very lengthy and uncomfortable journey when no contour of event occurs to form a shape or boundary to the monotonous passage of time. It's like drifting weightless in space while needing a pee.

The bus was a grim, unforgiving old single decker, a dark filthy green; as a bus, it had the aura of being a deeply unpopular outcast, even among other buses. If it had been human, it would have been foul-tempered and functioning only to seek the opportunity to exact retribution for some humiliating suffering it had endured. Its seats were hard and were spaced meanly so that one's knees touched the seat ahead in an uncomfortable position that kept the front of one knee under constant pressure. This pressure can only be relieved by hunching oneself upright in order to be able to straighten one leg under the seat of the next bench. This, in turn, causes the shins to grate against the metal bar at the base of the next seat – the effect is that no position can be found that suggests relaxation and sleep. I sat not exactly by a window but at one edge of one, so that when I leaned my head against it, I touched the beading around it, which was raised and uncomfortable. By this beading and between each window was an aluminium knob whose purpose I could not fathom, and each time my head rested against the window's edge and the bus hit a bump, my head was jarred backwards and hit the knob.

The bus left Adana sometime in the afternoon and it was not long before I got my anorak and sleeping bag out of the base of my rucksack to fend off the cold; I wrapped myself up and settled down for the long haul. As the day darkened, it became colder and colder and such heat as could be sensed did not linger or increase. Often on journeys there are the small encounters between passengers that bind them into one entity – even small courtesies open the door of human contact. There was none of that on the bus – the passengers seemed locked into their own bubbles, and that was that. Every few hours we stopped for a break. The men would piss on the ground by the bus and clamber back in; the women would disappear behind a wall or bush and scurry out of the cold back to their seats. I allowed myself one cup of tea where there was an extended stop in the early evening and eyed the food with envy, because I was truly hungry. We lumbered off into the night and I tried to sleep to forget the cold and my growing hunger.

I awoke in the early morning from half-sleep, desperate for a pee – my legs were aching, my back was stiff and sore, and I imagined the perfect tea and toast. The day wore on with unrelenting dullness and boredom; the windows were so filthy I could not see out and make something of the landscape. Then it began to rain. My feet were freezing: a leak trickled water down the inside of my window and began to form a puddle at my feet. More water was coming into the bus from the roof and other windows, and it was not long before the floor had a layer of water through which bits of food and paper began to ebb and flow at my feet.

We crawled into Istanbul in the mid-afternoon after a 24-hour marathon. I got off the bus without any plan or intention and, as I have always done, I began to walk the city. I had a few dollars and six two-pound traveller's cheques to survive on, and my first need was for tea. There was a profusion of small cafes on every street and alley, and the warmth and humanity of one that looked welcoming lifted my mood.

I followed the stream of teeming humanity of Istanbul and relaxed in its flow, walking where it took me without regard to direction or destination. I turned one corner and before me was the Galata Bridge over the Bosphorous – Asia beyond me, Europe at my feet. I wandered onto

the bridge and leant over the rails to watch the scenes below. Beside me
were men fishing, and at their sides were charcoal braziers. It took me
some time to realise that people were buying the fish that the fisherman
hauled up. I moved among them and found one that showed a card
with a price; it was very cheap, so I motioned that I wanted a fish. He
just pulled in his line, at the end of which was a good sized wriggling
fish. He pulled the hook out of its mouth, chopped off its head, slit its
belly from tail to gills and pulled out its guts; with a flick of a knife, he
tore out the bone and he had made a fillet. He poured a dash of oil onto
a big black pan, placed the fish on it and cooked it over the charcoal
in a couple of minutes. When it was cooked, he slid the fish onto a
piece of paper and handed it to me. I suppose between its catching and
my eating, only three minutes had elapsed, and my goodness, it tasted
wonderfully good. Exactly what the fish had been swimming in before
it had been caught, I preferred not to contemplate.

Energised by the fish, I set off to find the main train station with the
idea that I needed to quickly get an idea of what trains might take me
towards Paris, and at what cost. Like many buildings in Istanbul, the
station was a magnificent Gothic heap rich in atmosphere and romance.
Of the possibilities that I discovered, the most interesting was a train
that went all the way to Paris. The fare was more than the money I had,
but I had enough that would get me to Trieste in Italy. Armed with this
information, I returned to the bus station where I had arrived but where,
in my urgent need to get out of the bus and back to humanity, I had not
taken the opportunity to find out what buses might run from Istanbul
north. At the railway station there was enough English spoken that I
managed to get a picture of what trains went where, but at the bus station this was not the case. I could only see timetables and maps, which
showed the internal bus routes in Turkey but nothing more. By the time
I had achieved this, it was getting late and I had nowhere to stay. In a
strange place, if you have little money and you have to find a bed, find
a YMCA.

I asked whoever looked like they might speak a little English, and the
letters YMCA are well known. People had been pointing towards one
direction, and when I asked an American couple they pointed at the
building they were standing in front of.

'You found it,' one said.

The cheapest beds in the hostel were in dormitories, where two lines of double bunks filled a large and bare upstairs room. Thankfully, a bed was very cheap and within my means. I left my rucksack at the downstairs desk for safekeeping and went out again to walk and to see the city by night. It was cool but not cold, and the streets were so full of people and arrayed with the open doors of shops, cafes and restaurants that it felt almost warm.

When I got back, it was late and there was no-one else in the dormitory. The hostel had the air of a deserted school, and I explored some of the corridors to see if I could find a blanket and pillow. These were easily found and I slept like a baby till the next morning. My day in Istanbul had begun in morose despondency, but the excitement of the city had lifted my soul and I felt confident in my ability to keep travelling.

In the morning, I was up early and went to seek breakfast somewhere near the hostel, and then I returned to it to pack my things and leave them at the front desk. When I had done this, I went to the hostel's lounge and went in – there were about 10 people there, travellers like me, but I didn't feel like speaking with them and went out. I had much to do that day. When I had been at the train station the day before, I had not taken a note of the route that the Istanbul to Paris or Trieste train took and I realised it would be wise to be sure what countries it went through – I didn't know what visas might be needed. I had also to find a bank to change a little of my sterling traveller's cheques and I had to go to the British Embassy. The reason for this was to find out what help might be available if I got absolutely stranded somewhere. My funds were so low I thought it wise to be forearmed and to know what I should do if the point came that I had to press the panic button. I knew from my talking to Tom McKillop in the embassy in Delhi that British embassies do not bail out impoverished or stranded travellers, but I suspected that they would get in touch with family or friends in order to assist those too destitute or in such trouble that they needed rescuing.

I got a street map and worked out my hike for the day – a circuit that would take me around to all my necessary visits by the most efficient single route. I had to get everything done as quickly as possible because I harboured the vague intention of leaving Istanbul that day, if possible.

My first call was to the city centre, where there were plenty of banks. There were travel agents too, and I asked those that had signs confirming that they spoke some English about the need for visa on the train from Istanbul to Paris. All said that none were required.

The British Embassy turned out to be a consulate general rather than an embassy, but was as British and grand as all British embassies are. Before entering, I dusted myself off and tried to make myself look more respectable.

'Yes?' said the girl behind the polished oak counter. I found it difficult to speak.

'To be honest,' I said, 'I'm here to ask what I should do if I find myself absolutely broke. I know you don't repatriate people, but if I got stuck, say in Bulgaria or somewhere on the way to the UK, what should I do?'

The girl looked at me critically. Though the muscles in her face did not move, I sensed a chilling of her demeanour.

'Just a minute, I'll get someone. What was your name?'

'Michael Hendry.' She scribbled the name on a piece of paper, got up and went through a door behind her. I admired the clean, rich, cool atmosphere around me; it was like being in comfortable outer space.

A few minutes later, a man appeared in a suit, white shirt, and tie.

'I'm Mr Douglas. Are you in trouble?' he asked.

'No. But I'm broke and heading home, and I thought it would be sensible to get advice as to what I should do if I get stuck somewhere absolutely without a bean…'

The man in the suit gave me the predicted verdict. I knew what I was going to be told and my reason for going through the apparent charade was to let the embassy know of my existence – so that if I had to scream for help, there would be a face behind the frantic phone call.

I thanked the man in the suit and he wished me good luck, his tone softened.

'We can't do anything really, but get in touch if you have to, that's my best advice.'

I turned to go and had almost reached the front door when my name was called out.

'Mr Hendry? Mr Michael Hendry?' said the voice. I turned. It was the man in the suit again.

'Yes?' I said.

'From Aberdeen?'

'Why yes...' I answered, curious. This was an odd question because it had not cropped up in my conversation with him that I was from Aberdeen.

'Hold on a minute, would you?' he said. He disappeared and I waited a few minutes. When he came back he was holding a letter in his hand, and holding it out towards me.

'There's a letter for you,' he said.

'For me?' I asked, entirely perplexed.

'Yes,' he said looking closely at the letter, 'Mr Michael Hendry, c/o the British Consulate, Istanbul...' He turned the letter over to its other side.

'It's from a Neil Hendry, in Queen's Road, Aberdeen...' I walked forward to the counter and took the blue Aerogramme from him and looked at the sender's address.

'It's from my Dad,' I said, 'how...' I was speechless.

'Why not sit down and read it,' suggested Mr Douglas pointing to a chair, 'I'll be back in a few minutes.'

I sat down and looked at the letter in a state of disbelief. I opened it and read the following:

'Dear Mike,

I hope you are well. You may wonder how on earth you are getting this letter. We have been desperately worried about you, so I have written to every British Embassy and Consulate I could think of that might be en-route from Bombay in the hope that you might for some reason or another call in for... well, we don't know, but I thought it worth the chance.

Madelaine sent a telegram confirming your departure from Bombay. She said she was very unhappy about letting you go ahead with your overland trip. I have to say I am acutely anxious for your safety, especially since Cyprus seems to be imploding and who knows what trouble may flare up again round the Middle East.

Would you please get in touch to confirm you are alive and well? If you need to get home urgently, just get somewhere where there is a bank and an airport (and a telegraph office if there is no long distance phone) and we'll get you home.

Your very loving… Faither.'

Mr Douglas came back.

'You alright?'

'Yes,' I sniffed, 'I'm okay. It's from my Dad. He's worried about me.'

'Not surprised the route you've been… how did he know you would come here?'

'He didn't. He's written to every British embassy and consulate between Bombay and Paris.'

'Good gracious,' said Mr Douglas. He stood for a moment.

'Well, good luck again,' he said, then left. The girl who had been at the counter when I had first presented herself returned and sat behind the counter; she cast a long and curious glance at me as though she was going to speak, but evidently changed her mind and started clacking away at her typewriter.

I left the consulate in a different state of mind than when I had entered. I felt a mixture of acute homesickness and to this was added the alternating guilt that I had not sent any communication home. At the same time, my own being felt altered – as though I had glimpsed myself in a picture of my greater surroundings that included my family and friends rather than those that were lonely, immediate and anxious. I felt both strengthened and weakened in the same moment.

I straight away found a postcard and then a post office and wrote the untrue words that I was fine, hale and hearty and had just tasted some great (if unidentified) fish. I indulged in an air mail stamp and posted it off.

On my way to the railway station I sat on a bench for no other reason than that I was feeling weak and tired. My health was not good and had been deteriorating for months, mostly because of chronic diarrhoea. I took my father's letter out of my pocket and read it again, sensing the home it had come from and savouring the associations of comfort and security. I didn't cry again, but I felt very tired and I leaned forward with my head in my hands. It was after a few moments in that portrait of despondency that I found the ring.

I spotted something gleaming in the dusty roots of a clump of grass close to my left foot and scraped it with the sole of my shoe – which revealed the object, without doubt, as being a ring. I looked cautiously to my left and right and casually pretended to tie my laces as I clawed the ring into my palm. I held it in my cupped hand and examined it as best I could; it looked golden and was set with a single clear stone. So that I did not attract any attention to myself, or to what I was looking at, I put the ring into my trouser pocket, got up and walked off. When I was well away from the scene, I pulled out the ring to have a closer look and for all the world it looked like a gold and diamond ring. The stone was about the size of a tiny pea, it was faceted and held in its seat by small claws, and its interior dazzled and sparkled. Of course, I did not know whether this was a gold and diamond ring or a piece of worthless costume jewellery. I realised immediately that the difference between the two would have a great influence on my circumstances – as gold and diamond it could relieve my distressed financial state, but as a piece of junk it would only cost me precious time and effort. It was mid-afternoon, and of my remaining set tasks I had had only to visit the train station to find out the route of the Istanbul to Paris train. This took me another hour, and the information on the trains was not as simple as I had expected because different trains went via different routes, though they all arrived at the same destination. I wrote down such departures, times and fares as I was absolutely certain of and headed back to the hostel. Normally, I would have walked and toured the city, but I was anxious to have a close look at my ring in private and to carry out a test which I thought would tell me if the stone was a diamond. When I got back to the hostel, I went upstairs and into the room where I had found blankets the day before; it was a shabby narrow room with bare floor boards and a small window screened from the outside by tree branches that shielded the room from any outside view. I closed the door, took out the ring and went to the window to hold it in strong light – then I tried to scratch the glass with the stone. I knew that if the stone was just a fake it would not be likely scratch glass, but scratch it did. My heart raced. I tried again more vigorously and the stone left a deep score; I looked closely at the stone after this scraping test, and I could see no sign that it was marked or abraded.

By now convinced that I had an asset, the question remained of how to convert it into hard cash, and with the idea that I would try to sell it I set off into the streets to see who might buy it. I headed off back towards the Galata Bridge, where my memory told me there were a number of jewellery shops.

Some people find it easy to sell things and have no difficulty in asking a price, haggling and making it look as though they're doing the buyer a great favour. But that did not apply to me. There were several jewellery shops near the bridge and I cruised backward and forward trying to estimate which one offered me the best chance of success in the easiest way – a shop that was neither too snooty where one felt like a dog's mess on the carpet, nor one that was too shabby and down at heel. I needed something middle of the road and preferably somewhere with some English spoken.

I wandered up and down the street, peering into jewellery shop windows and feeling intimidated by them all.

I left feeling awkward and made my way to Turkey's great bazaar, the Capal Karsi, an astounding labyrinth of arched hallways, twisting alleys and narrow passages. I entered with a concentrated intention to do business, but my curiosity and fascination got the better of me for an hour of wandering before I brought myself back to the job in hand. Among the thousands of shops and stalls that sell everything from carpets to clothes to hookahs, one section was for jewellery, and I felt more at ease in this more informal atmosphere. The market teems with people, shuffling and peering, haggling and chatting, and I felt no-one was looking at me and suspecting my predicament. Why is it we feel ashamed in these circumstances? I chose a small stall where a young man stood alone behind a glass case full of jewellery – amber, turquoise, rings, necklaces and bracelets. I went up to his counter and he came forward.

'This?' I said, producing the ring. He pulled out an eyeglass from behind the counter, took the ring and examined it. I waited for his verdict. He shook his head and handed the ring back to me.

'No,' he said simply and smiled.

'Gold?' I asked. He shrugged his shoulders and displayed a well prac-tised disinterest.

I tramped the bazaar for hours, half-lost in its miles of shops, and came to a stall selling a jumble of second-hand stuff that was halfway be-tween the antique and the vaguely useful; there was a small glass counter cabinet filled with rings and other jewellery. Polishing a pot at the back of the shop was a thin, small man with a spectacular moustache. I got his attention, he came forward and I showed him the ring. He looked at it quickly and said, '200 lira.' He held the ring towards me.

'Okay,' I said, 'I come back?' He nodded. I took the ring now in the knowledge that it was worth something. I made a note of where the shop was and found my way outdoors again mighty relieved.

It was late in the afternoon when I emerged into the daylight and headed back to the hostel. I was nearly back to the YMCA when it dawned me that I had made a grave mistake in not accepting the offer on the ring at the first occasion; people change their minds. It was late afternoon and I headed back to the Capal Karsi. I began at a brisk walk, then, in a growing sense of urgency I began to run, the ring firmly clenched in my hand. I was near the bazaar, flying round a corner when I banged full force into a great big fat man. I ricocheted off his bulk at such a speed that I was knocked off my balance at an angle propelling me straight towards the traffic to my close right. I grabbed at a lamp post to save myself and stopped, panting and winded. The man I had crashed into was behind me and his face scowled at me with dislike. I was not concerned by him, but by the fact that the ring was no longer in my hand. I raised my eyes to heaven with an instant prayer that the ring might be found. I peered in the gutter, looked at drains and did everything but get on my hands and knees. I came to the conclusion that the ring had been projected into the street proper and under the wheels of the speeding cars and buses. Catastrophe.

I walked back to the YMCA and immediately packed my things, paid my bill and went to the main station. I had just enough money for a ticket to Trieste, and it was the thought of being in Europe that spurred my decision to act quickly.

12

Banknotes in a chicken, a helpful policeman, Paris and home

I BOARDED THAT DAY'S TRAIN TO TRIESTE WITH ONE TRAVELLER'S cheque for £2 and a few coins in Turkish Lira. It was the 19th of December, just six days to Christmas, and I was determined to get home. It was just after 10:00 at night when I clambered on to the train; I was hungry and cold. I found a seat in a compartment and was joined by a middle-aged man in a blue plastic cap. He did not communicate with me and instead established himself behind a newspaper. The train left Istanbul into the night, and since there was nothing to see, I snuggled myself into my seat and tried to sleep. I had a vague night of waking and sleeping, half-aware when the train was stopped and ready to show a ticket and a passport.

In the morning when I awoke we were in Bulgaria and it was numbingly cold, there was no heating and I constantly had to rub my hands to keep any feeling in them. I tried to get comfortable, but the seat was too narrow to sit cross-legged on and my feet were permanently frozen. I was hungry and desperate for a hot drink, but none was available. The train rolled onward, through a landscape I was hardly seeing – through Plosive to Sofia and towards Belgrade, where I had to change. The day passed and when the train stopped people got on and off; my compartment sometimes crowded, sometimes empty. After Sofia, the compartment was full and I began to talk to an English-speaking Swede, a geologist in a neat grey tweed suit who was on his way to Belgrade. We exchanged the small stories of where we had been and where we were going, and after this, he sat quietly opposite me reading a book.

When we neared the border with Yugoslavia, border guards accompanied the ticket collector and there was a fearful stiffening of necks and backs as their intimidating presence entered the compartment. The guards were two young soldiers, both armed; one carried a rifle and the other a machine gun slung over his shoulder. The one with the machine gun asked each of us in the compartment for their passport and ticket. My turn came and I handed over my passport and ticket. The soldier examined it more carefully than anyone else's and showed it to his partner, who said something I did not understand. The guard then motioned me to get up and to give him my rucksack. I got up and heaved down the rucksack, which he took out into the corridor; his partner took his gun while he searched it. The guard had emptied my clothes onto the floor. He pointed at me, then at the station. I edged out of the compartment, stuffing my things roughly back into the rucksack. The soldiers were behind me and I felt something prodding my back – I turned and it was the soldier pushing me with a finger. My heart suddenly started thumping. It seemed I was being arrested.

I was taken to a tiny room in the station with a window overlooking the platform; by the window there was a small table and a chair. I was made to sit down and the soldiers took everything out of my rucksack again and started going through my things in great detail – feeling the hems of clothing and shaking everything. When they had done this, one snapped his fingers and wiggled his finger to signify that I should empty my pockets. I laid everything out on the table and he picked up my wallet and took out the thin folder of traveller's checks. He opened this and showed the single £2 cheque to his partner.

The two of them conversed and I was getting very concerned that the train might leave without me; I would be stranded and in very unfriendly custody. The headline came flashing quickly to mind:

'N.E Man in Bulgaria Arrest Shock – Only Had £2! City Appeal Launched.'

'I must go,' I said to the soldiers, my shaking finger pointing to the train, my voice strained with tension 'must go!!' One shook his head, and said something that again I could not understand. There was a knock at the door. One of the soldiers opened the door and I could see the Swede I had been speaking to on the train; he pointed at me and held something in his hand which he handed to the soldier. What had been handed over at that stage, I did not know, but it provoked words between the soldiers. A minute or so passed and I heard the train's whistle blow. I looked anxiously at the soldiers and then at the Swede, who yanked his head in the direction of the train. I threw my stuff into the rucksack and grabbed my things from the table and made for the door. The soldiers just stood there and let me go. The train's whistle blew again – the Swede and I ran hurriedly towards the carriages and managed to clamber on as the train drew slowly away.

We worked our way down the carriages to the one we had been in. Before opening the sliding door to take our seats, I said, 'What happened? Why did they take me?'

'They want money,' said the Swede, shrugging his shoulders.

'Money? You gave them money?'

'Ten dollars… it is enough. I know; I come by this train often.'

'But why, why did you pay?'

'I see you are in trouble,' he said.

'But I cannot pay you – I have no money, no 10 dollars.'

'It is not a problem. Please. It is not a problem.'

We went into the compartment and retook our original seats. The Swede just smiled in a kindly way and went back to his book.

As the train worked its way north, the landscape and the buildings began gradually to take on a more European character; though the impression was sensed subconsciously, I began to feel I was entering more familiar surroundings. Some houses by the track were pure alpine, their roof lines, their proportions, their tiles and ambient air were Western European rather than Eastern European. The land too seemed to be getting richer and more precisely organised. Fields were fenced with familiar posts rather than odd metal ones, the telegraph poles were as telegraph poles ought to be, as were the sheds in gardens and as were the front doors of the houses. The landscape, the cultures and the very details of Turkey and Bulgaria were so different in their tiny details that they felt, illogically, more alien and different than those of India, Kuwait, or Nepal. The feelings of alienation are subtle and full of prejudices. In

India, the Westerner feels the invisible power of an imperialist past – an unfair, unearned feeling of (not quite) invincibility that is prejudice at its worst, particularly if assumed by a 19-year-old youth. I hope I never used this overbearing attitude and whenever and if I saw it in action, it riled my sensibilities and raised the hackles of my egalitarian north-east of Scotland upbringing. Yet for all that the self-moralising voice denies the presence of prejudice, the honest man would admit that one of the reasons that I felt more ill at ease in Turkey or Bulgaria was because this background superiority was absent and of no value. In a difficult situation, there was no bluster or posh voice that would have any sway, no power of association that would assist any difficulty.

The day wore on, slowly, interminably, monotonously. The sky, which had begun clear and cold, became cloudy and dull and still it became colder and colder, though the full compliment of bodies in the compartment helped. Snow began to drift past the window and the yellow neon lights in small towns seemed depressing and lonely as night fell. I had been on the train for almost 24-hours and I was feeling shaky from the cold and lack of food.

When the train pulled into Belgrade at the dead of night, I dragged myself out of my seat and pulled down my rucksack. I thanked the Swede again and again for saving me, but he made little of the event, only wishing me luck before he disappeared into the crowds that surged up the platform to the main concourse. I knew I had very little time to find the train that was to take me to Zagreb and Trieste. When I stepped out of the train, the cold air hit me in the nostrils and ears. It was so cold that I thought the inside of my nose would freeze – I reckoned it must have been about -20 degrees centigrade. I could not find an information board, so went to the main ticket office and waited impatiently in line to see if I could find out what platform would have my train. Everyone was huddled up in coats and scarves. I got to the grilled counter and said, 'English?' The woman behind the grill shook her head. In my desperation to communicate my needs as quickly and clearly as possible, I half-shouted, 'Whoo-whoo! Toot-toot ! Trieste?'

The woman smirked and said something.

'No understand!!' I said, straining to hear her among the din of the station and the blaring of loudspeaker announcements in the ticket hall.

She wrote something on a scrap of paper and pushed it through the grill to me – it was the platform number of the Trieste train.

I ran helter-skelter through the mass of people, my breath steaming and billowing in the intense, frosty cold, my rucksack bouncing wildly, my feet slipping in the ice and snow on the stairs and corridors of the station. After showing my ticket and confirming at the ticket barrier that the train was for Trieste, I jostled through the busy platform and jumped on. The train was packed to capacity and drew out of the station as I wandered up and down the carriages looking for a seat. I could find none and so stood frozen and miserable in the corridor as the train rattled into the night, the blowing blizzard visible from the windows. After an hour, the train stopped – in the exchange of passengers, I found a seat and slumped into it. I took out my sleeping bag, unzipped it, wrapped it around myself, and nestled into it to sleep. Sometime during the night I was prodded awake by a hand on my shoulder for a showing of tickets and passports as we left Bulgaria and entered Yugoslavia. There was no drama this time.

When I awoke to daylight, the compartment was empty. I wiped the window and watched the snowy landscape pass by. My surroundings were filthy, the seat was ripped and there was a layer of ice frozen on the floor. I moved to the seat by the window and hunkered down. I was dozing when the compartment door opened and suddenly filled with people; I was shoved and pushed as they installed themselves. There were three older women, one young woman and two teenage girls accompanied by a great quantity of baskets, suitcases and boxes, which they stashed on the upper racks, on their knees and on the floor. Their arrival in the compartment woke me up fully and I tried to make some communication with a smile and a nod, but they ignored me completely. It always helps a group of people travelling together if some pleasantry or politeness can be contrived – helping someone with a case from the luggage rack, or lending them a newspaper – because the effect is to relax the atmosphere. But these people would not entertain any such move. They exchanged a few words now and again among themselves and one of the teenage girls looked at me coyly from beneath her red hair and her plastic head band. In the circumstance where one's attempts to be friendly are ignored and rebuffed, there is nothing to do but retreat into one's corner. The train steamed through gentle rolling hills and the sun began to shine like polished silver between the clouds.

As we neared the border to Italy, the atmosphere in the compartment became tangibly frosty. The women looked tense and agitated, and fidgeted every few seconds with some detail; doing up buttons, re-arranging the top contents of a basket, rummaging in a handbag. They looked afraid and nervous. The train slowed and the trackside signs showed that we were approaching the border proper; the train stopped to let on border guards, who could be heard working their way up the carriages towards us. The women opposite me sat motionless, rigid, unmoving, their hands clamped tightly around their passports and tickets, their faces tight with fear. The door slid open and a military looking guard came in with one hand outstretched for papers, tickets and passports. I handed mine over and it caused no comment. The women handed over their papers in turn and the guards asked questions that I did not understand. To each question the women shook their heads. There was a moment when it seemed the guards were unhappy about something, and seemed to be weighing up what to do when there was a call to them from further down the carriage. They handed back the papers they had been examining and left.

The train was stopped for about 20 minutes, and then with a clanking of doors and a blowing of whistles, it drew slowly away from its halt and rattled through the border to Italy. As the border receded behind us and the train picked up speed, the women in the compartment got up from their seats and crowded round the window to look out; one left the compartment and came back just a few minutes later, chattering excitedly. At this moment, there was a great commotion between them – coats were unbuttoned, headscarves were unknotted, noses were blown and the elderly woman sitting opposite me wiped a tear from her eye. As the mood of relaxation swept around us, some of the baskets which had been up on the luggage rack were taken down, and from these great quantities of food and wine were produced. I was offered a cooked leg of chicken and had a paper cup thrust into my hand... and then a sandwich laden with salami and salad.

'Eat! Drink! Enjoy!' said one of the women to me as she poured my cup full to the brim with wine. I was astonished she spoke some English as she had ignored all my attempts to speak to her. As I gorged on the chicken, I saw that more than food and wine was appearing from their possessions.

The woman who had handed me the chicken had the carcass on her lap on a small towel; she pulled from its innards a small plastic bag and from that bag she withdrew a tightly bound roll of banknotes. She undid the rubber band and the wodge of cash flapped open.

'Shopping!' she exclaimed with unbridled glee.

Cash appeared from the insides of the children's shoes, headscarves, a vacuum flask, and from a baguette loaf.

'Shopping! Italy!' repeated the same women again, 'Yugoslavia shopping no good...' she gulped down a cupful of wine, 'Italy good shopping! Skol!'

From then until we arrived in Trieste, we had a party in which I managed to describe where Scotland was, and in a happy mood I ate my fill and I felt good and wonderful again. I managed to understand that there were severe restrictions on the holding of foreign currency in Yugoslavia, and that the journey between there and Italy was a hotly contested battle between the Yugoslavs who brought goods back from Italy and the guards whose job was to ensure that the regulations were observed in full. Partisans 1, Guards Nil.

The train pulled into Trieste in the early afternoon of December 20th. My ambition was to get home for Christmas, but I had doubts that I could get from the most easterly point in Italy to the north of Scotland in four or five days. I realised too that I had to make as quick progress as possible, because I ran the risk of trying to travel at the very holiday time when trains and ferries would be closed down between Christmas and New Year. At the station I changed my last traveller's cheque for £2 into French francs, reckoning that I would have more need of money there than in Italy, especially since I had eaten so well on the train. Without delay, I got my bearings and headed for the road west. The day was cold and windy with intermittent scurries of snow and sleet – not good weather for getting lifts.

I tramped for an hour through Trieste and came to the main trunk road to Venice. When hitchhiking, it's important to choose your spot to seek a lift so that a driver sees you as well as a safe and easy place to pull in ahead of you. A driver may consider giving a lift, but the decision to stop or not is a very quick one – a driver will slow to get a quick indication of the appearance of the hiker, and that will take a second or so; if there is a natural place to pull in ahead, the chances of a driver stopping are greatly increased. I found my spot just before a layby and stuck out my thumb.

I've always found it better to stop and face the traffic with thumb out clearly, rather than to walk back to the traffic with thumb out. Drivers want a quick look at the hiker.

I was quick to get a lift from a van; luckily he was heading west, and luckier still he was going all the way to Bergamo to the north-west of Milan. As a hiker, it is important to judge how to be the passenger that the driver wants – if he wants to chat and tell you about his weight lifting, then you must fit in with this and aver that you find weight lifting very interesting and have often wondered about steroids and so on and so on. Many drivers prefer a quick hello, where are you going, where are you from and, actually, if you just sit there and keep quiet, we'll be fine. If this consideration is not implemented, the hiker can find himself suddenly stopped at a layby wondering why the driver has discovered suddenly that he must change his destination in order to justify getting rid of you.

My van to Bergamo was a small orange furniture van and the driver just a few years older than me. He liked to talk and his English was fair, though my Italian was nonexistent. We stopped along the way to deliver a sofa, and I helped him humpff it into a very posh house. We got to Bergamo at about 4:00 and he kindly took me to a service station on the road that he reckoned was the best place to get a lift west. He dropped me off, gave me a cheery wave and disappeared.

I wandered round the car park and looked to see where the lorries were from based on the names and towns written on their sides. There were two parked together that appeared to be from Turin, so I hung about until their drivers appeared. Two men walked towards me and approached the two lorries and I managed to convey I wanted a lift. One nodded and I clambered up into the cab. We pulled out of the service area onto the road and I found to my relief that the driver was quite content for me just to sit there rather than talk. I was weary and cold, my feet were wet and I was glad just to get myself into a huddle in the warm cab and feel small and invisible.

Darkness came and the roads were covered in slush. We ploughed on. The lorry pulled off the main road a few miles to the east of Turin in an area of industrial estates, and there the driver pulled into a layby and motioned that I should get out. I thanked him as best I could and got out. As he trundled off, I tightened the straps of the rucksack and started walking. It was about seven in the evening. I walked along the roadside, watching out for road signs that would keep me heading either west or north-west. I had been dropped on one of the arterial roads that lead into Turin, but it was a poor place to get a lift because it was difficult for any vehicle to stop, such was the volume of traffic and the lack of stopping places. I plodded on for another hour through dismal districts, through industrial areas and anonymous road ways – I walked and walked and walked.

The night was becoming bitterly cold because of a biting, freezing wind that seemed determined to find every gap in my clothing. I had no gloves and no matter how deeply I thrust my hands into my anorak pockets, they seemed to become colder and colder so that I could hardly make them move. I thought of Madelaine in that Bombay shop, trying to persuade me to accept a pair of fine, warm gloves. By 9:00, the volume of traffic was distinctly thinner and patchier, and by 10:00 only an occasional vehicle was whizzing past and, in that cold wind, unlikely to stop.

I kept on walking and tramped along the roadside, sometimes where there was no verge or bank and where I earned angry hoots from some cars as they swerved to avoid me. I walked on, my mind numb and focussed solely on the job of walking. By midnight I had still no lift, and by 1:00 in the morning I realised that I had walked the entire length of that outer ring road that skirts Turin to its north and had left that city's boundary. Exhausted, frozen and hungry, I came upon a small service station that was open. It was a very small shed set back from a muddy, slush-filled car park in which there was but one car. I walked up to it and went in.

There was a short counter overhung by four big orange plastic lights and upon which was a cabinet of sandwiches and cakes. Behind the counter was the coffee machine and beside that was a short, bald, and very fat man in an apron. There were a few tables set opposite the counter, and at one was a man in a heavy overcoat.

When I walked into the cafe, the man behind the counter eyed me as I blew upon my hands and unslung my rucksack. I said to him, 'Perfavore, signor, un cafe?' then I lapsed into French, saying, 'Mais j'ai seulment l'argent francais, monsieur,'[but I have only French money] and at this I dug into my pocket and produced my French coins – I had no lira.

He said nothing, but turned to the coffee machine and made it whirr and hiss. He handed me a big mug of coffee and when I held out the money, he shook his head.

'No?' I said.

'It's okay,' he replied, 'just take'.

I sat down at one of the tables with my coffee and held its warmth to my hands. I was shivering like a leaf.

The man who was sitting at one of the tables when I had entered spoke to me in French.

'Where are you going?'

I replied that I was going to Scotland, and that I was trying to get a lift. 'You will get no lift tonight, jeune homme. I tell you. There is no-one.' I said I would walk.

'No, and you cannot stay here. This place will close soon, yes Bertrano?' he spoke Italian to the man behind the counter, who looked at a clock and nodded.

'No, you will come with me. You will stay the night with my wife and with me. It is sensible, and tomorrow you will get a lift.' There was silence for a minute or so, emphasising the fact that there was no traffic pounding the roads. I looked at him, summing up his character, mindful that people of any age can disappear from the face of the earth – but I judged him to be a good man from those traits of the face that we all read and have no logic but that of some distant, vague genetic instinct. He picked up my rucksack and led me to his car, an old Fiat.

I was very, extremely, exceedingly anxious. It was well past 1:00 in the morning, only the man at the cafe had seen me and this man together, and my official existence (or otherwise) was tenuous and vague. Though I was fearful, I still relied upon my judgement that this was a good man.

We drove for about 15 minutes and came to a row of small neat houses with tiny front gardens. The man turned at one and drove slowly up a narrow driveway and came to a halt. He switched off the car lights and then the engine, got out, and got my rucksack from the back seat. We went through a narrow passage, then through a gate, and he produced a key from his pocket to open the front door of the house – there was a light coming from inside. He let himself in and I followed behind him.

He put the rucksack down in the small hallway and bade me wait. He went down the hallway and went into the room from where the light was shining. From there, I heard a woman's voice and then a conversation between the man and the woman in which expressions of incredulity could be discerned. After a minute or so, the woman appeared in the hallway to inspect me. She was in a dressing gown and slippers and her hair was in curlers. She regarded me with the air of someone who has found a rat in close proximity to somewhere it should not have been. There then followed a heated exchange between the man and the woman, and though I could not understand Italian it was clear that the conversation, begun by her, was along the lines of: 'Are you stark raving mad? Do you mean to say that you brought this… this tramp into our home at 2:00 in the morning because… because you felt sorry for him!? Look at this bedraggled good for nothing that you choose to bring to me!'

'But Carla… he looked so cold. He has nowhere to stay!'

'So we become the sanctuary for every down and out you take pity on, eh? Oh, you've really done it now, what on earth were you thinking of… you and that cafe owner… it's just… it's just intolerable!'

'Oh come now, my dove, he is here now, let us get him to bed, so we can all get to bed can we?'

The lady of the house paced up and down, gesticulating wildly and pacing around me as though I was the unintended purchase at an auction. Finally, she sighed deeply, resigned to my presence, and she stomped off. The man led me to a small bedroom and pointed to the single bed there and I waited as he then brought my rucksack. I was about to close the door when the lady of the house arrived with a pillow and thrust it heavily into my hands. I closed the door and listened while a more muted but inaudible conversation took place elsewhere in the house. The bed had no sheets, so I clambered under its cover and went to sleep immediately.

The next morning, the lady of the house was quite a different animal and was as pleasant and cheerful as could be. I was breakfasted on eggs, coffee and croissants with honey and jam, and I caused minor offence by refusing, in sign language, the cereals. After breakfast, and with the man fussing over the time, I was bidden farewell by the lady in an awkward moment of half Italian and half gestures. The man drove me back to the main road, a few miles beyond the cafe where we had been the night before, and dropped me at a layby. I thanked him as best I could and, as he sped off, I realised I did not even know his name.

It was December 21st and the day was very cold, but the sun was trying to make its way through puffy pillows of clouds and I felt revived and optimistic. In this mood, lifts come easy and just an hour and half later, via a Citroen 2CV van and then a Renault, I was at the border with France at Montgenevre. I walked across, and as I presented my passport at the border, I was in high mood. The sun was now shining brightly and warmly and I felt in safe territory for the first time in weeks. My French has always been rotten, but it's competent enough that I can express my needs and understand the replies. The road from the border crossing is a small road that winds through the ski resort that is Montgenevre, which has a sweet and intimate atmosphere, so I set off feeling that I was on a hiking holiday. The pleasure was immense, the road felt friendly, and my goal was markedly nearer. From Montgenevre I walked for an hour or so and came to Briancon, and from there stuck out my thumb again, hoping for a lift that would take me towards the motorway that runs, basically, from Turin to Lyons.

Whereas in paid public transport there is the certainty of a bus a train or a plane, in hitchhiking there is no assurance of getting where you want at such and such a time. There is a mysterious ether that permeates the roadside and the hitchhiker – it is capricious and unpredictable; there are days when the vehicle you want to stop kindly obliges and takes you to where you want to be. There are other days when the lift-God has his or her attention elsewhere: at such times no car, truck, van or any other vehicle is going to stop and pick up a hitchhiker. Such was that day. A Citroen did take me a few miles, but only a few miles and those to nowhere in particular. As I walked, the blue Alpine sky became populated with a few streaky high clouds that became thicker and more solid, such that when the sun was obscured, the temperature plummeted and revealed a wind whose character changed from refreshing to chilling. By mid-morning there was no sky at all, just a spotted curtain of rich slow snowflakes that quietly spattered from above in slanted swirling waves through a grey disorientating gloom. Walking became more and more difficult because of the snow that lay deeper at the road's edge than at its centre so that it was necessary constantly to step into the slush from the bare tarmac every time a vehicle came near. As I became more and more a snowman, the less desirable I became as an object to transport. Who in a warm and cosseted in a car wants to suffer a freezing draught of snowy air in order to pick up someone who will cover their seats and floor with snow? A man in a blue Renault 4L was such a person.

The Renault drew up ahead of me and I ran forward. The passenger door was opened and before I got in, I put my rucksack onto the back seat, shook off as much snow as I could then I got in next to the driver – a middle aged man. He was pleasant and patient with my poor French and asked where I was headed; I explained that I was trying to get to the motorway. He said he knew a shortcut and it would not be a problem and he would take me there but, in the meantime, he had to call at his mother's house on the way and would be there just a few minutes. This was fine by me, and he chatted away about where I had been and where I was headed and did I have family and so on and so forth. And then, just after we had passed through a small hamlet, the hand slid onto my thigh. He had been looking straight ahead at the road, but then looked at me, smiling. I reacted instantly with a 'Non!' and reached for his hand, which was wandering quickly towards my crotch. He was not to be deterred by my unequivocal rejection and I realised in an instant that my predicament needed stronger force.

The man was stronger than me, but I managed to exert enough muscle to make it clear that I would resist him – far from discouraging him, his response was to grip my thigh so tightly that I was in sharp pain. I cried out and began shouting and, with my right hand I began to punch him. At this, he got the message that he was not going to succeed in his desires without a serious struggle. He slammed on the brakes and slewed to a juddering, screeching halt.

I wrenched my door open, leapt out and hurled the door closed with a mighty, slamming bang and in the same instant he revved the engine and accelerated forward and drove off. I went to the verge to try and find something like a rock to throw at him, but there was nothing at hand so I just held up a fist and shouted obscenities, more to the sky than to him. At this same moment dawned the dreadful realisation that my rucksack was still in the Renault. This elicited a full throated 'oh fuck', because though I kept my money in my clothing, my passport was in the inside back pocket of the rucksack – the old British passports were substantial board-bound things not easily squeezed into a pocket. The prospect of having no passport was a dreadful set back. I didn't doubt that after due process and enquiries I could establish and confirm my identity, but I knew that such a complication and wrangling of my timetable would delay my journey by many days, if not weeks. I would have to go to a police station, explain myself, and tell them what had happened and that I had no money. Sometimes, days that begin in too high a mood of happy anticipation crash because the anticipation cannot be sustained – the crash sinks to a low level that is equal to its high and is therefore deeply depressing.

I stood by the roadside, motionless and in a trembling state of confusion and fear. There was nothing I could do but walk ahead in the hope that I would get to a place where there was a police station. With this bitter determination, I set off, dejected and cowed. The snow had stopped and the sun blinked a few brilliant spotlights; I felt resigned to the failure of my little odyssey and at the end of some mental road and at the crossroads of another. I could feel the phone calls to home, the rescue, the well-you-tried, the return through the front door of my house, not in quiet triumph, but in the sense of failure that would lurk behind the eyes of my parents, my brothers and sister and the person looking at me from the mirror.

As I walked, I came to see that I had been very foolish. I realised that I had embarked on my journey because I had not found the direction in life that I had gone to India to find. The overland trek was a bluff, it was a sleight of hand, a trick of smoke and mirrors in which I could hide from a gigantic truth which I could not face – I did not know what I wanted to do with my life.

I tramped on and saw in view a small village, which was preceded by a road sign that indicated that the motorway to Lyons was but 8 kilometres beyond. The thought occurred to me that I should try to get to Paris rather than give up at the next police station. I had got into France after all, and in Paris there were close family friends with whom I could stay while my mess was sorted out. At least that way, I would be closer to home, airports and embassies and I would be in secure and friendly circumstances. Although my thoughts had spanned a great distance, only some 10 minutes had elapsed since my encounter with the Renault and its spooky driver and as I headed down towards the village before me, I saw my rucksack. It was half sitting in a cattle trough that was set into a fence at the side of the road. I ran forward, stepped over the ditch and fished it out of the trough. I examined it hastily and found my passport dry and intact.

By way of celebrating the finding of that which once was given up for lost, I walked quickly to the village and there in a cafe spent the last of my money on a sandwich, a coffee and a packet of Gauloise. I was now completely without money except for a few centimes.In France, like many other countries, it is forbidden to hitchhike on motorways. To get a lift onto a motorway, it is necessary to wait at the point where a trunk road turns into a motorway, or to get to a service station on the motorway. I continued walking towards the motorway and was given a lift by an elderly lady in a smart Panhard; she took me to within walking distance of the motorway, where I waited by the roadside with my thumb out. A Peugeot stopped and asked if I wanted to go to Macons – I had to decide very quickly whether this would get me to Paris more quickly than via Dijon, which was more directly north. Going to Macons meant going a little more west than I had planned for, but I calculated the volume of traffic on the Lyons-Macons-Paris autoroute would be greater, which meant that the chances of getting a lift to Paris were better, so I accepted.

By 4:00 in the afternoon I had been dropped off at Macons at a big service station and soon thereafter got a ride on a British lorry from Margate to Montceau-les-mines, away from the Autoroute, but still close to it. I had a long tramp from there until a 2CV driven by a beautiful and charming young teacher took me to Cahlon sur Soame at about six.

It had been my intention to keep to the autoroutes as much as possible, but in my anxiety to keep moving I hiked a mile or two and was offered a lift to the next village, which I accepted. This turned out to be a big mistake – though I was geographically closer to my destination, I was on a tiny country road at a village where nothing moved except the net curtains. I was also lost. I had enough knowledge of the geography of France that I had brought no map; I had my little notebook with all the major routes to Paris carefully planned out and I knew all the big cities, but I found myself in a tiny village in a maze of minor roads and lanes. I searched for a garage because many French garages have fine enamelled maps on their forecourts. This I found at the extremity of the village, and, thankfully, there was a map and just enough light to make it out.

My error in landing there was immense; I was some 20 kilometres away from the beginning of the autoroute, and I was in a deserted village and it was dark and it was snowing again. I cursed my judgement and began walking again until, just a few hundred meters from the village, I had to accept that in the dark and snow I could not see where I was going. I turned back. I was standing forlornly by the road when a big Citroen van approached me. Rather than just sticking out my thumb, I flagged it down and begged the driver for a lift if he was going anywhere nearer the direction of the autoroute. The driver said he was going to Autun, but I didn't know where that lay in relation to the autoroute. But the driver said that if I wanted to get onto the autoroute, I would be more likely to get a lift from Autun than by staying here. He was looking at his watch and seemed to be getting impatient at my questions, so I accepted his offer and gratefully climbed aboard. We got to Autun at about 10:00, and I was relieved that there was plenty traffic on the roads.

The snow had been getting more persistent and had begun properly to lie and accumulate. It was getting late so I stationed myself at a prominent road intersection at the north westerly exit of the town and held out my thumb. I was there until midnight when, finally, a doctor in a black Mercedes gave me a lift to the beginning of the autoroute. He said I was mad, wished me luck and bade me goodbye in perfect English.

My spot at the beginning of the autoroute was a sort of a big lay-by, at the back of which was a yard for motorway maintenance. The lay-by was lit by high neon flood lamps that cast their light quite strongly upon me. I hoped that by standing beneath a light, drivers would see me, and, by dint of being in a lay-by, feel safe to stop. There was a little traffic coming from the trunk road, which became a motorway at that point. There were a few lorries flying by and the odd car, but the frequency of vehicles was slight and thin.

As midnight became half past, I was still there lamenting the fact that my chances of getting a lift were small indeed. It was snowing heavily and I would periodically have to shake myself to get rid of it. I had been waiting for just about half an hour when I saw a motorcycle approach. As it came closer to me, it slowed down and I wondered if this might be a lift. The bike came right towards me, and as it did so I could see that this was a policeman. He stopped right by me, switched off the engine, rested the bike on its stand and raised his snowy goggles. He came up to me.

'Papiers,' he said, holding out his big gloved hand. I got my passport out and showed it to him; he held it up to the light.

'Anglais?' he said.

'Ecossais,' I replied.

'Hmph,' he said. He gave me back my passport, went back to his bike, reset his goggles and puttered off down the autoroute. An hour later, I was still there. On the road there were mostly trucks and lorries; there were few cars. I tried every conceivable technique to get a lift – jerking my thumb energetically, leaning into the road, with the rucksack and without, coolly, pretending to be unconcerned, but nothing worked. I paced, I made patterns in the snow with my wet shoes, I jumped up and down to make giant rabbit footprints going round in circles. An hour after the policeman had left me, he returned. Again, he drove right up to my side, dismounted and asked me for my 'papiers'. Again I showed him my passport. He said nothing but got back on his bike and roared off. By that time it was something like two in the morning and the snow was falling very heavily. There was still some traffic roaring past, but since getting a lift seemed unlikely I considered whether I oughtn't to go to the works yard behind me, where there might be a sheltered corner where I could sleep for a few hours. But I decided I would just wait.

Another hour later, I had no energy to do anything but stand as close to the road as was safe; I just stood there with my thumb at half cock so that anyone seeing me would know at least I was looking for a lift. As well as being as cold as I had ever been in my life, I was ravenously hungry. In this state of half-life, I heard the unmistakable sound of the police motorcyclist approach me again. In anticipation of his arrival I got my passport out, ready to show him. He once again drove right up to where I was standing and dismounted. Once again he demanded my passport, which once again he examined with intense interest. He said nothing, got back on his bike and left for the third time. Only 10 minutes later after his third visit, I saw him coming from the direction he had just left by, on the opposite side of the road. He slowed, crossed the road and came to a stop at my side.

As before, he rested the bike on his stand, but this time instead of asking for my papers, he touched me on my shoulder and nodded. He then walked into the middle of the motorway, right at the centre of where traffic would meet him head on and he stood there, facing the direction of the oncoming traffic – at that moment the road was absolutely quiet and empty. A minute or passed and I could see the lights of a vehicle coming towards him – at this sight, he held up his hand to signal the driver to stop. It was a brave thing to do: although there were strong neon lights illuminating the scene, he took a risk by standing in the middle of the road. In a moment of rapid braking, a huge dark and dirty lorry came close into view and, seeing the policeman with his hand raised, it began to brake and pull in to the roadside. It stopped and as it did so, the policeman motioned to the driver to wait where he was. The policeman came over to me and grabbed my shoulder and pulled me towards the waiting truck, whose driver was now leaning out of its nearside window. The policeman addressed the driver (with his hand still firmly gripping my shoulder).

'I don't know where you are going, but wherever it is, you will take this man with you,' he said.

The policeman led me to the opposite side of the truck, where the passenger door was already open. I climbed up the two steep steps to the cab and got in. The policeman retook the centre of the road, checked that the lorry was safe to pull out and waved the lorry away. The lorry driver said little, but he was friendly enough after we had exchanged a few words. I fell fast asleep.

On the morning of December 23rd, I was awoken by a shake on the shoulder by the driver of the truck as we pulled into a large service station near Auxerre. He explained that he was heading for Chatres and that if I wanted to get to Paris, it would be better for me to disembark to try for another lift. Although he had been forced to take me, he was a kindly, sympathetic man who was amused by the whole thing. He gave me a cheery wave as he thundered out of the service area in a plume of thick diesel smoke. I went to the service area cafeteria and found out I was well south of Auxerre and within about six hours of Paris. The coffee smelled delicious and the food mouth-watering, but I had absolutely no money. Before going to the car park to trawl for a lift to Paris, I went to the toilets to wash and refresh myself. In the echoing of that space and above the whirring and whining of hand driers I could hear English voices.

'Jeb, we gonna go with that madman… you sure?' said one.

'Gotta – need to get to Paris tonight otherwise won't get the ferry,' the other replied.

'Suppose you're right, Jeb, but that man's a madman.'

'I know, wild bastard.'

I went up to them because they had rucksacks too.

'Do you know of any lifts to Paris?' I asked, 'I've been on the road for days, and I need to get there as soon as I can.'

'Dunno mate. Jeb, think there's room for one more?'

'Who for? You?' said the other looking me over, 'we can ask. You of a nervous disposition?'

'No, not especially. Why?' I said.

'Better not be – this man's a mad mad bastard, 90 all the way. White knuckles.'

I followed them out to the car park and a new blue Peugeot 405. Standing by it was a man in a suit wearing leather driving gloves. He seemed agitated, speedy and nervous, like someone on amphetamines.

'Go on, ask him,' said Jeb.

I went up to the driver and asked if he could manage another passenger. He gave me the quick eye then said, in heavily accented English, 'Sure, why not. Get in the back. Your bag in the back luggage.' He motioned to the boot of the car and I lifted the lid and threw in my rucksack.

I sat in the back while the other two placed themselves, one at my side in the back, the other at the front.

'Okay? We go? We ready?' asked the driver. Without waiting for a reply, he roared off and onto the autoroute, accelerating all the way. My hiker companions were not wrong in their description of the driver. He drove at full speed, maximum speed in the outside lane, overtaking everything. It was not relaxing. It was frightening and we three passengers peered nervously ahead from the edge of our seats, judging every car ahead, how much time there was to overtake, and drawing in our breath as silently as we could. And in the blink of an eye, I was in Paris, set down, a shivering, quivering wreck just off the Peripherique near Vincennes.

The friends I was seeking lived in the 17th Arondissement in the north of Paris – as I had no money for the Metro, I began my hike. I had got to Paris about 5:00 in the evening. I walked north-east, towards my destination, and by 7:00 was near the Basilica of Sacre Coeur; among its small tourist-sweet streets I stopped by a cafe. I was trembling with hunger. There were a few small tables outside sheltered by awnings and potted plants, all decked with Christmas lights. The savoury smells of food wafted from the open door. There were a few people seated, and pretending that I was a potential diner, I unhitched my rucksack and sat down gratefully at an empty table and looked over the menu. A waiter, a young man, came up to take my order but I said that I wanted more time and he left me to my rest. The smell of the food was causing me to salivate and my hunger was intense. The waiter came back and I knew my time was up when he asked me what I wanted. I confessed I had no money and was just resting. The waiter was in no hurry and the restaurant was not busy so he began to chat and asked me where I was going and where I had been. I said that this was the last leg of my trip from India and that I was heading for Calais.

'Ah bon,' he said. '…Well sit for a while if you like, I'll tell you if you need to go – 5 or 10 minutes is okay.' I thanked him and he went back into the restaurant. I relaxed and felt my tiredness roll over me. Just a few minutes later, the waiter came back and placed before me a plate of food and a glass of red wine.

'But I have no money...' I protested, 'I cannot pay...' He said nothing, shrugged his shoulders and left me to gaze in dizzy delight at the coq au vin before me. At the moment I picked up the fork and pierced a potato covered in rich tomato sauce and brought it to my mouth, so did that plate of food become embedded in my mind as the best meal of my life. I ate slowly, and as a few sips of wine went to my head, I was elevated to a mood of exultant high ecstasy. I managed to elongate this heavenly experience for half an hour and when finished I rested heavily against the back of my chair and felt enervated, replete and... and triumphant. As I got up to leave, I slung my rucksack on my back as the saintly waiter who had brought this feast to me came from the inside of the restaurant to serve another table outside. Though he had been approaching his table to serve a tray of food, he stopped as he saw me preparing to leave. I bowed, long and low before him in the only act of gratitude that came to mind, and in answer to this, he held his tray level to one side of him and he bowed to me. I set off to find the family friends whose address I knew by heart.

It took me until 10:00 that night to find the building I was looking for. I scanned the list of names on the bells for the flats and pressed the button. I pressed my ear to the grill to await an answer, but none came. I rang several times but there was no reply. I rang the bell for the concierge, and without any voice coming from the speaker, the door buzzed and clicked unlocked. I went into the dim hallway and looked at the mail boxes by the door to learn where the flat was and climbed up the stairs to the third floor. I knocked on the door, praying for a response, but there was no reply.

The absence of help at this point caused me the returning anxiety that I would have to press the emergency button and seek help from home. I was absolutely without money and had nowhere to stay that night. I was not averse to finding some street corner or bench where I could sleep, but it was not that immediate problem that sharpened my worry. It was the late evening of December 22nd and so near to Christmas that in two days the city would be deserted and closed to its private celebrations – a period of days in which access to help would be almost impossible. I did not want to wander about a deserted city with no money and with nowhere to stay. The hallway was quiet and I wondered for a moment.

It came to me that the crucial thing was to find out whether the people I had been hoping to get help from were to be away for the whole Christmas period, or perhaps just out to dinner. I went down the hallway to the next flat's door and, having memorised the name by the nameplate, rang the bell. The door opened and there stood a small middle-aged lady in her dressing gown and slippers; she held the door open just a crack.

'I am very, very sorry to disturb you Madame… Lavalle,' I said, 'but I wonder if you know if Monsieur and Madame Verney next door are away, or if they are coming back soon? My family in Scotland are good friends with them and I was anxious to see them.'

'Oh no, they have gone to Montreuil,' she explained, 'it will be after New Year that they return. You are from Scotland? And what is your name?'

'Hendry, Michael Hendry,' I said.

'Ah Monsieur Hendry, I have heard Jacqueline talk of your family… please come in, please…' She opened the door and led me to a sitting room. After I had explained myself and my predicament and after she had given me a mug of cocoa, she said: 'But tonight at least you can stay here on the couch, and in the morning… oh, we shall see.' Though I protested that this was an unreasonable burden on her, she insisted that she was close friends with Madame Verney and that I should stay.

And so I had found refuge for the night, and under a warm blanket and quilt I slept soundly until morning.

I had drawn the curtains open and was peering at the street view below me when Madame Lavalle appeared, dressed and immaculate. In her kitchen we had breakfast and chatted of this and that as best as my limited French would accommodate.

'Now Michael,' she said, 'I have decided. How much money do you need to get home?'

'Oh Madame, I could not possibly expect you to…'

'No,' she interrupted, 'I am very good friends with Jacqueline, and I know that if she were here she would give you the money, and because I know she will give the money back to me, I think you must accept it. Otherwise, where will you stay, and how will you eat? I have money here, so it is not a problem. If you leave this morning, you can get to see your family for Christmas... and I think they would be very pleased to see you!'

Even though I knew in the privacy of my own mind that I would accept her help, I was ashamed and felt the need to go through the motions of resisting it. But in the end, I could see that I had no alternative but to accept her help, and within just half an hour on that morning of the December 23rd, I made my way down the flights of stairs with two hundred francs in my pocket.

I found the Metro and got to the Gare du Nord, and there found the train for Calais. By the late morning I had my ticket for the crossing and I was being sick into the English Channel by 2:00. I was in Dover by 3:30 and breathed the chilly must of British air for the first time in a year. It seemed so familiar, but the detail that made it different from other smells and atmosphere was beyond my ability to find the words to describe.

At immigration, my passport was inspected with suspicious interest, and at customs I was invited to accompany an officer to a small anteroom where my rucksack was emptied and my effects and person were examined with forensic intensity. It was with an air of frustrated disappointment that my examiner finally permitted me to leave, and I was at Kings Cross station in London in time to catch the overnight train to Aberdeen a few hours later.

A year from home is not a long time in the grand scheme of things; in the 18th and 19th centuries, men, women, boys and girls travelled across the globe to India, the Far East, the West Indies, Australia and the Americas as the consequence of a life's circumstance – in which, often, they had no choice. In this, they likely missed and regretted the leaving of their homes but set to in their lives and accepted what fate had laid before them – mostly, in the knowledge that they would not see their old homes again. But those were not my circumstances; I had anticipated getting back home as a central thought for much of the time I was away.

The night train was packed to capacity with people getting to Aberdeen for Christmas and I sat wedged uncomfortably in my seat and slept little. The train lumbered through the night, and in the early Sunday morning of Christmas Eve the familiar coast of Tayside, Dundee, Montrose and the cliffs and coves by the line came into view with the wintry dawn. There was a delay just past Montrose and we arrived in Aberdeen sometime after 9:00.

I had enough money for a taxi, but in the elongation of the anticipated pleasure of getting home, I walked from the station to Union Street – which, being a Sunday, was absolutely deserted and empty. I tramped most of its length until I saw my bus and jogged to the nearest stop – Holburn Junction, Albyn Place, Queen's Cross then Queen's Road, where the houses were residences rather than offices. The windows were adorned with the reds and blues and oranges and greens of Christmas tree lights. My stop came at Forest Avenue and a chilly wind whipped through me. A few steps more, past the big house on the corner, across the road, and there before me is the family house – a tall three-storey Victorian house with a lawn and gravelled driveway at its front. I stood in front of it for a long moment – in the upstairs first floor windows of the drawing room, the Christmas tree stood. I walked up the drive and into the front porch and opened the glass door to the hall. I quietly put my rucksack down and went to the kitchen. My mother was there and she stopped dead in her tracks and ran to embrace me, breaking into tears. She left to find my brothers and sister and I stood by the fire in the front room as they came to see me. Half an hour later, my father drove up the driveway in his car and walked into the front room, where I was standing.

He just said, 'Mike,' and embraced me. I was home. As my father's arms closed around me, so too did my journey come to an end and another began.

Appendix 1

Background to the Tibetans in India

VERY SOON AFTER THE INCEPTION OF THE CHINESE REPUBLIC IN 1949, China's ambitions to annex Tibet came to a head in 1950. Like the stalker who has fooled its prey with earnestly expressed statements of good intentions, China removed the smiling mask of its diplomatic pretences and used military force to impose its sovereignty on the whole territory of Tibet. Tibet's leader, a young man just 25-years-old, had to flee to India and from there (and to this day) watched the destruction of a country that had been an independent state for many centuries, albeit with vague boundaries and a loosely organised society. Faced with the violently imposed strictures of the Chinese, many Tibetans chose to leave Tibet rather than live under the Chinese, whose occupation was never benign. A strong state can legitimately protect a weak neighbour in its own interests, but when that neighbouring state dismantles a government and the mechanics of social administration, substitutes its teachings in schools and shoots anyone who objects to the destruction of a thousand years of its neighbour's peaceful evolution, no other judgement can made than that a full-scale invasion and subjugation has taken place. And despite the international condemnation that followed and still rumbles on in the UN, the Chinese attitude has always been: 'so who gives a damn?' The answer to that challenge is that nobody ever will give a damn, because what sovereign state would risk seriously offending China? The bully has just clouted your best friend off a wall – but the bully is seven feet tall and his Dad is owed money by your Dad. The exodus of the native Tibetans from Tibet has occurred in waves coinciding with periods when the Chinese acted to further impose their authority over them. Those Tibetans who left did so in circumstances of great hardship; most crossed the Himalayas into Sikkim, Bhutan, Nepal and India, and many deaths occurred, especially among women and children when crossing the snow-bound passes of the Himalayas. It was Prime Minister Jahwal Nehru who was responsible for the Indian state's position on Tibet at the time when Tibetan refugees were streaming into India in the early 1950s; he had acted diplomatically to bring agreement between China and Tibet but had been duped by the Chinese. Because of the impossibility of stopping refugees from infiltrating through obscure mountain routes and passes into India, Nehru sanctioned the arrival of the Tibetans – to this day, India has been home to the majority of Tibetans. In the town of Dharamsala, the seat of the Tibetan government in exile still survives. The Dalai Lama, the same boy and now the man who fled from Tibet's capital Lhasa in 1959, has been the leader of Tibet in two senses – the spiritual and the governmental. In 2011 he retired from his governmental role, but he remains the Tibetans' spiritual leader.

From the beginning of this process, Tibetans had been drifting into India and establishing unofficial settlements; although the Tibetans are a respectful and gentle race who caused very few social problems in their new environment, the settlements were a problem for the Indian government. The Tibetans wandered around the northern areas of India looking for work or selling craft wares, and very often they were filthy and riddled with disease – and just by their sight and plight, they were a social nuisance. There was a natural resentment from local Indian inhabitants, and in the early- and mid-1960s, in concert with worldwide organisations and charities, the settlements were formalised and organised with their own, linked, camp-based governance. The Palabir camp and others were administered from Dharamsala, and, in the case of the Palabir camp, by an office in Delhi: the Tibetan Rehabilitation and Relief Agency, the TRRA. The camps quickly became more solidly established and integrated. A cluster of these camps was, and still is, centred around the town of Dharamsala. In India as a whole there are some 40 Tibetan settlements.

Appendix 2
Bihar 1967

THE POLITICS OF BIHAR HAVE BEEN TROUBLED BY BETRAYALS, corruption and incompetence for a generation. Against this background, Bihar suffered a uniquely savage disaster that had its beginnings in 1965.

There had been flooding to the north, which had swamped the rice crop; in the middle and south of the territory, there was drought. As the year progressed, food became scarce. When this happens, it is the poor who are first affected – the middle classes have to adjust to a lower calorie intake, but they survive. Because the poor are at the bottom of the social heap, they have no opportunity to seek alternative incomes because have already checked into the last chance saloon. The middle classes survive by taking on tasks that previously had been beneath them, working harder, and perhaps reverting to a state they had worked themselves out of over a period of years. But the poor are stuck.

Although by the autumn of 1965 Biharis were suffering from severe drought and food scarcity, nobody paid attention to their plight. It is a well-known phenomenon in famines and droughts that until the middle classes are severely affected, no political assistance swings into action because the political classes are unaware of the condition of the very poor – because, well, they're the poor and are always such; what's wrong with them now? Also, the poor, being largely illiterate, do not buy or read newspapers. The middle class will write to a newspaper to complain of a crisis or scandal, but the poor do not see that external world as having any relevance to them. So, the middle class must be affected by famine before there is any public and political acknowledgement of its extent.

Late in 1965, the Bihari middle classes were registering their discomfort, and newspapers were sending reporters to investigate. This spurred the Bihari government into action – they related the growing problems to the Delhi central government. In this task they were at a severe political disadvantage because nobody in Delhi believed them. The Bihari government was in disrepute for shoddy and incompetent governance. Still, the newspapers were publishing photos of the sad sights seen throughout the stricken areas – young children, ragged, dusty, naked, with distended bellies, women begging, and groups of listless, exhausted men just lying motionless in the terrifying heat.

When the central government finally acknowledged that Bihar was suffering from a severe, life-threatening famine, the situation was so advanced that India recognised it needed international help – even its own substantial resources would not be enough to avert a major humanitarian disaster. Even though it was but one region of India facing catastrophe, that one region had 50 million people at risk of starvation. As the disputes dragged on, another year passed and the situation in Bihar was not improving; 1965 became 1966 and still there was little aid.

International help really meant American help in the form of gifted grain imports on a huge scale. At that time, the American president, Lyndon B Johnson, was enmeshed in the Vietnam war and was in conflict with Indian Prime Minister Indira Ghandi because she refused to support the American war. A period of stalemate followed. America refused aid except on a limited and short-term basis and the poor Bihari people were victims to events a thousand miles away, in Vietnam.

As the situation deteriorated and Biharis began to die of starvation, the international community swung into action – Bihar's drought became a big media story, both nationally and internationally. In April of 1967, a young Marlon Brando, looking sullen and grim, toured the areas of desperate human suffering. The world's newspapers and TV stations took up the story, and by the spring of 1967, the 'story' of Bihar's famine became a world issue. Lyndon B Johnson relented and the USA sent 14 million tons of grain to India, in exchange for which, India devalued its currency and changed its international trade and agricultural policies, this to open its markets to American fertiliser companies. Well done, Lyndon. Although America had insisted that India change its foreign policy on the Vietnam war as an additional precondition for aid, Indira Ghandi refused this and stood her ground. The grain came nevertheless.